LEADERSHIP CHALLENGES FOR EFFECTIVE MANAGEMENT

*Tesfa G Gebremedhin and
Peter V Schaeffer*

West Virginia University

BLACKHALL
Publishing

This book was typeset by
Gough Typesetting Services for

BLACKHALL PUBLISHING
26 Eustace Street
Dublin 2
Ireland

e-mail: blackhall@tinet.ie

© T Gebremedhin and P Schaeffer, 1999

ISBN: 1 901657 82 5

Printed in Ireland by
Betaprint Ltd

LEADE CHALLENGES FOR EFFECTIVE MANAGEMENT

About the Authors

Tesfa G Gebremedhin is a professor in the Division of Resource Management, College of Agriculture, Forestry and Consumer Sciences at West Virginia University. He has authored and co-authored three books and published four book chapters, a number of journal and miscellaneous articles, experiment station bulletins and research reports.

Peter V Schaeffer is a professor and Director of the Division of Resource Management, College of Agriculture, Forestry and Consumer Sciences at West Virginia University. He has co-edited a book and published a number of book chapters, numerous journal and miscellaneous articles, experiment station bulletins and research reports.

TABLE OF CONTENTS

TABLES

PREFACE

Leadership and management theory and practice continue to capture the minds of a wide variety of people across business corporations, governments, the military, international organizations, academic institutions and religious organizations. These institutions continue to explore the secrets and mysteries of effective leadership and management because the need for effective leadership and efficient management is stronger than ever. This book gives insights into how to address leadership problems and provides a practical guide to the acquisition of new leadership skills required for the changing business environment. It provides the skills and guidance on how to successfully accomplish the initial transition from being a follower to being a leader and on how to establish interpersonal relationships for successful leadership. It covers a wide array of leadership issues in a straightforward fashion and uses many practical examples to illustrate ideas and principles of leadership. The book is specifically directed at individuals who are aspiring to, or have only relatively short experience in, a leadership position. The "everyday' quality of the situations presented in the examples will also increase the confidence of new managers in their own ability to provide effective leadership. The format of the book makes it suitable for classroom use, primarily as a textbook or supplementary text in a college course on leadership and management. The book stands out as a unique text in a professional training course for aspiring or newly appointed managers. The emphasis on practical applications is useful for self-study initiatives or as a valuable workbook for professional reference. The book is not intended solely for business management; it also relates to other professions.

The book is organized into four parts consisting of sixteen chapters. Chapter 1 discusses the importance of investing in human resources development and stresses the role of leadership in this regard. It also presents the acquisition of leadership skills as an investment that we make in ourselves. In Part I, Chapters 2–5 discuss steps that one can take to become a leader. These four chapters compare different leadership styles. They also consider roadblocks to leadership and the essential traits and behaviours of effective leaders and the transition from being a follower to being a leader. The reader will learn how roles change as one assumes positions of leadership and management. In Part II, Chapters 6–12 each deal with specific leadership and management skills, such as decision making and problem solving processes, the art of communicating, delegation and empowerment, techniques of team building, styles of conflict management, and the practice of performance appraisal. In Part III, Chapters 13–14 discuss moral dimensions of leadership with particular reference to the problem of discrimination in management and the need for professional ethics in management as they relate to the promotion of a positive work environment. In Part IV, Chapters 15–16 provide a guide to the strategies for advancing the power of networking and promoting personal leadership careers. An appendix provides leadership and management related cases for discussion and reflection suitable for self-study or use in classroom situations.

Tesfa Gebremedhin
Peter Schaeffer

July 1999

ACKNOWLEDGMENTS

It has taken us longer than we thought to write this book mainly because much research was needed and we learned a great deal more about the subject as we wrote. We benefited from discussions with colleagues and individuals in management positions. Their ideas and suggestions complemented ideas based on our research and own professional experiences. In writing this book, many authors and friends have encouraged, empowered, excited and educated us and we are thankful to them. We would like to extend a special thanks to Arefaine Berhe, Minister of Agriculture, Eritrea, who first opened Tesfa's mind to the possibility of creating this book. If Mr Arefaine Berhe (when he was the Deputy Ambassador of Eritrea in Washington, DC) had not asked Tesfa to go to Eritrea and conduct workshops on management to upper-level and mid-level managers and administrators, this book would not have been created. We are also grateful for constructive feedback and encouragement from West Virginia University colleagues and other friends. A special word of thanks is extended to Neil S Bucklew, College of Business and Economics, for his review on the draft of the manuscript. We want to record our thanks to our colleagues, Dale Colyer and Gerard D'Souza, for their valuable comments and helpful editing suggestions of the final version of the manuscript. We are indebted to the Division of Resource Management and College of Agriculture, Forestry, and Consumer Sciences, West Virginia University, for staff support and facilities we used in preparing this book.

The preliminary version of this manuscript was used in a series of workshops in Eritrea at the Institute of Management of Asmara University, Ministry of Trade and Industry and National Union of Eritrean Women. It was also used in a workshop at the Embassy of Eritrea in Washington, DC. We have obtained useful feedback from workshop participants and from discussions with colleagues and students at West Virginia University.

Finally, we want to recognize our families who have been very important in our work. We extend our special gratitude and appreciation to Meheret Ghebremeskel, Abnet, Luwam and Adam Gebremedhin and to Patricia and Joseph Schaeffer, for sharing with us and giving us the space, time and emotional support we needed to complete the incredible time-consuming task of writing this book. We thank you very much for your love, patience, inspiration and for the stimulus you have provided us throughout the preparation of this book.

CHAPTER ONE

INVESTMENT IN HUMAN RESOURCES

The future belongs to those who believe in the beauty of their dreams.

Eleanor Roosevelt

Many managers, if they were asked to list their organization's assets, would probably mention buildings, land, equipment, facilities or financial assets. Too often however, an organization's most important assets, its human resources, are omitted from the list. Regardless of the quality of physical and financial assets, it is the way people use those assets that determines an organization's success. If managers fail to view employees as the primary and key assets, they may fail to invest in human resource development. Organizations that view human resources management as simply a routine matter of filling positions and keeping them filled, may never reach their full potential, no matter how much effort managers spend to develop their organization's physical resources or products. We need to remind ourselves that each person has unique needs, feelings and emotions. Because we deal with individuals, human resources management is complex, but mastering it can yield high dividends in satisfaction and lead to productivity gains and financial success.

The importance of human resources is not limited to business and other organizations. The potential for sustained growth and development of a whole country is influenced not only by its natural resource endowments and physical capital, but also by the productivity of its human capital. The productivity of all of these assets depends also on available technology and the institutional setting under which these resources are employed (Gebremedhin, 1996). Although natural resources can play an important role in economic development, few countries have ever been able to sustain economic growth because of their rich natural resources. However, the spectacular successes of natural resource-poor countries, such as Israel, Japan, or Switzerland, indicate that a lack of natural resources need not hinder development, just as their abundance does not ensure rapid and sustained growth and development (Tweeten, 1972). Israel, Japan, and Switzerland have in common a well-trained labour force, strong managerial and entrepreneurial abilities, and stable social and political institutions that make growth and development possible. Societies that are equipped with strong human resources can also afford to take reasonable risks with their energies and capital in the pursuit of economic and social gains. South Korea and Taiwan, two countries that have made the transformation from traditional to modern economies, are also poor in natural resources, but have achieved economic success through a strategy of human resources development.

The accumulation and creation of a large pool of skilled human capital, as measured by the educational attainment of the population, has been recognized as an essential feature of economic growth and development. Human capital theory, the economics of investment in people, argues that education augments cognitive and other skills, which, in turn, increases the productivity of labour (Schultz, 1961; Becker, 1964). Human capital theory has been extensively tested. Schultz (1988) and Strauss and Thomas (1995) review the evidence from dozens of empirical studies. The results consistently show that more educated individuals receive higher wages and are more efficient in managing the health and general well-being of their households. The higher wages reflect the value of human capital in the workplace. There is also empirical evidence that a large stock of human capital facilitates the production of new ideas and technological progress, and facilitates the relatively rapid adoption of new ideas and acquisition of technological capabilities (Nelson and Phelps, 1966; Romer, 1990). Thus, the benefits of human capital development are not limited to the most technologically advanced economies. Rates of return to human capital investments may even be increasing over some range because of beneficial spillover effects: just one well-trained worker may make an entire group of workers more productive. In summary, it is likely that the combination of greater educational and training opportunities and a growing demand for skilled workers sustains the economic growth of many of the fast-growing developing countries (Birdsall, Ross and Sabot, 1995).

In any country, the work ethic and aspirations of its people influence, and are influenced by, political institutions. Strong and democratic institutions provide an atmosphere of stability, freedom, justice, and security which is necessary for people to realize their full potential and to contribute successfully to the structural transformation and development of the economy and the maintenance of a just society. In a just society, human resources constitute the basis for economic development and social progress. The wealth of a nation is more dependent upon the development of its people than upon the accumulation of physical capital and lies in the wisdom, knowledge, and skills of its people. Although capital and natural resources are positive factors of production, human beings are the active agents who accumulate capital, exploit natural resources, build social, economic and political organizations, and carry forward national development. That is why development has to start with people and the careful planning and development of human resources.

Leadership and management are very important factors in the development of human resources. Sound management and effective leadership help achieve goals and objectives and maintain the efficiency and productivity of an organization. Management and leadership are not the same. To manage is to bring about, to accomplish, to be in charge of or assume responsibility for something. By contrast, to lead is to influence, guide and provide direction. Of course, not everyone is good at both leading and managing. Some people have the capacity to become excellent managers but not strong leaders. Others have great leadership potential but have great difficulty becoming strong managers (Kotter, 1998). One can be a leader without being a manager. Conversely, one can manage without leading. Nevertheless, the two jobs often overlap; at times leaders must manage and managers must lead (Gini, 1998). Leadership is not just good management, but good management is part of the overall job description of every leader. The difference between management and leadership may be summarized as efficiency versus effectiveness. Management is about coping with complexity and operational functions. Leadership, by contrast, is about coping with changes and challenges. Managers "do things right' and leaders "do the right thing' (Fiedler and Chemers, 1974). According to the definition and distinction made by Abraham Zaleznick (1990), "the crucial difference between managers and leaders is their respective commitments. A manager is concerned with *how* decisions get made and *how* communications flow; a leader is concerned with *what* decisions get made and *what* the leader communicates". This definition implies that leaders are involved in strategy, and that managers are more concerned with operations. In other words, leadership and management are two distinctive ingredients, but complementary systems of action in the life of every organization. The real challenge is how to combine strong leadership and strong management, and use one to balance the other to accomplish goals and objectives, to broaden career prospects of employees, and to achieve success in the increasingly complex life and changing environment of most organizations.

Everyone whose work involves the direction and supervision of other people is in a leadership position. Therefore, all managers who supervise people hold leadership positions. However, not all leaders are managers. Some may have power and influence without having a formal managerial position. Likewise, the functions of some managers may not include leadership responsibilities. In general, however, leadership represents one of the most important dimensions of management (Bennis and Nanus, 1985; Fiedler and Chemers, 1974). Thus, although the terms "manager' and "leader' are not perfectly synonymous, we use them interchangeably. This book is a guide to the practical application of contemporary leadership principles by administrators of public and private organizations in a changing business environment. The fundamental aim of this book is to enhance managerial capabilities at work by presenting valuable leadership ideas and practices. It is designed to appeal to a wide range of people in management positions, particularly (Miller, 1988):

(a) those who have been managers or supervisors for a while but have had little or no formal management training and want to learn new ideas and skills;

(b) those who have been recently appointed or promoted to a management or supervisory position for the first time and need contemporary leadership skills;

(c) those who hope to be promoted to the management team soon and know that improved leadership skills will help them achieve their career goals;

(d) technical, scientific and other specialists with leadership responsibilities but with little formal training in management and leadership skills;

(e) individuals who are involved in teamwork and who play an important role in leadership and management;

(f) employees who desire to know more about leadership in order to be good followers.

This book provides a step by step pathway for effective leadership with fairness, integrity, honesty and human dignity. It lists principles that help leaders to adapt to change, and teach them how to take advantage of opportunities that result from change. Its practical, interactive, proven content helps managers get better results. It focuses on important problems regularly faced by managers, and on difficult situations and unique challenges. A considerable literature about successful techniques and methods of management exists. This book seeks to combine our knowledge of basic principles of management with that of effective leadership. The book covers topics that are important for the management of dynamic organization, such as how to:

(a) build cohesive and spirited teams in order to motivate employees to give their best effort to increase efficiency and productivity in the organization;

(b) recognize and eliminate potentially destructive workplace conflicts and create positive interpersonal relationships;

(c) form powerful partnerships with colleagues and followers inside an organization, handle employees performance problems with greater ease and confidence, and confront employee performance and attitude problems tactfully and firmly without arousing resentment and creating stress and frustration;

(d) create an environment without conflict, hard feelings or game-playing by demonstrating self-respect and confidence, and encouraging others to take pride in their work resulting in higher productivity, greater quality and a bottom-line boost for the organization;

(e) delegate and empower people by expanding their authority and enabling them to have more time to explore new ideas and practices;

(f) boost the credibility, impact and confidence of the management team and become more "bottom-line' oriented without losing "people focus';

(g) improve supervisory and communications skills, and enhance communications among employees by creating an atmosphere that encourages co-operation and the sharing of ideas;

(h) assess your weaknesses and strengthen your personal leadership style to succeed in accomplishing goals and objectives;

(i) achieve a higher quality of work life through the creation of a workplace characterized by openness and fairness in which everyone is treated with respect and integrity;

(j) motivate yourself and inspire your fellow employees to improve their job skills through on-the-job or off-the-job training for new innovations and technological changes, thereby enhancing greater career success.

Developing the right leadership strategy for an organization is crucial to management success. The success of an organization depends on the abilities of the people working in it. Appointing the right individuals to key management positions is, therefore, critical to any organization's long-term success. However, without building their skill for handling management challenges, new appointees will not be well prepared. Some leaders believe that their experience is sufficient to deal with new challenges. Others believe that they are fully qualified on the basis of their educational credentials. Of course, experience and education are valuable and help prepare us for new assignments, but we should be aware that few things remain the same in this changing business environment. New opportunities and challenges often require new approaches and contemporary leadership skills to successfully deal with the changes in business management. Organizations are now evolving toward team-based institutions characterized by the concurrent transition of managers into leaders, the transition of employees into team-mates, and the transition of functional hierarchical organizations into those of team empowerment with all team members sharing the ownership of goals and responsibilities equally. It is, therefore, important that even experienced leaders cultivate and nurture their leadership and management capabilities in order to cope with the fast-changing business environment.

PART I

BECOMING A LEADER

The future is not a place to which we are going. It is a place we are creating. The paths to it are not found but made. And the activity of making these situations changes both the maker and the destination.

Brenda Rogers, 1991

CHAPTER TWO

TRADITIONAL VERSUS CONTEMPORARY LEADERSHIP

Great minds talk about ideas;
Average minds talk about things;
Small minds talk about other people.

Anonymous

The effort to understand the concept of leadership and relate it to reality starts by asking questions such as: What is leadership? What purpose do leaders serve? What do followers expect from leaders? What do leaders expect from their followers? Why do people believe in some leaders but not in others? And why do some people choose to follow one leader while others reject that same leader? There are at least three important factors involved in understanding leadership: (i) the characteristics of leaders; (ii) the attitudes, needs, and other personal characteristics of the constituents; (iii) the characteristics of the institution, such as its purpose and structure.

Leadership is a dynamic relationship, exhibiting complex patterns of interaction among the leader, followers and the organization. Leadership is everyone's business. Everyone is a leader; at least the leader of oneself and most are followers more often than they are leaders. Leadership is the highest component of management and perhaps the most important managerial function because it is through leaders and followers that the goals and objectives of an organization are accomplished. The proper co-ordination of individual efforts is the prerequisite for effective leadership in any organization. Thus, there is a need for a concrete understanding of leadership and management. This section discusses the basic requirements for effective leadership and the characteristics of an effective leader from the point of view of contemporary principles of leadership and management (Bennis and Nanus, 1985; Conger, 1992; Fairholm, 1994; Kouzes and Posner, 1987, 1995; Miller, 1988; Terry, 1993).

Leadership: Myth or Reality

There is the traditional belief that leadership skills are inherited at birth: leaders are born, not made. Leaders respond to their calling through some mystical process. Biographies of great leaders sometimes read as if they had entered the world with an extraordinary genetic endowment, that somehow their leadership role was preordained. According to this school of thought, the power of leadership is vested in a small number of people whose inheritance and destiny make them "natural' leaders. The myth portrayed is that those of the right breed can lead; all other people must be led. This view is sometimes referred to as the "Great Man' theory of leadership in which gold parents produce gold children and silver parents produce silver children. In its extreme form it implies that no matter how much you learn or yearn, you cannot change your fate. Such a view fails to explain the true meaning of leadership. Contemporary management theory believes that great events turn ordinary people into outstanding leaders. As Max De Pree indicated, "we can not become what we need to be by remaining what we are". We can be leaders only if we learn to be leaders. Leadership is just an art that we can learn. Leaders are not born but made through learning, experience and opportunities. Experience demonstrates that leadership skills can be learned and that nurture is far more important than nature in determining who becomes a successful leader.

Traditional approaches to management view leaders as charismatic individuals who possess some special traits of character, skills or talent. In other words, leadership is thought of in terms of the personality and capacity of individual leaders, and defined as something that only leaders have. This view implies a hierarchy with the leader at the apex of the structure, charged with the task of shaping the organization. At best this view distorts our appreciation of what leadership is; at worst it can lead to hero worship. There is virtually nothing in terms of physical appearance, personality or style that sets leaders apart from followers. To be sure, leaders must be energetic and enthusiastic but a leader's dynamism does not come from special powers. It comes from a strong belief in a purpose and a willingness to express that conviction. Charisma is the result of effective leadership, not the other way around. It is also normal that outstanding leaders are granted a certain amount of respect, and even held in awe, by their followers, which increases the bond of attraction between them (Bennis and Nanus, 1985).

Traditional management approaches assume that leadership exists only at the top and that those at the top of an organization automatically are leaders. Leadership is neither a property nor a place; it is an active process of bringing forth the best from oneself and others, not focusing exclusively at the top of an organization. Leadership that exists alone at the top of an organization may be sufficient to provide an organization with a vision but is usually not sufficient to turn that vision into reality. Leadership is needed at every level of an organization. Leadership involves skills and abilities that are useful not only in executive positions, but also on the front-line. Effective leaders assume responsibilities and engage in activities that shape the culture of an organization so that it becomes capable of realizing its institutional vision (Bennis and Nanus, 1985).

Traditional management thinking also promotes the idea of power as a fixed sum. This means that if leaders have more power, employees have less, and vice versa. Naturally, leaders who hold this view are reluctant to share power but hold tightly onto the power they perceive themselves to have. By contrast, in contemporary management practice, leadership is a shared responsibility between leaders and the people whom they aspire to lead. Of course, this is possible only if leaders and followers also share power. A failure to understand that leadership is a shared responsibility has led many leaders to act alone, without any involvement of those whom they lead. This view of leadership thinking actually prevents the building of strong and effective organizations, the promotion of co-operation and teamwork and the achievement of the goals and objectives of the organization. Shared power and leadership responsibility result in higher job satisfaction and better performance throughout the organization. The key to doing well lies not in the competition for power or in dominating fellow employees, but in sharing power and gaining their co-operation (Kouzes and Posner, 1987).

For a long time, it was thought that the primary job of leaders is one of control: the control of people, facilities, machines, materials and money. Managers used to be trained in giving orders and putting the good of the organization and its business profits before the good of individual employees. Tight controls, however, impede creativity by those who are controlled and may, therefore, reduce an organization's productivity; they also reduce the ability to adapt to unusual circumstances. Very tight controls imply the absence of trust between managers and other members of the organization. A modern view is that leaders do not command and control but serve and support. Leadership is not so much about telling people what to do but the ability to inspire them to share a common goal. This is more readily accomplished if followers trust their leaders. The followers' trust, respect and loyalty allow leaders to engage in collective and collaborative action. Although we often focus on individuals who are particularly successful leaders, leadership is not an expression of individual action but of collective action.

So far we have argued that leadership is the result of the collaboration between leaders and followers. It is not so much the exercise of power as it is the empowerment of employees. Leaders should be able to translate vision (intentions) into reality by sharing responsibility and delegating authority. Successful leaders pull rather than push; inspire rather than order. They create challenging but achievable expectations, reward progress toward reaching goals and objectives, and encourage individual initiative. The most effective leaders are often involved and in touch with those they lead and care about the values of their followers, their beliefs and their feelings. Insensitivity and disregard for the humanness of their workers are major causes of professional failure of leaders. Thus, leaders should have passion for what they believe in; they should inspire and challenge; but they should also show respect and demonstrate trust, caring, kindness and even love. According to Craig Pace, a senior consultant with the Covey Leadership Center, "People do not care how much you know – until they know how much you care" (Heasley, 1997). Caring behaviour comes from deeply held beliefs. Leaders should care deeply about their followers, not just as employees, but as human beings and friends.

Some leaders often refer to those with whom they work as family. In fact, nowadays there is a movement towards training managers to care about people in organizations; to understand their feelings and to try to make their jobs and workplace interesting and rewarding (Kouzes and Posner, 1995; Rogers, 1991).

Leaders are sometimes also represented as individuals who magnetize a band of followers with courageous acts or by creating a state of hostility and fear. Leadership is not about heroism or playing a starring role. Heroic leaders, who assume sole responsibility for the organization, are in danger of attempting to control too much; seeking full control can lead to obsession. A very tightly controlled environment is an unpleasant place to work, and very strict controls reduce the ability of employees to react creatively when unusual situations arise. To the leader, the exercise of control is a constant burden that requires information and knowledge of all situations to be dealt with. The more control a leader retains, the more information and knowledge is required, and the more difficult and stressful the leadership role will be. Leaders who are obsessed with controlling everything are likely to end up engaged in constant crisis management with little or no time for anything else.

Traditional leadership theory focuses so much on the role of the leader in creating success that it ends up undervaluing the roles played by followers. Modern organizations are designed to be flexible so that they can react quickly to challenges and opportunities. This is not possible if the organization relies on leaders alone. Contemporary leadership theory therefore examines the roles of followers in the dynamics of organizational success. Followers are partners with their leaders in accomplishing goals and objectives as well as defining goals and a path to the future. True leadership is leaders and followers working together to achieve common goals. If leaders are to achieve success, they must encourage participation of followers in the creation of the vision, mission and goals. We mentioned above that leadership is a form of collective action. Credible leaders attract followers if they understand and demonstrate respect for their aspirations. Effective leaders know how to motivate and persuade others to join in the search for shared aspirations and the pursuit of common goals. Leadership involves shaping the social, emotional, and spiritual dimensions of interpersonal work relationships, in addition to system, structure, and strategy formation (Rosenbach and Taylor, 1998; Bennis and Nanus, 1985).

The traditional notion of leadership does not allow for mistakes because, if everything depends on leaders, then their mistakes could be very costly. If we adopt a different view, one where leadership responsibilities are shared, then mistakes by one person are far less likely to cause serious harm to the organization. In such an environment the long-term success of a leader does not depend on a record that is free of mistakes and leaders can, therefore, afford to take risks. An organization that is structured so that it can afford to take risks, will be more innovative, more dynamic, and, therefore in the long run, more successful than organizations that expect their leaders to be perfect.

It follows from the above that the long-term success of leaders of modern organizations does not depend on a mistake-free record. Every successful person has an imperfect record. Some have accumulated huge failures before they achieve success. Some of the greatest leaders failed many times before they succeeded. Some famous leaders even had to struggle to win leadership position, as their talents were not recognized at first. Abraham Lincoln was defeated eleven times in state and national elections for public office before being elected president of the United States. Perseverance is an expression of conviction, an important quality in a leader. Thomas Edison failed in 3,000 laboratory experiments before he succeeded in his electric light and other inventions. Abraham Lincoln and Thomas Edison both realized that mistakes and failures played an important role in their success. Without the lessons learned from those experiences, they would not have been able to achieve their aspirations. Failure breeds success because we can improve only if we accept that we might fail and try again and again. Charles Jones said it well: "You weren't put on earth to make right decisions – you were put here to make decisions and then work like hell to make them right" (McLean and Weitzel, 1992). Obviously, we are not advocating that failure ought to be the goal of an endeavour. However, unless we are willing to accept mistakes, we will shy away from taking risks and we will never have the opportunity to learn from our mistakes. Only if we take risks and step out into the unknown, will we progress beyond the present state (Kouzes and Posner, 1995).

If leadership is not shared the organization cannot afford leaders who make mistakes. For leaders not to make mistakes, they have to be knowledgeable about every aspect of the organization. This can easily cause some leaders to believe that they must be able to perform the jobs of their followers. This may be feasible in a small organization but is impossible in complex organizations. Fortunately, it is not necessary that leaders know about every job in the organization. On the contrary, enlightened leaders seek out individuals with talents and skills that complement their own. They do not feel threatened by followers with superior qualifications in some areas. While proficiency in a wide range of skills is not necessary for effective leadership, experience with a variety of situations is desirable. Experience is often a good, and sometimes the only, guide for making decisions under conditions of uncertainty. Experience is more valuable for effective leadership than the ability to perform the jobs of the followers (McLean and Weitzel, 1992).

For a long time it was widely accepted as fact that women could not lead and that employees would not accept a woman leader. Similar myths existed about the leadership capabilities of African-Americans and members of other minority groups. Although these myths have been proven wrong many times, there are still some people who cling to them in spite of much evidence to the contrary. The ascendancy of women and minorities in every profession has been one of the most important trends of the 20th century. Women are gaining recognition for their leadership abilities and accomplishments in politics and corporate businesses. Women have been effective leaders in spite of the lingering prejudice against them. The accomplishments of women as leaders are documented by a quickly growing body of evidence (see McLean and Weitzel, 1992).

Leadership and Followership

There is no simple definition of leadership and there even is some confusion on how to define, describe and analyze leadership. Perhaps this is because there seem to be contradictory demands made of modern leaders or there are so many perspectives reflecting the many differences in people, organizations and societies. Another possible source of confusion results from the common use of the term leadership to refer both to actions and to personal qualities of leaders. There is, therefore, a diversity of opinions on what leadership is and this requires a quest for a broader and deeper understanding of the meaning of leadership as well as followership.

Common terms describing aspects of leadership that are found in the literature include: personality, a form of persuasion, a power relation, initiating action, developing attention, arousing enthusiasm, creating inspiration and maintaining structure. Together these terms suggest that individuals are accepted as leaders because of the quality of their ideas, their character, strength of will, ability to arouse and motivate and ability to help others achieve more than they could do on their own. Leaders influence human behaviour by imposing their will upon others in a manner that commands respect, instills confidence, and elicits co-operation (Wishart, 1965). Thus, leadership is the ability to capture the allegiance and devotion of individuals or groups and direct them toward accomplishing common goals. In other words, leadership is a transaction and interaction between leaders and followers for the purpose of accomplishing the common goals and objectives of an organization. In the relationship between leaders and followers, influence and power are unevenly distributed as a result of respect for the leaders. Leaders earn, and must continue to justify, their influence and power. Rockefeller makes this clear when he reminds us that, "the only justification for power is service" and, as Martin Luther King added, "everybody can be great because everybody can serve".

Leadership is not only about leaders; it is also about followers. Modern organizations can no longer depend on the leader alone because leadership does not exclusively reside in the leader. Rather it is a dynamic relationship between leaders and followers alike. The achievements of an organization are the result of the combined efforts of leaders and followers (Gini, 1998). Leaders need followers and neither one could exist without the other. A person without followers is not a leader because leadership does not exist in isolation. Leaders are only as good as their followers make them. Effective leadership strongly depends on a complex pattern of interaction among leaders, followers and the situation. Aristotle's *Politics*, Plato's *Republic*, Homer's *Odyssey* and Hegel's *Phenomenology of Mind* affirm the mastery of followership as the *sine qua non* of leadership (Rosenbach and Taylor, 1998). Without the commitment and devotion of his armies, Napoleon was just a man with grandiose ambitions. Without the trust of those who came with him, Christopher Columbus could not have sailed to America. Mahatma Gandhi would not have been noticed without those willing to follow his strategy of non-violence. These three leaders had a vision of what could be achieved, and the confidence and energy to pursue their vision, but each needed followers to turn the vision into reality. Although leaders and followers have distinct characteristics, styles and functions, they share similar roles in accomplishing goals and objectives. Qualities that we associate with effective followers are the same qualities that we find in effective leaders. In fact the dichotomy between leaders and followers has become less relevant in a contemporary work setting dominated by highly educated professionals (Rosenbach and Taylor, 1998).

If a person has initiative, self-control, commitment, talent, honesty, credibility and courage, it is commonly said, "here is a leader". The stereotype is that a follower cannot exhibit the qualities of leadership. This stereotype is wrong. Effective followers and effective leaders are often the same people playing different roles at different times, sometimes during the same day. Organizations stand or fall on the basis of how well their leaders lead and on the basis of how well their followers follow.

While most organizations teach and encourage leadership, they assume that followers do not need to be taught how to follow.[1] It is commonly assumed that everyone knows what it means to be a follower. This assumption is based on three faulty premises (Kelley, 1998):

1. Leaders are more important than followers.

2. Following is simply doing what you are told to do.

3. Followers inevitably draw their energy and aims, even their talents, from the leader.

Although followership dominates our lives and organizations, a preoccupation with leadership has kept us from considering in detail the nature and the importance of the follower. Followers differ from leaders not in their intelligence or character, but in the roles they play. Effective followers do much more than carry out orders from their leaders. Followers are as important as leaders and can offer as much value to the organization as leaders do. Relationships between leaders and followers vary. Some relationships are hierarchical with leadership authority at the top. Others consist of a partnership

---

1. It is worth noting that the armed forces teach their soldiers how to accept and follow commands.

between leaders and followers. In either case, followers and leaders work together for the benefit of their organization.

Sometimes the term "follower' has negative connotations because of instances where people blindly followed unethical leaders, such as Adolf Hitler in Germany in World War II or the cult leader Jim Jones in Guyana in 1978. We may view followers differently when we remind ourselves that leaders come from the ranks of the followers. In fact, few leaders can be successful without first having learned the skills of following (Rosenbach and Taylor, 1998; Kelley, 1998). Although followership includes the willingness to accept the authority of a leader, this is not enough. Followers who end up helping organizations prosper beyond the short-term are those who are enthusiastic, reflective, intelligent and self-reliant. These are characteristics of effective followers and leaders alike. It is therefore not surprising that strong leaders emerge from among the followers and that all leaders, at some time and to some degree, are followers. It bears repeating that many of the traits and characteristics of an effective leader are the same as those of an effective follower: trustworthiness, friendliness, enthusiasm, positive attitude, vitality, democratic attitudes, perseverance, sympathy and credibility.

Effective followers must be open-minded and willing to accept change. They should be willing to listen to ideas and carry them out, even if they do not agree with them. Effective followers serve a vital role in creating organizational change, they take responsibility for getting their jobs done and take the initiative in fixing problems or improving processes. It is critically important, however, that followers maintain sufficient independence from their leaders to be critical thinkers. The organization should be structured such that followers feel comfortable expressing their thoughts and identifying problems; they should not have to fear rejection for expressing their opinion. In an environment that encourages the exchange of opinions, followers often provide important information to the leadership. It is particularly important that followers feel that they can question leaders when they think the leaders are wrong. When they do so, they assume leadership responsibilities themselves. Chaleff (1995) claims: "It is the willingness not to follow the leader on every issue that makes for outstanding followers". He uses the analogy of championship teams, which are composed of individuals who know when to follow the game plan and when to be innovative and deviate from the plan. Effective followers, like effective leaders, must be self-accepting, good communicators, and assertive, but not aggressive. Ideally they also are capable of self-management, assume responsibility for their own work and feel involved in the activities of the organization. Followers must be willing to address issues that would otherwise take up much of the leader's time and attention which can then be devoted to other important issues pertaining to the organization's goal (Lee and Kelly, 1988; Bennis and Nanus, 1985; Fiedler and Chemers, 1974). In other words, effective followers and leaders have many characteristics in common. What are considered leadership traits in one situation may be considered followership traits in another. Despite the fact that most of the characteristics for effective followers are considered those of leaders and effective leaders are more often followers than they are leaders, there still exists a line of distinction between leaders and followers.

The lack of a clear difference between followers and leaders is not a cause for concern but, as we will show, provides organizations with flexibility in how they deal with different issues. There are instances when a follower must become a leader. Even in a formal hierarchical organization, such as the military, expertise may temporarily outweigh rank. For example, in military exercises in a rugged mountain environment, the expert mountaineer will be expected to provide leadership and direction regardless of the presence of officers without such expertise who hold higher ranks. In this situation, these formal leaders become followers. In less formal hierarchies, individuals may change even more frequently from being followers to being leaders and back to being followers. In other words, most of us are simultaneously followers and leaders. For example, principals provide leadership to their schools, but they look for leadership on larger policy issues to the superintendent of the school district. At the work place, in the family, and elsewhere, individuals are leaders to one group or in one situation, and followers in others. If followers and leaders did not share important characteristics, such role changes would not be possible. The flexibility that results when members of an organization can switch roles has great value because it allows an organization to call on the person with the best qualifications to deal with a particular situation by assuming leadership responsibilities.

As indicated above, individuals frequently switch from being followers to being informal leaders. Although such informal leadership is very important to the smooth operation of organizations, there are functions and situations that require formal leadership. As we have shown, leaders do not emerge suddenly; they develop from the ranks of the followers.

Example 2.1

The career of Jim Perdue, son of Frank Perdue, owner of Perdue Poultry Farm, Inc., is an excellent example of a follower becoming a leader. While Frank was building the family business, Jim (son) followed closely in his father's footsteps. Jim was attentive to every detail that made his father a successful businessman and exhibited the traits of an effective follower. Upon his father's retirement, Jim inherited the family business. As the new formal leader, the characteristics that had made him an effective follower are now serving him in his leadership role.

Leadership is the ability to co-ordinate diverse groups of people and deal with different tasks in a changing and, sometimes, unstable environment. Leaders provide direction and vision, while keeping the mission of the organization in mind. The power of leadership derives from values and principles. Leadership is future-oriented; it looks ahead. This makes it the most important function for the long-term success of an organization. As Edward Barlow said, "The moral obligation of leadership is to think beyond your experience and plan beyond your tenure" (Heasley, 1997). This quotation expresses the importance of a clear vision for effective leadership.

Followers also determine the quality of leadership. Leaders can accomplish their goals only when followers accept the vision and agree with the goals. To gain acceptance, leaders must know their followers and understand what motivates them. Thus, leaders must develop good interpersonal skills and be able to work with groups. They need these skills because leaders at times have to teach, train and motivate their followers. The ability to work with groups is needed when there are inter-group or intra-group conflicts and to build effective teams. How managers lead their employees and delegate tasks and responsibilities determines the success of the work unit and, ultimately, the organization (Barge, 1994; Covey, 1992; Fairholm, 1994).

Successful leadership is measured by team performance and by the nature of the relationship between leaders and followers. Effective leaders create an environment characterized by mutual respect and establish the direction for the group. They have the capability of motivating others to work with them in pursuit of common goals and gain the group members' commitment to follow them. Some leaders have vision but lack team-building skills. Other leaders can inspire, motivate people and build teams, but lack vision and direction. The most outstanding leaders combine these skills. They plan, organize, co-ordinate, supervise, direct, communicate and delegate. They also accept responsibility for achieving the organization's goals.

Leaders are concerned with the future. There are no reliable road maps and no signposts to look forward to the future. Pioneering leaders, therefore, rely on a vision, dream, mission, or a personal agenda to focus and direct their actions. A vision is an ideal image of what the future could be. It spells out the destination and defines the guiding philosophy of the organization. To create a vision of the future, the leader must understand the environment in which the organization exists today and the one in which it will exist tomorrow. According to the Chinese proverb: "A vision without an action is a daydream, and action without a vision is a nightmare." To this effect, vision remains the hallmark of effective leadership, the element that creates opportunity for each individual to participate in the collective future of the organization. Without a vision leaders cannot ignite the flame of enthusiasm in their followers. A leader has to see things farther than a telescope and deeper than a microscope. The ability to develop a vision and to gain support for it is, therefore, an important quality for effective leadership.

Communication is another very important quality of effective leadership; leaders must communicate the vision in a way that attracts and excites members of the organization. This is particularly important if the vision entails significant departures from the status quo. Many members will view such a vision as risky and will be reluctant to accept it without information on how change could benefit them and the organization. The past holds many lessons for the future and reflecting upon the past experience will enhance a leader's ability to think about the future. Effective leaders are also skilled at recognizing the good ideas and learning the perspectives of followers and are willing to support them. Ideas from employees should be given serious consideration. Employees have detailed knowledge of the organization that may not otherwise be available to the leader. Followers who know that their ideas are being taken seriously will also be more willing to make the leader's vision their own and assume responsibility for change. A vision that is clearly communicated and explained results in a sense of shared purpose, identity, and unity within the organization. Acceptance of a vision depends on the respect of the leader among the followers. Respect is earned and based on past actions and behaviours. Leaders can be tough and demanding, but they must have credibility and be trusted. Honesty and integrity are, therefore, two important characteristics of leaders. There is also evidence that leading by example and/or persuasion is more successful than leading by command. In other words, asking employees to follow seems to work better, to energize and excite employees toward a vision of the future, than ordering them to follow a path determined by the leadership (Miller, 1988; Barge, 1994; Kouzes and Posner, 1995).

It takes practice to become a good leader. In today's fast-changing environment there is much demand for leadership. When the world around us changes, we welcome those who have a clear vision. Thus, in today's work there are many opportunities for practicing effective leadership (Barge, 1994; Covey, 1992).

Leadership Personality Types and Styles

Many readers may already be familiar with the personality types developed by psychologists. The Myers-Briggs test is the most popular among a number of commercially available personality tests. It is important to note that there is no single "best' personality. Each personality type has strengths and potential weaknesses. In fact, a characteristic that is considered strength in one situation can be a weakness in another. Leaders have distinctive personality types, it is possible, however, that most leaders share certain common characteristics.

According to the results of the study by Myers and Briggs (1993), leaders are usually extroverts, interested in getting the job done and seeing results. The term "extrovert' describes individuals who receive their stimulation from interaction with others. By contrast, introverts derive stimulation and satisfaction from working by themselves. All of us have characteristics of both the introvert and the extrovert. It is not all that surprising that leaders tend to be individuals who obtain satisfaction and stimulation from working with other people and who like action and variety.

Myers and Briggs also describe different characteristics related to problem solving. They distinguish between intuitive types, thinking (analytically minded) types and judging types. Those with intuitive-type personalities like solving problems but tend to be impatient with routine and details. Leaders with thinking-type personalities prefer analysis and logical order. They are analysis-oriented and respond more easily to people's thought. Judging-type personalities work best when they can plan and make programmes and complete their work as required (Myers and Briggs, 1993). All three characteristics have value. An intuitive approach often reveals creative options to approaching an issue. A thinking approach may prevent mistakes because of careful analysis that takes into consideration all relevant information. A judging approach may be best for implementing plans. In other words, the traits and characteristics described here are complementary. Good leadership sometimes consists of making sure that they all are present and used when important decisions are being made.

Leadership is about getting to know oneself and the organization and its members. It is also about learning from the past, and learning how to recognize and evaluate opportunities. Leadership is, therefore, related to how we learn. Learning styles are usually divided into four basic types.

1. *Divergers thrive on taking time to develop good ideas.* They tackle problems by first reflecting alone, then brainstorming with others. They need people who are supportive and share their sense of mission.

2. *Assimilators thrive on assimilating disparate facts into coherent theories.* They tackle problems through rational and logical thought. They work best with people who are well organized and follow through on agreed decisions.

3. *Convergers thrive on planning and tackle problems by making unilateral decisions.* They work best with people who are task-oriented.

4. *Accommodators thrive on crisis and challenge.* They tackle problems by looking for partners and scanning possibilities. They need others who provide follow up on planning details (Kolb, 1985).

As in the case of personality types, there is no single preferred learning style. Most people use different learning styles at different times but have one style that dominates. The variety of learning styles is one reason why important information should be presented in different forms, so that it may appeal to learners relying on different styles.

An individual's leadership style is the result of dominant personal traits. For an individual to be a successful leader these personal traits must be acceptable to followers (Bogardus, 1934). Just as there are different personality and learning styles, there are also different leadership styles. In this text only the most distinctive leadership styles are discussed:

(1) authoritarian;

(2) democratic;

(3) laissez-faire leadership.

Authoritarian Leadership

Authoritarian leadership, also called autocratic, is a leader-centered style. The leader makes all the important decisions. Followers obey reasonable and customary requests without questioning them. The leader's thoughts, ideas, and wishes are accepted and employees follow prescribed procedures strictly. Authoritarian leaders seldom consult those working under their supervision. They mould the actions of others to suit their own plans; they know what they want and forge ahead to accomplish it.

Autocratic leaders often exercise great personal power and seldom disclose any doubts that they might have. This leadership style can deteriorate into a coercive relationship with followers. The leader may feel threatened by them if followers do not live up to the leader's expectations. This leadership style may result in an unpleasant work environment for employees. Research findings indicate that the number and degree of aggressive acts are greatest in autocratically led groups. While autocratically led groups spend more time in productive work activity than groups using other leadership styles, they do so only when the leader is present. When the leader leaves the workplace, the amount of work-related activity drops dramatically. This is to be expected since the autocratic leaders leave little room for independent thought and work and achieve results as much through intimidation as motivation.

Authoritarian leaders are usually not dictatorial (although they can be ruthless and devoid of feelings). Such leaders may instead be benevolent autocrats and manipulative autocrats, respectively. Benevolent autocrats persuade employees to follow their orders by being so well liked that no one wants to be disloyal or "let the boss down'. The benevolent autocrat gives so much praise that employees are shamed into obedience. The manipulative autocrat creates the illusion that employees are participating in the decision making by "making them think they thought of it'. However, all decisions originate with the autocrat, who maintains firm control over the organization.

The only real difference among autocratic leaders is the manner in which they exercise control: through fear, personal charisma or manipulation. Over time, all autocratic leaders tend to surround themselves with "yes men', that is, followers who assume no responsibility but do what they are told. This combination of strong leaders and weak followers is often quite productive but is limited completely by the individual autocrat's ability. Success of an autocratically led organization, therefore, often lasts for only a limited period of time. If a leader becomes incapable of leading or leaves the organization, the result is often chaos and disintegration. An autocratically led organization is in particular danger in a fast-changing environment. When conditions change quickly, the constant need to collect and process new information and make decisions to adjust to change, are too demanding for one person. An autocratic leadership style may, however, work well when the leadership wants to effect dramatic change in an organization. Dramatic change can often be achieved only at a significant cost to some current members, or other constituents, of an organization and may, therefore, require a strong leader who is willing to accept negative feelings from at least some of the followers. In practice, once the adjustment to change is achieved and secured, the autocratic leader is often replaced by a leader with a different leadership style. The autocratic leadership style is not uncommon and is perhaps found most frequently in owner-managed businesses or in public institutions, particularly those organizations in developing countries.

Democratic Leadership

The democratic or participative leadership style grows out of the needs of the group. Democratic leaders encourage group members to assume leadership responsibilities. They suggest rather than order, and depend upon personal contacts and persuasion. They favour a shared decision making process, with the leader maintaining the ultimate responsibility for decisions but actively seeking input from followers. The leaders may delegate some decision making power to the group. Decision making mechanisms include consensus or majority vote; the participation of all members is encouraged. Needless to say, this style of leadership requires considerable skill working with groups. Without knowledge of group dynamics and the ability to lead a group in problem solving, decision making can become deadlocked. Followers must be ready to participate or intervene in group processes. A group that is experienced with participatory processes and is skillfully led, can be very effective. Participation in the decision making process stimulates employee involvement, identification with the organization and favourable attitudes toward work. Research findings (Fiedler and Chemers, 1974) indicate that employees with democratic leaders are usually the most satisfied and function in the most orderly and positive manner. The biggest disadvantages of a democratic leadership style are the skill requirements to make it work and the time it takes to reach decisions in a participatory process. This leadership style is, therefore, not appropriate for all institutions and situations.

Laissez-faire Leadership

Laissez-faire describes a free-rein leadership style that encourages employees to assume many of the leadership functions. To work well, this leadership style requires strong organizational skills. Leaders stay behind the scenes, allowing employees to work with minimal supervision. Since leaders cannot relinquish all decision making to followers, however, they must remain well informed of important developments. Leaders using this leadership style need to develop effective personnel evaluation techniques. If employees are en-

Table 2.1 Leadership Styles Comparison

Characteristics	*Autocratic*	*Democratic*	*Laissez-faire*
Decision making	Quick	Slow and expensive	Quick
Dealing with emergencies	Excellent	Poor	Unpredictable
Co-ordination of actions	Easy	Slow	Slow and difficult
Creativity	Depends on leader	Potentially high	High
Effecting organizational change	Can be done quickly	Difficult and slow to accomplish	Difficult and slow to accomplish
Employee "buy-in'	Unpredictable	Excellent	Can range from poor to excellent
Long-term organizational stability	Low beyond tenure of current leader	High	High
Supportive of delegation of responsibility	No	Yes	Yes
Supportive of teamwork	No	Yes	Unpredictable
Employee satisfaction	Tends to be low in the long-term	Tends to be high	Can be either high or low

trusted with many decisions, it becomes very important that employee skills and experience are well matched with their responsibilities. *Laissez-faire* leadership may work well in complex organizations that are engaged in the production of non-standardized products or services. In such organizations decisions, have to be made frequently and about many different issues, such that centralized decision making would be impractical. Colleges and universities are examples of organizations that use a free-rein leadership style. Among its costs are the time and effort necessary if they wish to co-ordinate decisions or to make significant organizational changes. This leadership style can lead to frustration among employees, particularly if they are unsure about the mission of the organization. In organizations that use this leadership style, one of the most important functions of the formal leaders is the development of a clear mission that translates into a vision and purpose common to all employees of the organization.

It is worth repeating that there are no typical behaviours and traits that are specific only to leaders. Although planning, organizing, controlling, and directing are thought of as typical leadership activities, they are also performed by employees who hold no formal leadership positions. Leaders and followers differ with respect to the frequency with which they engage in leadership activities and the extent to which they are held accountable for the results. In addition, leaders are held accountable not only for their own actions, but also for the actions of their followers.

As the comparisons in Table 2.1 demonstrate, there is no one best way to lead. Different decision situations and different organizational missions call for different leadership styles. All leadership styles have one requirement in common, as expressed in the following quotation.

> You can only lead others where you yourself are willing to go.
>
> (Bennis and Nanus, 1985)

In a similar vein:

> If you want to know whether you are a leader, see if there is someone following you.
>
> (Fiedler and Chemers, 1974)

Using an appropriate leadership style may be the key to obtaining the cooperation of those we wish to lead. We mentioned above that one leadership style works well in some organizations or situations but not in others. Therefore, as organizations (or the work environment) change, the leadership style may also need to change. Sometimes this is possible only if new leaders assume responsibility for the future progress of the organization, as not all leaders are able to adapt to a changed environment. A person's leadership style is not independent from their natural characteristics and personal traits. For a leadership style to be effective, it must therefore be compatible with the leader's personality.

Example 2.2

The following statement by Ted Turner, television station owner and general manager, is compatible with the personality he projects: "Leadership is a choice. The choice is yours, either to lead, follow or get out of the way of those who are doing it." It would not have the same impact if it did not come from a leader who has repeatedly demonstrated his willingness to assume great risks to forge ahead and who has kept trying to commit people to action and convert followers into leaders.

Former British Prime Minister Margaret Thatcher stated in a speech, that "you may have to fight a battle more than once to win it". Her statement conveys a message similar to Ted Turner's; to be a leader you must believe in what you do. You must be willing to take risks, even fight for your beliefs to accomplish tasks successfully.

CHAPTER THREE

TRANSITION TO LEADERSHIP

We cannot become what we need to be by remaining what we are.

Max De Pree, Leadership is a Performing Art

The transition from being a follower to being a leader is not always easy. There are differences in expectations and responsibilities. To be a good leader takes skills, experience and dedication. This chapter offers advice to those new to leadership and management positions, for making the *transition* successfully. In several respects, the role of the leader differs fundamentally from that of the follower. Behaviours that are appropriate for followers are not always appropriate for leaders. The purpose of this chapter is to explore the most important role differences between followers and leaders. The materials and organization of this chapter have been influenced by the ideas of Gmelch and Miskin (1993).

From Individual to Group Concerns

Followers tend to have little experience beyond their own work and responsibilities. Therefore, they tend to view the organization from their work's perspective. Leaders must adopt a more general outlook. They cannot afford to adopt a narrow point of view but must understand the organization and its needs as a whole; their decisions must reflect a broad view of the roles of the organization. In addition, whereas followers are expected to "do their job' and are not held responsible for what others do, leaders assume responsibility for the actions of those whom they lead. To be a leader means to act in ways that enable followers to serve the organization more effectively. Thus, the performance of followers reflects on the organization's leaders. The responsibility for collective performance also means that leaders get their satisfaction from the success of those whom they lead. By contrast, those who have no leadership responsibilities derive most of their satisfaction from their own accomplishments. Below are three examples of how leaders can facilitate the work of those in their charge.

1. *Keep followers informed*. Leaders must keep their followers informed of important goals and objectives, rules or events. If followers are ignorant of important information about the organization, it is often a sign of a weakness of the leadership. It may indicate lack of communication from

top to bottom and vice versa. The result is frustration and inefficiency.

2. *Remove institutional obstacles*. Managers may have to use their power to assist an employee. Particularly in organizations with well-developed hierarchies, employees may encounter obstacles that can be overcome only with the help of a manager.

Example 3.1

In early December John was preparing a bid on a project and needed the assistance of accounting to complete a budget. The deadline for submission of the bid was early–January. The accounting office was very busy getting ready to produce the annual financial report and gave John's request low priority. When John mentioned this to Veronica, his supervisor, she called the manager of accounting. She explained the importance of the task. Based on this information, the accounting manager assigned a staff person to work on John's budget so that it would get done quickly.

---

3. *Co-ordinate group efforts*. In most organizations employees do not have the authority to compel other employees at the same rank to work cooperatively with them. The co-ordination of efforts between employees and the establishment of teamwork and co-operation among employees will often depend on the support and initiative of the manager.

Unlike employees without leadership responsibility, leaders are held accountable for their actions and for the actions of their followers. They are also assigned responsibility for the welfare of their followers, as the following example illustrates.

Example 3.2

Jim is a scout leader. He recently took his troop on a backpacking trip. He was well aware that he assumed responsibility for the safety of the troop. In preparation for the trip, therefore, he carefully studied the map of the area he was planning to visit and marked places on the map that had hazardous terrain. He also called a friend who had visited the same area the year before to discuss the planned route with him. To help the scouts to get ready for the trip, he provided them with a list of items to bring along. This list included food, clothing and equipment. He also made a list for himself. His list included a first aid kit which he had put together with the advice of a friend who was an experienced scout leader and medical doctor. During the week before the scheduled trip, Jim checked the weather forecast every day. Before leaving on the trip he gave a copy of the planned route and schedule to his wife and another copy to a fellow scout leader. When he assembled his troop the day of the trip, he checked their equipment, shoes, and made sure that they had made the necessary preparations. Only after checking and making sure that everything was in order did they depart on their trip.

Jim's preparations and precautions reflect his responsibility for the welfare and safety of his troop. A manager in a business firm also assumes such responsibility. For example, if employees have to work with machinery, the manager is responsible for their training. If an employee is assigned to work with equipment without first having been properly instructed, the firm may assume greater financial liability if there is an accident. The manager's leadership responsibility in such cases extends beyond training of employees and includes appropriate supervision.

There are other reasons why leaders often have to put their own interests second to those of others. To lead sometimes requires acts of unselfishness. Managers and leaders must consider how their actions affect customers, employees, other departments and other managers. Employees tend to have considerably more leeway.

Example 3.3

A few months ago Robert was promoted to supervisor of his department. Before his promotion he would sometimes criticize decisions by the firm's leadership when talking with colleagues. Although he still does not agree with all decisions handed down, he no longer comments on them in public. Robert fears that his employees will not back him when he tries to implement the management's decisions unless he supports the management and only voices his concerns and disagreements privately in meetings with his superiors.

Leaders who fail to take the concerns of others into consideration will lose the respect of their followers, the support of other leaders within the organization and the support of their constituents. To lead means to inspire others toward the accomplishment of common goals. This definition of leadership really summarizes why leaders must understand *and* serve the concerns of others. Leaders who are perceived as selfish will not persuade many to support them in achieving their goals.

Although there are times when leaders must put their own interest behind that of others, it is important that they do not neglect their personal needs. To be unselfish all of the time will lead to burnout and the feeling of being taken advantage of. Over time, leaders must be able to meet their most important needs (and those of their families). Leaders may have to postpone satisfying their own needs in the interest of the common good of the organization but they should not ignore them. While employees may also be occasionally asked to make sacrifices for the common good, leaders have a special responsibility in this regard.

Example 3.4

John was the manager of the accounting department of a manufacturing firm. A member of the department was seriously ill and other staff members had to work extra hours to ensure that the department did not fall behind in meeting the needs of the firm. Thus, when Labor Day approached, John reminded all staff members that he would not approve any requests for taking an extra day off. Without his knowledge, however, John's wife had arranged a surprise weekend at a resort that would require him to take an extra day off. She told him about it only a week before the Labor Day weekend. John, who had been working long hours himself, felt guilty for not taking more time to be with his family and decided that he would spend the weekend with his family.

John's desire to spend more time with his family was justified. Likewise, it was also justifiable for the staff members of the department to spend more time with their families. As the leader of his department, however, John set a poor example by requiring a commitment from his employees that he was not willing to make himself. Actions like this undermine the credibility of the leader who will be perceived as self-serving by others.

From Focused to Fragmented

Most occupations without leadership responsibility are focussed on a relatively small set of well-defined tasks. This is not true for a typical leadership position. It is a paradox that the most powerful individuals with the most responsibility have the least control over their time. To function well they *must be* responsive to their constituents and cannot afford to ignore their legitimate needs. Leaders meet with clients, discuss concerns of employees, give advice on technical problems, approve funding for a new project, represent the firm at public events, evaluate a new marketing strategy, judge an idea for a new product, participate in a strategic planning meeting, etc. The diversity of tasks increases with the level of responsibility. To remain effective when there are so many diverse demands on their time and expertise, leaders must have good work habits and effective time management. They must also learn to empower and delegate responsibilities to their followers, a skill that we discuss in Chapter 9 of this book.

Example 3.5

Ruth had recently been promoted to manager of a large department. She had been looking forward to her new responsibilities. She was well aware that she had been chosen over other applicants because she had presented plans for improving the processes and products of the department. A few weeks into the job, she felt the pressure to implement some of her ideas but had difficulties finding the time to plan the necessary actions. Her daily schedule was fragmented. It often started with a meeting, then one or two hours in the office, lunch with a client, etc. She also had to respond to correspondence. Even when nothing was scheduled she was frequently interrupted by phone calls. Ruth felt frustrated. She was fortunate that her predecessor in the office had taken an interest in her success. Ruth decided to ask for her advice.

The advice she received was simple. If possible, come to the office an hour earlier, when few people are around and the phones are not yet busy. During those quiet hours work on the items that have the greatest impact on the department's long-term success. When you are in the office at other times during the day, have your secretary answer and screen the phone calls. Return calls later, after you have accomplished what you needed to get done. Prepare an agenda and time schedule for those meetings that you control. Allow some time for "small talk' at the beginning of the meeting, but make sure you get to the agenda items in a timely fashion and deal with them efficiently. If an agenda takes much longer to deal with than initially planned, it may be best to schedule a follow-up meeting to finish the business.

New leaders are often unprepared for the many diverse demands on their time. They sometimes think "it will get better' once they have adjusted to their new responsibilities. Unless the new leader recognizes fragmentation of the schedule as a normal part of her role, however, the situation is more likely to get worse, not better. Only if she accepts and adjusts her work habits to the diverse demands of her new position, will she be able to regain a reasonable measure of control over her time.

From Autonomy to Accountability

Within many organizations, individual members retain a fairly high degree of de facto autonomy, i.e. if they complete their tasks in a responsible fashion, their actions will not be scrutinized. To formally make every individual member account for their actions would be too time consuming. The actions of leaders are more likely to be noticed. Leaders, therefore, no longer enjoy the relative autonomy they were accustomed to before they assumed leadership responsibilities. They are more likely to be held accountable by superiors and by followers who observe their leaders' actions. Accountability without control is stressful. Although leaders cannot exercise complete control over everything, they may be held accountable for actions of their followers. While this may seem unfair to some, it serves a useful function, as the following example illustrates.

Example 3.6

George was the manager of a pharmacy. His pharmacy business had grown significantly and he had, therefore, hired another pharmacist to assist him. The new pharmacist was a fairly recent graduate with little professional experience. One of George's clients was an elderly woman, who came regularly to have her prescription filled. George was aware that she had some allergies that prevented her from taking certain medications. He had been too busy, however, to show his new assistant where all the records were kept. When the customer came to the pharmacy, George had just left for a quick lunch. His assistant filled the customer's prescription. He gave her a generic brand because her medical insurance paid for it in full whereas it paid only a portion of the brand name medication. The assistant did not know that the generic brand contained ingredients that triggered some of the customer's allergic reactions. It was very fortunate that George returned from his lunch just as the assistant was ringing up the order. George remembered the elderly woman's allergies and checked the order. He noticed the error and quickly corrected it. After the customer had left, he talked to the assistant. George was not angry with him, only with himself because he realized that he had not given the assistant all the information he needed.

Although the assistant should have asked the customer about allergies, George realized that the responsibility for the mistake was his. It was his job to properly train the assistant and give him the necessary information before letting him make decisions without supervision.

Former United States President Harry Truman was aware of his responsibility as a leader; he realized that he would be held accountable for his decisions and actions. He expressed his acceptance of this with a sign on his desk: "The buck stops here.' Such an attitude is important for a leader's credibility. Because they hold responsibilities that others do not, leaders are given special privileges and powers. If they do not use their power for the benefit of the organization, or if they reject the accountability that comes with power, they will lose respect and stop being effective.

From Private to Public

There is anonymity in numbers. Individual members of an organization, therefore, enjoy a great deal of privacy. By assuming a leadership role, they step out from the crowd into a position where they are much more visible. The result of taking this responsibility is a loss of privacy. Leaders are much more in the public eye than other members of the organization. Therefore, they have to be more careful about what they do, say and even how they dress. Leaders represent not only themselves but also the organization. Representing one's organization is an important leadership responsibility. To be effective representatives, leaders should seek contact with constituents, other leaders within the organization, and anyone else whose actions might impact their organization. In other words, leaders play a public role if they are to be effective.

Example 3.7

Monica had recently been promoted to manager of her department. She was surprised when a friend told her what she had heard from others. Monica was hurt by some of the critical comments because she had put a lot of thought and effort into her first few weeks in the new position. Worse yet, the comments were inconsistent. Some employees liked the informal style she used to conduct the weekly staff meeting; others, however, interpreted her openness to the ideas of staff as a possible weakness. Opinions were also divided about her plans to give employees more authority to make decisions. Monica felt confused and frustrated. How should she react to these situations?

This example illustrates several issues. First, you cannot react to all comments you hear about yourself, if for no other reason than that they are often incompatible with each other. Second, it is very dangerous to take comments personally, particularly those based on hearsay. If you are concerned about an issue identified in a comment, follow it up and find out more about the causes of the negative comment. You must be careful, however, about how you follow up. Confronting the person who made the comments is appropriate only if the comments are defamatory and/or hurt the efficient working of the organization. Otherwise, individuals in positions of power and visibility must develop immunity to irrelevant criticisms, even if they are unfair.

Example 3.8

Jane tends to be a somewhat critical judge of the work of others, including the work of her supervisor. She has never expressed herself inappropriately, however, or in front of customers. The comments are usually based on facts and usually identify real weaknesses. Her performance evaluations acknowledge that Jane also sets a high standard for herself. The evaluations make no mention of her critical nature as a detriment to her work. A year ago John became her supervisor. He likes her work but cannot stand her critical comments, particularly those that reflect on work in which he was involved. On several occasions he confronted her in front of others. Jane felt intimidated by his reaction and has become worried that John might punish her by giving her a poor performance appraisal. She has therefore stopped offering her opinion and keeps much more to herself. She now only rarely offers comments and never when John is around.

Because leaders hold power over their followers, they must be careful how they interact with them. John may feel that Jane is disrespectful to him when she comments critically. By confronting her in front of others, however, he has intimidated her. As a result, she no longer offers him her advice and has become a less active team member. If John had reason to be concerned about the way in which she offered her comments, he should have focussed on that, and not in front of others.

Finally, do not expect yourself to be perfect. Everybody will occasionally make mistakes. Rather than listening and reacting to haphazard comments, ask a trusted friend or a mentor how you are doing; rely on solicited feedback from people you trust and who have demonstrated sound judgement in the past.

From Joining Teams to Building Teams

Many tasks in organizations require teamwork. Leaders are responsible for the formation of teams. While some teams may form at the initiative of a few employees, teams need resources and other support to be effective over a long period of time. Very often only managers can command the necessary resources. They generally also have a broader perspective on the needs of the organization and can, therefore, better assess what responsibilities should be assigned to a team rather than individual employees. The leader's knowledge of their staff's strengths and weaknesses can also be very helpful in selecting team members who complement each other and work well together. When teams experience conflicts, leaders may serve as facilitators and arbitrators. Finally, leaders have the responsibility to assign appropriate goals and authority to teams. They also ensure that team members understand the role and know the limits of their power to implement decisions. Techniques for team building are discussed in detail in Chapter 10 of this book.

It is possible for a formal leader, such as a department manager, to be a member of a team that consists of members of her staff. It is important, however, that she play the role of team member, not that of "boss'. Therefore, the manager should be clear of the role she wishes to play on the team. Does she want to be the team leader or would she prefer that someone else assume the leadership? In the latter case, the team leader must be made to feel comfortable that she will accept her role as just another team member. It is difficult to drop the primary role and assume a new role. The leader may not be able to let go of her power. The other members of the team may worry that opposing their leader may have repercussions outside of the team. It is therefore probably best if leaders do not join teams consisting of their followers, unless it is in the leadership position.

CHAPTER FOUR

ROADBLOCKS TO EFFECTIVE LEADERSHIP

Our greatest glory is not in never failing, but in rising every time we fall.

Confucius

There are behaviours of leaders or followers that diminish a leader's effectiveness. An example of counterproductive behaviour is that of a manager who tries to capitalize on past achievements that are unrelated to current leadership responsibilities. Counterproductive behaviours also include attempts to gain an advantage from the name recognition and reputation of a parent, other relative or friend. These are not legitimate criteria to claim a leadership position. What matters is who *you* are or what you know. The following are relevant criteria because they reflect the skills and insights necessary to be or become a good leader.

1. Experience enables leaders to anticipate opportunities and problems and may have provided them with insight in how to deal with them.

2. Communication skills help leaders express their vision and persuade others to follow them.

3. Formal training prepares individuals for leadership roles.

Leadership training should enhance positive skills. In addition, training can help overcome weaknesses by identifying behaviours and attitudes that diminish leadership effectiveness. Four of the most common negative behaviours of leaders are (Miller, 1988):

(a) trying to be perfect; avoiding mistakes at all costs;

(b) trying to please everyone; avoiding conflicts;

(c) failing to adapt a broader perspective, being involved in details of the organization;

(d) being a follower instead of a leader.

Avoiding Mistakes by Trying to be Perfect

Perfection is a desirable standard but expensive or even impossible to achieve. We should measure the results of efforts against the best outcome possible, not to determine how far we have fallen short, but to decide whether or not we *should* have done better. That is, the highest known standard, an ideal outcome, is used as a benchmark but not necessarily as a goal. Deviations from ideal outcomes may be unavoidable because of time and/or financial constraints. Further improving an already outstanding product is often not cost-effective. In other words, it may be more beneficial for an organization to trade off quality for timeliness and lower cost.

Example 4.1

Alexander is a high achiever and hard worker. Everyone says, "give him the project if you want it done right". His excellent work is the reason he was promoted to manager. But because Alexander dislikes substandard performance, he gives his employees only a few small tasks at a time and checks everything they do. Whenever possible, he completes most of the important assignments himself. There is only one way to do things in his department and that is his way. Alexander does not tolerate deviations from what he considers standard procedures. He is a stickler for details.

Such behaviour can easily lead to problems with employee morale. It also is likely to result in a manager who is burdened with more work than he can handle. We have often observed that employees who feel themselves "up to the neck' in work are reluctant to accept change because they do not want to add to their stress.

A few months ago Alexander's senior manager ordered the installation of a new computer system. All of the department's employees were asked to complete a training programme to become familiar with the new system. *Alexander* did not like the introduction of the new system; he was already working at full capacity.

The example illustrates what problems may arise if a manager is so concerned with avoiding mistakes that he does not trust his employees with important work. Even if a leader assigns important work to employees, the effects of perfectionism are negative.

Example 4.2

George had been a manager at another firm before joining his current department. In that previous position he had experienced failure. It was clear that the failure was not related to his performance but was due to events

---

that nobody in the firm had anticipated. George's supervisor did not blame him for the failure. On the contrary, his performance appraisal was positive and he commended George for efforts that averted even more damage. George, however, blamed himself and resolved not to let something similar happen again. When he had the opportunity to move to his current position, he quickly took it. After half a year on the job, however, he was encountering serious morale problems among his employees. They resented the very tight supervision and complained that George was constantly looking over their shoulders. They felt that George did not trust and respect their professional skills.

According to Miller (1988), the following are common characteristics of perfectionists.

1. Doing everything yourself results in stress and low productivity. In fact, you are not going to get very far until you stop trying to do everything yourself.

2. Not asking for help from fellow employees results in inefficiencies.

3. Difficulty in adapting to change results in lack of progress.

4. Excessive use of rules or following the formal organizational red-tape results in "doing it the hard way'. It pays off to respond flexibly to different situations.

5. Fear of being wrong results in lack of initiative and reluctance to exploit opportunities.

6. Not delegating tasks and authority results in lack of opportunities for training and development of employees.

7. Over-supervising or over-controlling results in lack of initiative exercised by employees.

8. Lack of respect for ideas of others results in low employee morale and motivation.

9. Uneasiness with uncertain conditions or functions results in lost time and lost opportunities.

10. Resisting constructive criticism results in a lack of feedback that could lead to better management practices and the full development of leadership potential.

It seems ironic that the desire to be perfect is likely to create inefficiencies and, instead, lead to low productivity. Aaron Miller (1988) offers this advice: "No one is perfect and no one can make it without help." Leaders should look to their followers for ideas, advice and help. The following are steps to help overcome too strong a tendency towards perfectionism (Miller, 1988).

1. Recognize that you are trading personal approval and personal rewards for effectiveness in your department. Managing is not doing everything yourself but getting work done. Leaders are evaluated on the basis of how well they motivate their followers to work with them towards common goals and how effectively they lead them to reach those goals. Your department's performance will improve and increase when you let go of the 'doer' role and assume the leadership role.

2. Evaluate your standards and judge the cost of achieving a more perfect result against the cost of doing so. Consult with members of your team.

3. Give yourself permission to be less than perfect, risk being wrong. Seek feedback from your employees. Their reaction can help you find your weaknesses, the first and most important step toward improving management and leadership skills. Change your goal from avoiding mistakes to obtaining better results.

4. Learn from the behaviours and traits of successful leaders. Use a role model, such as a father/mother, an outstanding teacher or an effective manager.

5. Show trust and confidence in your employees. Give them responsibilities and opportunities to develop their skills.

According to Stenmark (1994), the greatest mistake a leader can make is to be fearful of making mistakes.

Example 4.3

A journalist and a Company Executive Officer (CEO) met at a social event. The journalist asked the CEO, "What does it take to be a good leader?" The CEO answered, "Good decisions." The journalist asked again, "How do you learn to make good decisions?" The CEO said, "Experience is a good teacher." The journalist added, "How do you gain experience?" The CEO confidently replied, "Bad decisions."

In addition, an old man who was dying said, "If I had my life to live all over again, I would try to make many mistakes." There is nothing dreadful about making mistakes. Forget perfection; perhaps it does not exist. Strive for excellence instead.

Avoiding Conflict by Pleasing Everyone

It is impossible to please everyone all of the time. Along the same line of thinking, Benjamin Franklin said, "I cannot give you a formula for success, but here is the formula for failure: Try to please everybody." This common knowledge should be enough to keep people from even trying to avoid conflicts by pleasing everyone. However, we all enjoy being liked. Individuals who have a particularly strong need to be liked, or individuals who cannot deal with conflict, are at risk of engaging in behaviours that are doomed to failure.

Example 4.4

Fletcher, a newly promoted branch manager of an insurance company, did not want to offend his superiors by telling them that his office was already working at capacity and would not be able to do additional work without being given more time. His senior supervisor therefore continued to give him additional assignments. When his employees complained of too much work, he did some of the work himself because he did not want to confront them. The inefficient allocation of work resulted in the deterioration of performance in his office. Senior supervisors began to doubt Fletcher's capacity to be an effective branch manager when assignments were not completed by the time promised. Morale was low and employees felt overwhelmed with work. Fletcher also felt frustrated and his self-confidence was low as he realized that he had lost the trust and respect of both his superiors and employees.

The following are some typical blocking characteristics that help identify behaviours of leaders engaged in avoiding conflicts by 'pleasing everyone' (Miller, 1988).

1. Inability to say no. Individuals who cannot say no are likely to over-commit themselves and experience excessive stress. When they become unable to keep promises because they have stretched themselves too thin, they lose the trust of their followers and senior managers.

2. Avoiding dealing with problems usually makes them worse. If the problem is one of employee performance, not dealing with the problem results in further deterioration and low morale among other employees who have to make up the slack.

3. Individuals who avoid confronting problems may instead resort to hints and illusions. Such indirect forms of communication are very ineffective and usually result in misunderstandings and missed directions.

4. Wanting to be liked is excessive when the result is avoidance of giving direction, feedback and guidance. The leader is shortchanging everyone when "not offending' takes precedence over the interests of the organization.

It feels good to be liked and being liked can help establish a strong power base for effective leadership. We already mentioned, however, the dangers of making the desire of being liked the primary criterion for guiding our actions. While the danger is obvious, we are often unaware that to be liked is one of the strongest motives for what we do. This is a positive motive. It prevents us from acting without regard for the feelings of others. Concern for how our actions affect others is a prerequisite for co-operation. It is only when the desire to be liked takes precedence over everything else, that it becomes a problem. The following are steps to deal with this problem (Miller, 1988):

1. Recognize that being liked is the result of integrity, fairness, effective leadership, and efficient management. If being liked becomes the goal, effective leadership almost always suffers and resulting problems will reduce how well the leader is liked.

2. Do not make promises you cannot keep. Broken promises always create mistrust among your followers.

3. Say no to unreasonable demands; do not feel guilty for saying so.

4. Confront problems and work to address them without having to "give in'.

5. Communicate your ideas, wishes and concerns clearly and directly with conviction but allow for feedback. Do not use indirect communication such as hints and allusions (they rarely work).

6. Implement decisions in a timely fashion.

7. Change your goal from wanting to be liked to being a fair and effective leader. If you accomplish this goal, you will at least be respected; being liked often follows.

8. Be honest. People like and respect honest leaders. Do not cover up problems or constraints but explain them. Superiors and employees will find it much easier to accept problems if they know about and understand them.

In the long run employees will like and respect those leaders who assist them in identifying and correcting their problems. Honest, respectful and direct communication is not offensive in the long-term, even if it causes hard feelings in the short-term. The potential for misunderstandings, conflicts and frustrations is reduced when expectations are clearly communicated. Do not trade being respected for being liked. Leadership without the respect of followers is not possible. In the long run followers respect leaders when they address problems in a professional manner and with honest communication.

Failing to Adopt a Broader Perspective

The transition into leadership can be particularly difficult for technical experts who are promoted into management positions. By definition, technical experts deal in relatively narrow areas. Their job responsibilities reflect their specialization. As they assume management or supervision responsibilities they must broaden their perspective. Specialists who focus on technical problems or processes often fail to see organizational or interpersonal problems (or opportunities). These characteristics may make them reluctant to assume responsibilities that do not rely on their technical expertise. The following example illustrates the negative impact of relying on technical skills instead of focusing on management skills to lead the organization effectively (Miller, 1988).

Example 4.5

Maria is an outstanding accountant. She is also a hard worker who knows her department better than the other accountants. When a supervisory position opened up, Maria was promoted on the basis of her outstanding performance record. She continued to work as hard on accounting tasks as before, in addition to serving as the department supervisor. After a while she began to lose personnel who quit or transferred to other departments. Her employees complained that she did not trust them to do the work as well as she could. They also suspected that she kept the most interesting and challenging accounts for herself.

This type of behaviour is not uncommon among newly promoted supervisors. It points to two issues. First, technical skills do not guarantee leadership skills. The selection of new supervisors must also consider interpersonal skills. Furthermore, leadership skills must be developed through proper training. A person should not be given responsibility without being first prepared for it. Second, the new supervisor must change her behaviour to reflect her new role. She cannot take on the leadership role without giving up some of her prior work responsibilities. When such adjustments are omitted, several problems may occur.

1. As demonstrated in the previous example, the supervisor's behaviour may create a barrier to employee growth and development.

2. Too much emphasis on the technical aspects of the job can result in neglect of other responsibilities, such as co-ordination of efforts with other units.

Maria was focussed on her work as an accountant and had not learned about "the bigger picture'. For example, she did not know what information other departments needed, when they needed it, or how to co-ordinate efforts with them. Maria was still stuck in her technical, specialist role. She continued to rely on her technical skills instead of broadening her perspective and learning about the role of her department in the organization and its relationship to other departments. What she needed were management skills, such as planning, organizing, co-ordinating, delegating and leading. Unfortunately, Maria had not developed the ability to see how each job contributed to the mission of the department or how her department fit into the larger organization. Maria can only become a stronger leader of her department if she leaves the detailed orientation and specialized work to her employees.

Following Instead of Leading

As we have stressed repeatedly, new supervisors and junior managers have to *learn* to assume leadership responsibilities. Making decisions can be intimidating. Often a decision has to be made without full information of all issues involved. This can be stressful for experienced managers; it can be outright scary for new managers. A junior manager is therefore well advised to ask for advice and help. However, it is important that the manager does not delegate the responsibility for the decision to those who advise him.

Example 4.6

Tom had recently been promoted and was worried about what others might think about his leadership. Rather than risk making mistakes, he let his boss, or sometimes others, make important decisions. At first his superior welcomed Tom's questions. He remembered his own difficulties when he first became a manager and was also flattered that Tom seemed to value his advice. Tom's superior became worried, however, when he saw that Tom did not make any important decisions without consulting with him. He therefore talked to Tom and told him that managers must learn to act independently and make important decisions based on their judgement, after evaluating the available information.

Tom was still acting as a follower. The success of Tom's department depends on his developing confidence in leading. Tom has to make the transition from being a follower to being a leader. Managers who find it difficult to be leaders may benefit from emulating the behaviours of an effective leader they respect. However, what makes a good leader in one situation does not necessarily work in another situation; 'one size does not fit all'. While it is true that what works for one leader may not work for another, we can learn from the experience and example of effective leaders. Many leaders became successful because a more senior leader took an interest in them and helped them when they first started in management.

In every organization there is a division of labour among individuals and departments. For the efficient working of the organization it is important that each member understands the assigned responsibilities and carries them out.

The analogy with the parts of the human body may help you visualize how each part of the body has its functions. They work together so well precisely because each part does its job well. Ears can only be ears to hear things. Eyes can only be eyes to see things. But eyes and ears can do many things together. Likewise, an employee is assigned to work as an employee and a manager to be a manager. Imagine what would happen to an organization if an employee without management training tried to take the place of a manager and a manager who did not have the necessary technical expertise, the place of an employee. It is evident that the organization would not function properly. However, a manager and employees, with good co-operation, can do many things together and the outcome is productivity and job satisfaction. The difference between a leader and a boss is explained in the following statement. The contrasts highlighted in the following parable can help us better understand the meaning of effective leadership:

> Be a leader not a boss.
> The boss drives his men.
> The leader inspires them.
> The boss depends on authority .
> The leader depends on goodwill.
> The boss involves fear.
> The leader radiates love.
> The boss says "I'.
> The leader says "We'.
> The boss knows who is wrong.
> The leader knows what is wrong.
> The boss knows how it is done.
> The leader knows how to do it.
> The boss demands respect.
> The leader commands respect.
> So be a leader, but not a boss.
>
> *Anonymous*

CHAPTER FIVE

ESSENTIAL TRAITS FOR EFFECTIVE LEADERSHIP

He who learns but does not think is lost.
He who thinks but does not learn is in great danger.

Confucius

What is the character dimension of leadership? To what standards should we hold our leaders? Common sense tells us that our behaviour is determined both by our voluntary intent, by what we would like to do or think we ought to do, and by factors which are to a greater or lesser extent outside our control. The behaviours of leaders are more strongly determined by internal drive and motivation than by external situations than is true for others. In other words, one of the characteristics of highly effective leaders is that they overcome external factors that may be barriers. Particularly creative individuals even manage to turn barriers into opportunities.

The ability to lead effectively is incremental and is accumulated one step at a time. As Posner and Kouzes (1998) indicate, the key to lasting improvement is small wins – the sure way to achieve extraordinary milestones is leadership development. Leadership is an observable, learnable set of practices. It can be learned just as one can learn to be a doctor or an engineer. Leadership is a performing art; the instrument is the self. All of us have the potential and capacity for leadership. The belief that leadership cannot be learned is a far more powerful deterrent to development than the nature of the leadership process itself. There are many opportunities to gain leadership experience in our daily lives. We acquire such experience without even thinking about it. Much of that experience is gained in fulfilling responsibilities to our families. Parents who are active in their children's schools or who serve as coaches of youth sports teams, assume leadership roles. Organizing a large family gathering often takes the leadership of one or more family members.

There are also opportunities at work. There is no clean break between followers and leaders. We have different expectations of a senior employee than of an employee who just started on the job. The difference is usually in how much leadership we expect. For example, we frequently ask senior employees to introduce new employees to their jobs. We give the senior employees this responsibility even when they have no formal leadership assignments.

We can question the relevance of leadership experience gained in one environment to our ability to provide leadership in a different environment.

Based on our experience we have come to believe that the basic nature of leadership does not change and that the experience can be transferred from one environment to another. It is intuitively clear that our basic personality affects how we act at work, when we are with friends, and when we are at home. We cannot be leaders with one set of standards when we are at work, and then become a different kind of person, especially with lower standards, when we are away from the work (Posner and Kouzes, 1998). Leadership is about the whole person because it reflects our values and attitudes.

Although everyone has a capacity for leadership not everyone will become a formal leader. Those who wish to lead, however, can transform themselves to become leaders, regardless of their age, gender or ethnicity. Becoming a leader is an act of free will; if you have the will to lead you will find ways to become a leader. Of course, not all who want to lead will be good leaders. Good leaders rise to the top in spite of their weaknesses (Abraham Lincoln) while bad leaders rise because of their weaknesses (Adolph Hitler). Bad leaders often use personal charm but also threats, coercion, and violence to impose their will and vision on others. However, effective leadership, which promotes the good of the organization, cannot be achieved in this fashion. Bad leaders are those who fail to address their weaknesses (Bennis, 1989).

Leadership traits are personal qualities that are helpful in leading others. The review of the literature indicates that 'good leadership traits' are: democratic values, vitality, a positive attitude, friendliness, trustworthiness, perseverance, alertness, bearing, courage, decisiveness, dependability, endurance, power (influence), humility, humour, initiative, integrity, intelligence, judgement, loyalty, tact and unselfishness. By contrast, 'bad leadership traits' are: indifference, narrowness, timidity, egotism, silliness, fickleness and stubbornness. There may be other traits that individual leaders possess that characterize them as good or bad leaders (Wishart, 1965; Brown, 1958). What is positive or negative depends on several factors, including the combination of traits and the extent to which they are present.

Traits are dynamic. They are important relative to the interpersonal context and the value of each depends on the situation and objective realities (Hollander, 1978). Good leaders are aware of the beneficial traits that they possess and those that they are lacking. They work on eliminating bad traits and refine and nurture their good traits. However, traits that we consider positive, others may view as negative. For example, you may think of yourself as determined and persevering. Others, however, may view you as inflexible and stubborn. The very desire to act as a leader may be viewed as negative. Richard Lynch (1993) writes: "One who begins to assume a leadership role is often seen as a disruptive influence and a threat to the established order." Because we are sometimes challenged when we try to lead, it is important that we believe in the validity of our vision and act with integrity and honesty.

Example 5.1

Mr Honda of Honda automobiles had a passion for change and a passion for improvements that made his company the source of many breakthroughs in automotive and engine technology. Although Mr Honda was not always liked by his peers, he is admired today as someone who has had a large impact on the automobile industry (Lynch, 1993).

Qualities of Successful Leaders

Essential management and leadership skills, like any other skills, are acquired through formal and informal training, and enhanced through practice. As David Kearns indicated, "in the race for quality, there is no finish line". Even the most distinguished leaders had to acquire the skills that made them effective. Leaders are made, not born. There are important behaviours and traits that make managers successful leaders. The following list of characteristics of effective leaders has been adapted from Miller (1988) and Kouzes (1993).

1. *The ability and personal commitment to develop and nurture co-operation and team spirit.* The intellectual and emotional commitment to working together as one team is important for promoting efficiency and productivity in an organization.

2. *The ability to help the organization make changes and transform itself to meet opportunities and challenges.* Leaders who do not encourage their followers to be innovative are unlikely to succeed in the long-term because today's dynamic environment requires adaptation and change from all organizations. Thus, effective leaders feel responsible for creating an organizational structure and a work environment that rewards innovation. They have a high level of involvement in formal and informal communication networks. This helps them to recognize and respond to challenges and opportunities.

3. *Effective leaders tend to have an anticipatory and positive attitude.* They are comfortable with uncertainty and ambiguity; the ability to plan and prepare for the unexpected or the low probability event is a necessary trait in management. Many decisions made in organizations (especially as one moves up the ladder of management) involve situations for which you may not have enough information to make a decision.

4. *Effective leaders know how to utilize personal power.* Power is the ability to influence others. Power is manifested in interactions and decision making processes whereby leaders select appropriate strategies to influence others and accomplish organizational and interpersonal goals. Good interpersonal skills are an important factor in developing and maintaining the power to influence others.

5. *To be an effective leader one has to be politically astute.* This includes good knowledge of the formal and informal communication networks of the organization. It is essential to be able to identify the 'movers and shakers' in the organization.

6. *The ability to give and receive constructive critiques (not criticism) is one of the most difficult skills to learn and also one of the most important skills leaders must develop.* One's instinct is to react defensively to real and perceived criticism. To give and accept evaluative comments is to provide and receive feedback; an organization that is effective at providing feedback up and down its hierarchies will learn of problems quickly and can, therefore, correct them quickly. An organization that has ineffective feedback mechanisms will often learn of problems only after they have developed into a crisis. In other words, feedback is a necessary part of organizational growth.

7. *Effective leaders are forward looking;* some people can see clearly with both eyes through a small straw or narrow tunnel because they have the ability to set and define the vision. They define vision and goals and motivate others to share their vision and help them accomplish the goals to make it a reality. Such leaders have a clear sense of direction; they know where they are now, how they got there, and where they want to lead the organization. Leaders make certain their employees know when they are doing well and how to do well by giving them guidance that ensures tasks are completed.

8. *Integrity is a key characteristic of respected leaders.* To have integrity means to be fair, truthful, ethical, consistent, and honest. Leadership is based on honesty and good morals. To be honest means more than not to lie; honest leaders say what they mean and act upon their beliefs. Leaders who have integrity set an example for others by behaving in ways that are consistent with their stated values; they value and respect the individuals who work with them, and they respect and adhere to the values of the organization. Followers look for trustworthiness (honesty), expertise (competence), and dynamism (inspiration), while personal credibility is the foundation of effective leadership.

9. *Competence is essential.* It includes being and acting mature, and being a positive role model. It goes almost without saying that competence is a key ingredient in effective leadership. Leaders do not necessarily need detailed technical knowledge. Instead, they need to be competent in the basic leadership skills, such as communication, and they need to have a good knowledge of the organization, the roles of the different parts of the organization, and their own role within the organization.

10. *Effective leaders have the capacity to inspire others.* They inspire by being dynamic, uplifting, enthusiastic, positive and optimistic. They are as-

sertive and confident in their ability to lead. They encourage their followers and have concern for themselves and others, and for the organization. To inspire others requires their respect and trust. Leaders who lack integrity will usually lose trust and will, therefore, cease to be inspirational and effective leaders.

11. *The ability to solve problems is an important practical leadership skill.* To solve a problem one must first recognize and properly define it. To recognize the true nature of a problem is, therefore, the most important skill in solving problems and one that is highly valued in leaders. Once the nature of the problem is known, it becomes possible to consult others with more specialized skills on how to solve it. Within an organization, the ability to recognize problems requires knowledge of the organization and its mission and goals. The ability to solve problems also requires decisiveness and the willingness to take risks. Creativity and strong technical skills are also helpful but less important; once the problem is properly defined, others who have those skills can be assigned to help solve it.

12. *Effective leaders have self-awareness, self-control, self-direction, self-knowledge and high self-esteem.* Erich Fromm (1974) argues that individuals who do not accept themselves, i.e. who do not respect their value as individuals, cannot accept others. Since respect for others is an important value and critical to effective leadership, Fromm's work implies that self-respect and self-esteem are very important to effective leadership. Leaders who have a healthy self-esteem will also be less likely to react defensively to critiques, and will not let suspicion of the motives of others turn into paranoia. Self-confidence enables leaders to act without constant approval and recognition from others (Bennis and Nanus, 1985). Self-control is also important. Individuals who frequently lose their temper will soon lose the respect of their employees. When they are 'out of control' and act impulsively rather than rationally, they are more likely to make mistakes. Decisions that reflect anger or other strong emotions are usually poor decisions that may serve their egos but not the goals of the organization. Thus, effective leaders need to develop discipline and know themselves better to help them make sensible decisions. They must learn not to become overwhelmed by their emotions when they face stressful situations.

Recognizing strengths and weaknesses is the first step toward achieving self-confidence. The second step is that of nurturing skills. With a disciplined approach it is possible to build on strengths to develop and improve leadership skills. We expect leaders to take responsibility for their own development, and to seek help and advice as needed. A third step is that of evaluating the fit between perceived leadership skills and the organization's needs. Some leaders are creative thinkers. Their creativity is a wonderful asset in an organization that is exploring new directions. Other leaders have great motivational skills. They can take an idea and persuade others to follow. Such skills are particularly highly valued after new ideas have been developed and need to be implemented. What are your strengths and how can they be used to help the organization?

A positive self-image is related to emotional maturity and wisdom. It is reflected in the way leaders relate to others. As Fromm (1974) argues, only when we accept ourselves are we truly able to accept others. How we relate to others, however, does not only depend on how we feel about ourselves. The literature identifies several skills that facilitate interpersonal relations (Bennis and Nanus 1985).

1. The ability to accept people as they are, not as you would like them to be; to understand what other people are like on their terms, rather than judging them.

2. The capacity to approach relationships and problems in terms of the present rather than the past. Although you can learn from past mistakes, use the present as a take-off point for improving the way you relate to others.

3. The ability to treat those who are close to you with the same courteous attention that you extend to strangers and casual acquaintances.

4. The ability to trust others, even if the risk seems great. The price of always being on guard is very high.

5. The ability to do things without the need for constant approval and recognition from others.

The following example illustrates the importance of starting with the present as a way to deal with interpersonal issues.

Example 5.2

Ellen was furious. She and Joe, her assistant, had met with a client. In front of the client, Joe had contradicted Ellen's statements regarding one of their company's products. Right after the meeting she had called Joe into the office to talk with him about the incident. She was still angry and accused Joe, "You have done this sort of thing to me before." Joe was surprised at first and then grew angry himself. "First, your claims regarding our products were wrong and I had no choice but to correct you. Second, I do not recall that something like this has ever occurred before."

It is pretty obvious that such a discussion will not lead to a fruitful conclusion. Ellen's first mistake was to confront Joe while she was still angry. Our ability to think rationally declines the angrier we are. Because of her anger she committed a second mistake when she brought up the real or imagined past. A more constructive approach is to deal with what happened, the present. Ellen can explain how Joe's behaviour impacted her, and Joe why he felt it was important to intervene. Together they can work to find an approach they are both comfortable with, should a similar situation occur in the future.

Skilled leadership behaviour is marked by two qualities: it is appropriate and effective. Skilled behaviour that is appropriate conforms to established organizational procedures and norms; it is effective when it allows the organization to achieve organizational and interpersonal goals (Barge, 1994). In our society, honesty and competency are among the established norms and we choose to follow leaders who are honest, competent, forward-looking and inspiring. As citizens, consumers, and workers, we express our leadership preferences through the means available to us: at gatherings or meetings, at ballots, through our consumption behaviour, and in the news media. The importance of leadership in our daily lives is underlined by the following statement by Bennis (1984): "As a person cannot function without a brain, a society cannot function without leaders."

Practical Steps to Effective Leadership

To become a leader you must get to know yourself and take charge of shaping your own life. Knowing thyself is a difficult task. A logical point of departure in this quest is the objective examination of your own personal characteristics and behavioural tendencies. This sounds easier than it is. Many thinkers have observed that one of the most difficult things in life is to know yourself. It requires separating who you are and who you want to be from what the world thinks you are and wants you to be. The reason it is so important that you should know yourself is because leading others requires that you know and understand them. It is difficult to conceive of how anyone can truly know and understand others without self-knowledge. Leadership is built on real life relationships with peers, followers and yourself.

As Erich Fromm (1974) has observed, healthy relationships require that we first know and accept ourselves. In Fromm's opinion, acceptance of who we are, which requires self-knowledge, is a prerequisite for the acceptance of others. Since we can build healthy relationships only with people whom we accept, Fromm's insight demonstrates the importance of self-knowledge. It is possible to lead those whom we do not accept, but such a relationship is unhealthy and incompatible with leadership in a democratic society. Democracy's foundation is the recognition of each individual's self-worth. It is difficult to see and respect the self-worth of those whom we do not accept.

Self-knowledge is also important in more immediately practical ways. Knowing our weaknesses allows us to work on and improve them; self-knowledge allows us to develop a leadership style that makes the best use of our strengths and relies least on characteristics and skills where we have weaknesses. Conversely, those who attempt to lead without self-knowledge may fail completely without ever knowing why. Because most of us feel that we know ourselves better than others know us, we may suffer from the illusion that we have all the self-knowledge we need (Bennis, 1989; McLean and Weitzel, 1992). Without working on self-knowledge, however, we end up knowing only very little about ourselves.

The following are some suggestions to help increase self-knowledge, maintain productive fellowship with superiors, establish strong relationships with peers and followers, and build their trust in you as a leader (Miller, 1988; Kouzes and Posner, 1987; Terry, 1993).

Have Confidence in your Leadership Ability

(a) Being seen by those around you as credible, confident, and authoritative is crucial to success. This does not mean that you cannot show weaknesses or that you must have a solution to every problem. Your credibility can be enhanced if you have the confidence to admit when you do not know something and are sure enough of yourself to ask others for help. Your ability to interact confidently and assertively with people both up and down the ladder is critical to your career success. As Larry Olin, captain of a college tennis team, learned: "You must be confident in yourself before you can expect others to be confident in you."

(b) Discover your weaknesses. Analyze your experiences when you succeed and when you fail. Your failures and successes may reveal strengths and weaknesses that you may not have been aware of. Use the insights to strengthen your leadership skills. Admit mistakes, learn from both your successes and mistakes, and keep a positive attitude about the future. Perfection is an ideal that is impossible to achieve; it may be wiser to develop the humility to admit mistakes, ask for help, and strive for continuous learning.

(c) Develop positive power skills that make people want to follow your lead. Remember that leadership and interpersonal skills can be learned and improved through practice.

(d) Stay away from common 'land mines' like drugs and alcohol that diminish your credibility and adversely impact your personal integrity, health and leadership performance.

(e) Find new ways to nurture your inner self. Learn to respect and like yourself. If you do not start respecting yourself first, you cannot really expect your followers to respect you.

Tune-up your Personal Leadership Style

(a) Being an effective, dynamic leader requires special skills. If you have only recently moved into a leadership position, have realistic expectations of yourself. Some skills take years to master fully. Strong leaders take time to develop and enrich their skills.

(b) Take a hard and honest look at how your personality affects and influences your followers. Cultivate those personality traits that help you and try to correct those traits that are a hindrance to effective leadership.

(c) Good interpersonal skills are important in any relationship. Employees, clients, and superiors value friendliness and honesty. Good manners earn respect and compliance. Employees are not motivated by financial rewards alone; acceptance and being respected are fundamental human needs.

(d) Master the art of asserting yourself without being pushy or disrespectful of others. Assertiveness skills are the key to building and maintaining strong business relationships, to leading others successfully, to increasing productivity and overall organizational success, and to improving professional and career successes. "Your job gives you authority, but your behaviour earns you respect" (Terry, 1993). Assertive leadership skills can be taught and learned. They include the skill to say no to inappropriate demands.

(e) Some individuals are nervous, shy, or uncomfortable when they are around a group of people. If you experience this problem, learn and practice the skills to improve your comfort level. It starts with recognizing and appropriately asserting your own needs when you are working in a group.

(f) Regularly assess your leadership style. Reflect on how you handled an important meeting, a staff evaluation, a presentation, etc. What did you do well and what would you like to change? Leadership skills do not come with the job position. Leadership style is learned and improved through reflective leadership practice.

Take Care of Yourself

(a) Leadership comes with many responsibilities, and it is easy to let those responsibilities overwhelm you. We all have limits to what we can handle. Listen to your body and recognize stress symptoms, such as frequent fatigue, irritability, sleep problems, etc. Take action to prevent damaging your family life, your health and job burnout. If you do not know how to deal with your stress, seek help.

(b) We often impose stress on ourselves through poor time management and exaggerated expectations. Set ambitious but reachable goals for yourself and then plan your time and other resources to achieve them. Use exercise and hobbies to relax and reduce accumulated stress. Take your personal needs as seriously as your work; do not allow your time with family or important friends to always come second to your job.

(c) Effective leaders take risks but are careful to distinguish between 'smart' and dangerous risks. The first step in avoiding assuming dangerous risks is to follow the rule that the greater the cost of an error, the more thought and information are required. Risky steps should not be taken when you are in an emotional state (angry, feeling peer pressure, etc).

(d) Your time is valuable: protect it. Do not allow frequent interruptions for unimportant reasons. Set time limits on meetings. Plan and schedule the use of your time.

(e) Show concern for your staff members. Help them balance their responsibilities with their personal needs. It will improve their long-term productivity, health and general well being.

(f) Do not become trapped into satisfying the needs of others but neglecting your professional goals and self-needs. Learn how to say no without causing hard feelings and feeling guilty.

(g) Leadership sometimes requires creativity. Learn skills that enhance creativity (for example, brainstorming and other group problem solving techniques). Try keeping an open mind when someone presents a new idea. It may be helpful to ask 'How could this be done?' instead of the much more common 'This is not practical' or 'We have tried this before and it didn't work!' Innovation is a hallmark of excellent leadership. Creativity is necessary to progress and requires willingness to risk failure.

Keep Open Communication and be Accessible to your Followers

(a) Learn to listen. The importance of this skill cannot be overstated. Listening is more than letting others 'say their thing'. Too often, when someone tells us something, we are listening with less than full attention because we are already thinking about how to respond to what is being said. Focus on what the other person really says. Some topics are difficult to broach and the person you are talking with may use hints, allusions, or may even talk about something else. For example, an employee may be very angry and give a reason that does not justify such anger. In such a situation it is likely that while the reason given may have triggered the anger, the true cause lies elsewhere. Encouraging the employee to talk about the concerns by showing that you take him or her seriously, may lead you to find out what the true cause of the anger is. Leaders who are good listeners can learn about problems before they become costly, and they may learn about opportunities that others miss.

(b) Listening is an essential function of leaders. People want to be taken seriously. The clearest signal we can send that we take someone seriously is by listening to what they have to say; listening demonstrates respect for the other person. If your employees do not feel respected by you, they are also less likely to trust you. People know they are respected when they are listened to and when they are encouraged to participate in a shared challenge.

(c) Get to know your employees. Hold some meetings with them in their offices. It demonstrates interest in them and the appearance of their workplace gives you some information about them. They may have pictures of family or decorations that tell you something about their hobbies. It may help you better understand what is important to them. You may see signs that work is going well or that a lot of work has accumulated that you were not aware of. You may then be better able to assess whether an employee needs assistance or is ready for more responsibility. Finally, meet regularly with key team leaders, supervisors, and senior and junior staff to discuss their situations.

(d) Learn to express your opinions and speak your mind whether you are dealing with employees, peers or supervisors. Good speaking skills are only a part of this. You often must express your opinions and expectations in private meetings, not in a public speech. For example, you may have to tell an employee that his performance needs improvement. Many of us find this an unpleasant and difficult task. By learning the right skills, which include listening skills, we can express our concerns, opinions, and expectations constructively and improve the chance that we can help correct a problem. Addressing problems is important, but if we confront a problem in such a way that employees feel threatened, we may get such a defensive reaction that the search for a solution will be difficult.

(e) In some organizations leaders become regular employees for a day by trading places with one of the employees. Experience is the best teacher and trading places may teach something to both the employee and the manager. By trading places managers also express respect for the work done by their employees. For example, it has been observed at West Virginia University when the president traded places with a food service worker at the student's cafeteria at one time and with a student at another time.

(f) Leaders must build consensus around core beliefs. They do so by finding common ground (which may first require listening) and building a sense of community. There may be conflicts that cannot be resolved through consensus. It is important that leaders resolve such conflicts on the basis of established principles, not on the basis of their position. It can be very helpful if leaders explain the process and reasoning used in resolving conflicts.

(g) Think about your position on important issues. This requires self-knowledge: What is important to you? What are your values? Once you have decided, communicate your stand on the important issues. People do not respect and trust those who frequently shift their position based upon the latest opinion or news.

(h) Communicate your confidence in your employees by entrusting them with responsibility. Effective leaders encourage their employees to show initiative, be creative and give them opportunities to succeed. They also provide appropriate educational and training opportunities. Such leaders build a team of confident and competent employees. Future leaders of organizations often come from the ranks of employees who were given opportunities to test their leadership abilities before they were given formal leadership responsibilities.

(i) Credible leaders encourage other people. They give people choices and latitude; they educate and build confidence. Work so that everyone can be entrusted with leadership responsibilities. Credible leaders keep promises, hold themselves accountable for their actions, and accept responsibility for the actions of their employees. They are optimistic and hopeful and inspire positive images and action. They seek and give the support and recognition that enable others to excel.

Think Creatively to Discover better Opportunities

(a) Most of us are creatures of habit. We find it difficult to think of new approaches. The longer we have been doing something, the harder it seems to think of better ways of doing it. There are schemes that specialize in creative problem solving and there is a growing literature on the subject. Creativity often comes from the interaction among several people, for example in a brainstorming session. Many creative ideas, however, are ignored or ridiculed. Good listening skills do not guarantee that we will find and adopt more creative solutions, but they do help us to respect the ideas of others so that we are more likely to 'give them a chance'. Creative ideas are often unconventional and seem at first 'crazy'; they are therefore often dismissed prematurely.

(b) We can teach ourselves to be more creative. When you have an idea on how to deal with an issue (it does not have to be a problem) write it down and put it in a file. When you hear an idea, do the same thing. Creativity does not usually come in a sudden inspiration but from the availability of alternatives.

c) Uncover the world of opportunities in every problem. According to John Gardner, "We are all continually faced with a series of great opportunities, brilliantly disguised as insoluble problems" (Miller 1988). Try to look beyond perceived boundaries; they limit your perspective. One way to do this is by asking questions that start with 'wouldn't it be nice if. . .'.

Challenge 'the way it has always been done' so that you may venture beyond old boundary lines. Determine when your background is clouding your perspective and explore what you can do to get a complete understanding of a situation before exploring the great opportunities.

(d) Try to develop a positive outlook and break negative thinking that can hold you back. Oprah Winfrey in the May 1997 commencement address at Welseley College told her audience that she keeps a journal. Every day she writes down five good things that happened to her that day. She said it changed her outlook on life and how she deals with problems. To have a positive outlook does not mean that we ignore problems. It just requires that we give the same weight to the positive things in our life and work as much on them as on the negative.

(e) Creativity may require taking risks. Doing something that has not been done before always entails some measure of risk. Evaluate and weigh risks against rewards carefully, but do not let fear of failure prevent you from taking steps that, while risky, may yield rich rewards.

(f) Tap into and build on the potential of every idea. Improve your decision making skills and generate more unique ideas that turn problems into opportunities. Keep your best new and original ideas alive to make sensible decisions. Give them the added attention they need to flow naturally, survive, and thrive to make changes.

(g) Avoid 'idea killers' that threaten breakthroughs. Avoid statements such as 'this has been done before and was a failure'; 'this is not our responsibility' or 'why would anyone want to try this?' Statements such as these will discourage your employees from offering their ideas in the future. Only if you take them and their ideas seriously will they develop and share their creativity.

(h) Once a solution idea has been evaluated and judged feasible, move to implement it. Not only does this solve a problem or take advantage of an opportunity, but also to see ideas become reality gives satisfaction to all who were involved and motivates them to contribute in the future.

> To know what to do is wisdom.
> To know how to do it is skill.
> To know when to do it is judgement.
> To strive to do the best is dedication.
> To do it for the benefit of others is compassion.
> To do it quietly is humility.
> To get the job done is achievement.
> To get others to do all these is effective leadership.
>
> *Anonymous*

PART II

DEVELOPING LEADERSHIP SKILLS

When you want to get a herd to move in a certain direction, you stand at the back with a stick. Then a few of the more energetic cattle move to the front and the rest of the cattle follow. You are really guiding them from behind. That is how a leader should do his work.

Nelson Mandela, 1994

CHAPTER SIX

THE DECISION MAKING PROCESS

Everybody is ignorant, only on different subjects.
But everybody is an expert on something.

Will Rogers

There are three parts to making good decisions in the process of solving a problem: preparation and analysis, decision and implementation, and assessment and evaluation. All parts of this course of action are important in the decision making and problem solving process. The first part, preparation, involves the collection and analysis of information. This includes learning more about the nature and characteristics of the problem or opportunity, the resources necessary to address it, and the exploration of alternative approaches to dealing with it. The cost of implementing a decision should be taken into consideration and evaluated as an important input into eventually reaching a decision. When enough information has been collected and evaluated the first part of the decision making process is completed. How much information is enough depends on the complexity of the issues, that is, the uncertainty involved in making a decision, and the cost of making a decision that, retroactively, turns out to have been wrong.

Secondly, reaching a decision to solve a problem is based on the information collected in the first part. However, the process does not end here. Decisions are not automatically carried out after management announces them. The implementation mechanism needs to be prepared. It may require that individual employees or a group of employees be given more or different authority and always includes the assignment of responsibilities, allocation of resources, and the establishment of dates by when certain parts of the decision should be completed.

Finally, the third part of decision making is that of follow-up. After the decision has been fully implemented, you should evaluate if it is working as anticipated or if additional action is necessary. Assessment is also valuable because it often reveals information about strengths and weaknesses that are useful for corrective action and may improve future decision making.

Successful leadership and management require the ability not only to make decisions but also to make the right decisions at the right time. Just as there are fundamental principles associated with leadership and management there are fundamental principles associated with decision making. The goal is to identify these principles and from them develop a sound decision making procedure that will make decision making easier, improve the quality of decisions, reduce the time necessary to make decisions, and increase the probability of making good decisions.

The Problem Solving Process

The fundamental principles of decision making involve: getting a clear understanding of a problem, weighing alternatives, making appropriate decisions, efficiently implementing decisions and attaining the best solutions, and subsequently evaluating outcomes. The following more detailed description of the decision making process and problem solving techniques is based on the writings of Beierlein *et al.* (1986), Downey and Erickson (1987), Castle *et al.* (1987) and Rogers (1991).

1. *Setting goals.* A goal is a target or desired condition. Goals are the outcomes anticipated or the promise to be achieved. Goals represent the desire for distinction and provide the direction for planning. They are realistic work plans and not just dreams. Work without goals is like a journey without a destination and an organization is aimless and unproductive without basic goals and objectives. Well-defined and well-stated goals reflect the philosophy and image of an organization. Goals and objectives should state what direction the organization should take. To identify and have a clear and consistent set of goals is to have a sense of purpose, or direction. Goal setting is a process that can be learned through reflection about needs. To be effective, goals need to be communicated and become accepted by the members of the organization. All decision making is at least implicitly based on goals. Something is a problem or can be an opportunity only because it either stands in the way of, or contributes to, our reaching the goals we set for ourselves. Therefore, clearly defined goals are a prerequisite to the decision making and problem solving process.

2. *Recognizing problems and opportunities.* Decision making always involves a *problem* or *opportunity.* A problem is a discrepancy between the management's desired or stated goals and what is actually achieved. Managers and supervisors become aware of a problem when there is a discrepancy between their accomplishments and stated goals, or when the results do not measure up to their expectations. If you can learn to look at even serious problems as an interesting challenge to be overcome, then you will acquire a positive attitude to problem solving and think about the problem logically and reasonably. Write down a concise account of what the problem is, who is involved, and describe the circumstances. Ask for help, if necessary. A person who is not involved with the situation can sometimes see a solution when you cannot. Define clear objectives and a strategy to overcome obstacles standing in the way. Sorting out objectives and obstacles helps to clarify the nature of the problem. Recogniz-

ing problems is not always easy. We often mistake symptoms for the real problem, as illustrated by the following example.

Example 6.1

A large increase in the number of accidents is a symptom. The reason why there are more accidents may be that the equipment is in poor condition (because of the equipment's age, abuse, or lack of maintenance), inappropriate equipment (because of a poor purchase decision or because the work load has outgrown the capacity of the equipment), or employee mistakes (because of poor training, lack of morale, poor supervision, or fatigue from working too many hours).

In other words, seemingly clear-cut events have many possible causes. The real cause may be only loosely linked to the observed event. In the above example, if the increase in the number of accidents is the result of poor purchase decisions, that may still not be the final underlying cause. The cause may be problems in the purchasing office. Recognizing the true nature of problems (and opportunities) can be a challenging task.

3. *Obtaining reliable information.* Once a problem (or an opportunity) has been recognized, information is needed on how to address it. Information is needed to define the characteristics of the problem and to determine alternatives for solving it. Breaking the problem down into more manageable portions may help identify information needs. Without a systematic approach, we are more likely to forget to ask the right questions, and overlook or misinterpret information. We need enough reliable information for analysis. The effort that goes into obtaining information depends on the perceived value of the information relative to its cost. The search for new information should continue as long as its perceived value is greater than the cost of obtaining it. As a rough rule of thumb, the higher the initial uncertainty and the greater the cost that results from making a poor decision, the more we should spend on information collection and processing, evaluation and analysis.

4. *Consideration of alternatives.* This is a critical step in the determination of the optimal course of action and involves the evaluation of alternatives, and weighing of the advantages and disadvantages of each solution relative to the goals of the organization, and an assessment of its costs. The problem is analyzed and divided into parts. Each part may need a different problem solving method and a different kind of solution. It helps to write down solution ideas, even if they seem unrealistic. List all the points for, and all the points against, each solution. When you have completed your list, add at the bottom any other factors that could influence the problem, even if they are not necessarily in favour, or against, that

alternative solution. Some possible solutions will turn out to have a great deal more in favour of adopting them than they have points against them and you can see at once which alternative would provide the best solution.

5. *Making decisions.* A decision is a choice selected from among the feasible alternatives. The most common reason for putting off making a decision is a fear of the consequences or the fear of making mistakes. Experience alleviates the risk involved in important decisions but cannot eliminate it. Timing of the decision is important but you should resist pressures to rush into critical decisions. While delaying a decision may result in lost opportunities, making a decision without appropriate consideration will usually result in poor outcomes. Only rarely do you face situations so urgent that you must act immediately.

6. *Taking action.* Once you have decided what to do, you must implement it. Unless we clearly communicate the decision, employees have little reason to implement it with confidence. If the decision is controversial, it may be necessary to explain it. This would consist of a listing of alternatives that were considered and the criteria that were used to make the final selection. In addition to clearly communicating the decision, it is also important that sufficient resources be made available to implement the decision. Unless the leadership provides resources, its decision will not be implemented. The leadership skill to take appropriate action on time always pays off.

7. *Accepting responsibility.* Managers must accept responsibility for their decisions. Failure to do so undermines their credibility and their employees will be reluctant to accept their leadership in situations involving risk in the future. Managers must even accept responsibility for failures of their employees. As leaders of their departments, they are responsible for the selection and supervision of employees who carry out the tasks assigned to them and are accountable for the actions (success or failure) of their employees.

Example 6.2

Jack is a junior consultant. He started his present job less than a year ago, fresh out of graduate school. He is working under the supervision of Walter. About two months ago, when Walter was very busy, he told Jack to work on a project on his own. It was the first time that Jack was working without direct supervision. When he encountered some difficulties with the assignment, he went to see Walter. Walter looked over the work very quickly, made a few minor adjustments, and then told Jack: 'It looks fine.' When Jack handed in the finished project, Walter accepted it without any request for changes. Yesterday the company received a call from the client. The client had found several mistakes in the final report. They were not very big mistakes but they reflected poorly on the firm. The senior manager of Jack's firm called Walter into his office to ask him about the problem because Walter had been assigned as project manager. In the discussion Walter accepted responsibility for the mistakes. Although Jack had made the mistakes, Walter felt responsible because he had not taken enough time when Jack asked for his help and had not read the final report carefully enough to catch the mistakes.

8. *Outcome assessment.* The decision making process is not complete until the outcome has been considered and evaluated against the stated goals. This step involves re-evaluating the decision on the basis of the outcome achieved. The evaluation will be effective only if standards and criteria have been developed against which the outcomes are to be judged. Such standards should consider both qualitative and quantitative aspects of the results. It is through the evaluation of past decisions that managers learn from experience, improve their decision making skills and build confidence in their ability.

Barriers to Decision Making

Rarely is a person skilled in all aspects of the decision making process. It is the development of the skills needed for all phases of decision making that makes successful leaders. However, even leaders skilled in the decision making process may have developed habits that reduce their efficiency. The goal is to identify habits that are roadblocks to good decision making.

1. Lack of self-confidence may have some leaders preoccupied with what others think about them or become immobilized because of the risks associated with decisions. They may underestimate their own ability to assess a situation and overestimate the ability of others who appear more confident. Such leaders run the danger of letting others tell them what decisions to make. If a leader thinks that he can do it, he has the confidence that he can do it. But if he thinks that he cannot do it, then he is right that he cannot do it.

2. Perfectionism is another obstacle to decision making; it is sometimes combined with fear of failure and assuming large risks and making mistakes. This habit may lead to a preparation phase that includes the collection of more information than necessary. The costs are a decision process that is longer and more expensive than it should be, often without any significant improvement in the quality of the decision made.

3. Any decision that would change the status quo is likely to offend some-

one. Leaders who are trying to please everyone will find it very difficult to consider responsibilities (accountability) and to make decisions that would change their organization.

4. Sometimes we hope that a problem will resolve itself (and sometimes it does). If the effects of a problem are serious, it should be addressed, even if it eventually goes away. The cost of waiting is too high.

5. Leaders are often busy and may feel that they too have too many other problems to deal with. Being too busy should not be used as an excuse not to deal with a problem or an opportunity that may have a significant effect on the organization. Leaders need to prioritize their time and may have to delegate some responsibilities and authority if they do not have enough time to address all-important issues themselves.

6. Maybe the most difficult habit to change is the refusal to recognize problems or opportunities. Even if only one person associated with the organization sees a problem, then there is a problem. Leaders need to take the concerns of others seriously. They may decide that the problem does not warrant any action, but they should not deny its existence. Similarly, leaders should be open-minded to descriptions of opportunities, even if they cannot see them. Leaders who have developed good listening skills will be in far less danger of overlooking or ignoring opportunities or problems that are brought to their attention.

Decisions are not always related to mechanical or technical situations, but often include intangible factors; to some degree the 'human element' seems to be present in all decision environments. The following is an illustration of the impact of human behaviour on problem solving.

Example 6.3

The occupants of a tall office building were complaining about the slow elevator. The property management sought to address these complaints through a technical solution but the tenants were not satisfied. After studying and analyzing the system further, it was discovered that the waiting times were in fact short. The complaints were the result of waiting in a dull environment, that is, of boredom. With this additional information, a solution that recognized the human factor was tried and full-length mirrors were installed at the entrance of the elevators. The complaints disappeared as people were occupied with watching themselves and others while waiting for the elevator.

The recognition of the human factor in decision situations is particularly important in our contemporary societies. Too often we look to technology to provide solutions to problems where technology cannot help.

Classification of Decisions

Decisions vary in their characteristics and it is helpful to classify them accordingly for proper implementation. The following list of characteristics provides criteria for a classification of decisions commonly encountered in management practice (Castle *et al.*, 1987):

1. *Importance.* Decisions vary in importance. The importance of a decision may be measured by the size of the potential gain or loss involved. For example, the purchase of computers is usually less important than the purchase of the networking and/or operating system. The purchase of the latter has a greater impact on training and the need for technical support staff than the choice between different brands of computers.

2. *Frequency.* Decisions also vary with respect to the rate of frequency with which they are made. Decisions that have to be made frequently become familiar as experience accumulates. Such decisions take up less time than infrequently made decisions, except when the costs of making a mistake are very high. For example, the purchase of a particular brand or type of computer will be a more frequent occurrence than the purchase of a whole new operating system.

3. *Imminence.* The penalty for delaying a decision is not the same for all decisions. Some decisions have to be made right away to avoid penalties. When the cost of a delay is low relative to the cost of making a poor decision, it will be desirable to obtain more information before committing resources to a particular course of action. If the costs of delay are low, it may even be desirable to wait and work on less urgent but more important problems that need your attention. One of the dangers faced by people in management positions is that their time is consumed by urgent but relatively unimportant tasks while important tasks with high long-term benefits that are not urgent are ignored.

4. *Revocability.* Some decisions can be revoked only at a considerable cost and others at minimum cost. This characteristic is directly linked to the cost of making a poor decision. If a decision can be changed quickly and at a low cost, it may be reasonable to act with relatively little information and learn from experience. For example, if a computer is purchased and you find that it does not work as well as you had hoped, we have a number of inexpensive options. You could assign it to another, less demanding task, you could upgrade it or you could sell it. By contrast, if you purchase and install a new operating and network system and that system does not work well, everybody connected to the network will experience reduced efficiency. The measures that are necessary to improve the system's performance will interrupt work, may require additional training, and will, therefore, be costly.

5. *Available alternatives.* In some situations many alternatives are available while in other situations there are only a few. When a wide range of choices is available, criteria must be developed for evaluating alternatives and choosing the one that is expected to contribute most to the organization's goals.

Characteristics of Goals

A goal is a target that the management of an organization wishes to reach. It is something that is desired and provides direction for the actions of the organization. Major goals and objectives should be stated in writing and should distinguish between short-term, intermediate-term and long-term goals. Short-term goals should be precise and measurable. Intermediate-term and long-term goals can be less precise if they do not require immediate action. Long-term goals, in particular, serve the purpose of setting the general direction in which to go. More specific goals are usually best determined around the time when decisions have to be made. The longer we can afford to wait the more current the information on which we base goals and the decisions to implement them.

Goals should be analyzed to determine conflict (competition), independence (neutrality), or complementarity (harmony) between goals. It may be possible to overcome conflict between goals if sufficient resources are available, but there will be cases when not all goals can be reached and trade-offs have to be made. The following list of points is helpful in understanding the characteristics of goals (Bradford and Cohen, 1984; Beierlein *et al.*, 1986).

1. *Goals should reflect the core purpose of the organization.* That is, goals must be compatible and consistent with the overall purpose of the organization. If achieving high quality performance (efficiency and productivity) is one of the core values of the organization, this value must be supported by the goals.

2. *Goals should be challenging and require effort.* Goals are vehicles of change. They can serve this function only if they challenge the organization and create a sense of excitement and ambition.

3. *Goals should have a larger significance.* Work is a central part of most people's life. It is part of their community and may define their sense of who they are. Because of the importance of work, people will enjoy their responsibilities more and work with greater dedication for goals that they see as important and compatible with their personal values.

4. *Goals should be specific and measurable.* If goals are to motivate members of the organization, they must be clear and specific. Unless we formulate specific goals, it may be impossible to determine when or if we reach them. If goals are measurable, it will be easier to compare and con-

trast what is achieved and what is not. Success is a powerful motivator and we should celebrate when we achieve it. We can only celebrate, however, if we know whether or not we have been successful.

5. *Goals should include deadlines.* Deadlines are part of formulating goals that are specific. Deadlines are important to determine resource needs, assess progress at regular intervals, and for the assignment of responsibility. If there is no deadline, any time can be the right time to accomplish the goal or the goal may not be accomplished at all.

6. *Goals should include assignment of responsibilities.* Goals are much more likely to be reached if we assign responsibilities to departments and individuals. The people involved in accomplishing the goals need to have commitment and persistence. They can only succeed if they understand what is expected of them, and they will be more strongly motivated if they are rewarded for success.

7. *Goals should be objective and realistic.* Goals should be feasible and attainable on the basis of the capabilities of employees and management capacities. It is often a good idea to formulate some goals that are quite easy to reach within the available quantity and quality of material and human resources. Success builds confidence. This is particularly important in a new organization. Starting out with goals that are very ambitious relative to the resources, ability, and experience of an organization is likely to result in failure. Starting with failure is detrimental to morale and may undermine team spirit. Experienced organizations have greater capacity because they have had successes that build their confidence in their abilities, and they have established trust among employees so that failure is less likely to result in assignment of blame than in an objective assessment of what went wrong. The goals of experienced organizations can, therefore, be more ambitious.

8. *Try easy goals first.* All goals are not the same. It is important to distinguish the easy goals from the hard ones because it helps to identify the most appropriate strategy and resource combination to accomplish the goals. Accomplishing easy goals will give encouragement and incentive to tackle more difficult ones.

Example 6.4

Many small rural towns in the American mid-west were hit hard by the farm crisis of the early-1980s. Even before the crisis, rural downtowns had deteriorated, reflecting the exodus of retailing businesses to strip malls and suburban shopping centres. One small community was not willing to see its downtown decline. Under the leadership of several community members, they set goals and explored strategies to fill thees empty stores. One of the goals concerned the appearance of the downtown area. They decided that one way to improve the appearance was to re-paint the facades of several buildings. This was easy to do. Most property owners agreed to have the facades of their buildings painted. The owners supplied the paint; community volunteers did the work. The effort was successful and highly visible. It motivated more citizens to join in the volunteer effort. Since then this community has moved on to more challenging goals. The confidence they built with first completing some easy steps has helped them succeed with the more difficult ones.

9. *Goals should be flexible.* This seems to contradict the advice that goals should be specific, as they cannot be specific and flexible at the same time. What we suggest is that goals should be specific but should be revised and altered as conditions change. Do not box yourself into a situation that will not allow you to change. As conditions change and you learn more about yourself and your capabilities, be ready to revise your goals.

10. *Recognize that all goals may not be attained.* When that happens, as it inevitably will, avoid the assignment of blame. Instead, objectively assess why you did not reach the goal, learn from the experience and make changes to the decision process, if necessary. If the goal is still important to the organization, try again.

CHAPTER SEVEN

FUNDAMENTAL MANAGEMENT FUNCTIONS

A little knowledge that acts is worth infinitely more than much knowledge that is idle.

Kalil Gibran

Management is the art of pursuing the best potential outcomes and accomplishing goals through the effective utilization of available human, material and financial resources. Managers provide structure and establish systems within which to work toward the goals of the organization. They do this by organizing resources and working with and through people to achieve desired results (Covey, 1992). Management is a process in which information is the input and decisions are the output. A key to successful management is accepting responsibility for leadership and making decisions through skillful application of management principles. The success or failure of any organization rests primarily on the way its management utilizes its resources. The ability to manage is a skill that can be learned. To some, management represents a land of mystery and games and they may, therefore, be too intimated to try to become managers and leaders themselves. As we have stressed before, however, there are many opportunities in our daily lives to apply and develop leadership and management skills.

Although management skills and principles can be learned, they must be adapted to fit the situation and management pattern of an organization and the personality and style of the individual manager. Managers practice management as doctors practice medicine or lawyers practice law, by combining technical know-how, logic, and judgment to fit the situation. Clearly, management is a process or art supported by science and logic (Downey and Erickson, 1987).

Today it is widely accepted that managers of successful businesses use principles and knowledge of management. The fundamental management principles and knowledge are the same for any type of business – private or public, large or small. The differences between two businesses rest on their specific situations. For example, a small business needs fewer formal structures than a very large business because employees are more likely to know each other and know to whom to go with questions or requests for help. Thus, although the basic principles of management fit all types of organizations, 'one size does not fit all'. All the functions of management discussed in this text are used in different ways by different business enterprises and public organizations.

To be a successful manager you must want to play the managerial role. When a successful manager looks in the mirror they see a leader, a person who is willing to accept responsibility for change and become the catalyst for action. Managers accept responsibility and power as a challenge rather than as a curse. The famous educator Nicholas Murray Butler once placed managers in three classes: "The few who make things happen, the many who watch things happen, and the majority who have no idea what has happened." Good managers are most effective in an environment that permits creative change as they obtain much of the satisfaction from their ability 'to make things happen'. Peter Drucker remarked that: "The ineffective manager concentrates on doing things right, rather than on doing the right things." Success as a manager, then, necessitates the ability to understand and be comfortable with the managerial role, to accept responsibility, and to provide leadership for change.

An exciting management technique called management by exception has been introduced relatively recently. Its basic premise is that managers should not spend time on management areas that are progressing according to plan. Rather, they should concentrate on those areas in which not everything is progressing as it should. Through delegation and team building managers can free up time from routine management tasks and devote more time and effort to areas where there are problems or opportunities. That is, managers can spend more time being creative and innovative.

There are two important dimensions to good management – the human dimension and the technical and material dimension. Of these two, the human dimension is by far the more important. This is because the ability of managers to achieve results rests on the co-operation of others in the organization. People are the basis for growth and development; effective human relations management is, therefore, one of the most critical skills for the long-term success of any organization. How managers deal with human resources ultimately determines the nature and character of an organization. Technical and material inputs, mainly capital and natural resources, are positive factors of production, but human beings build and run the institutions that accumulate capital and put natural resources to work. Investment of time and energy in human resources can pay large rewards. Human resources development is one of the most important aspects of this, but human resources management should also include the establishment of organizational structures that encourage employees to make the fullest use of their talents. By communicating confidence and by assigning responsibility, management can encourage personal growth in employees, making them stronger contributors to the organization's goals and objectives.

Management consists of four essential functions: planning, organizing, controlling and directing. A vehicle wheel symbolizes the concept of management. The four functions of management are represented as the spokes of the wheel that connect the manager with the objectives and results that are sought. It is through planning, organizing, controlling, and directing that managers achieve goals and objectives. Overall management is only as strong as the weakest spoke in the wheel. The wheel illustrates the need to view management as a whole, with each function tied to the other functions, and all overlapping one another. Now add motivation as the torque, or speed, with which the functions are accomplished. Motivation provides the motion by which the wheel moves. Strong motivation results in speedy and successful forward movement; poor motivation can result in discouraging backward movement. The axle on which the entire wheel of management turns is communication. Without good communications, the wheel of management soon begins to wobble and squeak; if attention is not given soon enough, the entire wheel is likely to break down and fall apart (Castle *et al.*, 1987; Downey and Erickson, 1987).

Planning

Planning is thinking about the future and determining courses of action directed at specific goals and objectives. Planning deals with all activities that determine the direction of the organization. It requires the setting of daily priorities and schedules, recognizing problem areas and seeking alternative solutions. Once we know what it is we would like to accomplish, we can collect and analyze information relative to reaching our goals and objectives. What resources will we need? Are those resources available? How long should it take to reach our goals? Are there legal constraints? With sound and sufficient information, management can develop a plan of action and start organizing the necessary resources. An organization that knows where it is going is much more likely to reach its goals and prosper than one that depends on chance. It has been said, 'If you do not know where you are going, do not worry at all, any road will get you there.' Planning is critical because it is the key function of management and the foundation on which all other management functions depend. A plan of action must be developed before all else. Without a plan of action, we do not know what resources we need. Without goals, we cannot evaluate the appropriateness of decisions. And without shared goals, members of the organization may not work towards the same ends. Thus, planning is the framework of management and proceeds through organizing, directing and controlling (Miller, 1988; Castle *et al.*, 1987).

Planning should be carried out at nearly all levels of management. It begins with those who have the overall responsibility for the organization and ends with managers of specific work units. The level of planning moves from the general to the specific. Plans concerning the organization as a whole tend to be broader, deal with more complex issues, be more flexible and have a longer range. Such plans may recommend shifting significant resources from one set of tasks to another. The smaller the unit and the less complex its roles, the more detailed and specific its plans; such plans are usually for immediate action and may be unwritten, in contrast to the very formal written plans for the whole organization. The extent to which smaller units can shift resources is usually very limited because of the small size of the resources allocated to them relative to the tasks assigned to them. Significant resource allocations are usually initiated and supported by the management of large units where senior managers set long-term goals for the whole organization. Junior managers translate long-term goals into intermediate-term objectives and develop implementation plans for their division or department. Supervisors translate the mid-range goals into short-term plans to assist in the implementation of the action plan. Employees should be consulted during the planning process. They often have special insights into the work programmes that can improve the chances of success, and their involvement also serves to inform them of the plan and make them feel part of it. All plans help meet the organizational objectives. All plans give guidance, direction and time schedules. Plans at all levels must be monitored and kept on track. The planning process involves the following concerns or questions (Castle *et al.*, 1987; Krueckeberg and Silvers, 1974).

1. *Statement of goals and objectives.* What do you want to accomplish? State what needs to be done. Establish objectives for each area of responsibility and set up benchmarks for achieving goals. Objectives are targets toward which goals are aimed. They are also the most neglected of all planning segments. This neglect occurs because managers either avoid the mental exercise needed to set objectives or fear the failure that might be evidenced by an inability to reach them.

2. *Analysis of past performance and resource inventory.* What resources would you like to have available to work with? What quantities and qualities of resources are needed to accomplish the stated goals? Make an inventory of all available human, material and financial resources needed and institutional regulations that affect the course of actions. What has been accomplished? An analysis of the past is made based on the organization's records and institutional memory. Adequate information must be available to formulate or synthesize fuzzy problems or opportunities. Information gathering is a recurring part of the planning process.

3. *Identification and selection of possible action plans.* What might be done? Choose alternative action plans and suitable courses of action. After the goals have been set, alternative courses of action must be developed, and managers must explore the different ways of achieving the goals. Then, select the best action plan to accomplish the stated goals and objectives.

4. *Designing an implementation procedure.* How will it be done? Develop a step by step implementation plan that states who will do what (delegation) and by when (timetable).

5. *Evaluation of outcomes.* Is it working? Evaluate the results to determine if the goals have been accomplished. If so, it is the end of this plan. If not, there is a need to go over a new idea or plan. State standards to judge outcomes (performance criteria). Compare actual results against standards (control). Evaluation shows whether the plan is on course, and allows both the analysis of new information and the discovery of new opportunities.

Some managers do not like to plan because they do not see the inherent advantages of guidance, action plans and goal accomplishments. Specialists in human behaviour tell us that what we accomplish depends on what we expect, on what we think is possible. Through planning, we first set goals. Goals should be ambitious but realistic. They should force the organization to 'stretch' to reach them. Challenging goals are important because we often underestimate the talent and resources at our disposal and, therefore, set goals that are too low. Planning that involves employees empowers them by giving them a voice in what the future might be like. Successful managers think ahead and involve employees and superiors in the process to make sure that they have a stake in the successful implementation of the plan. By providing a vision and defining goals, they shape events. Without planning we do not anticipate change and are forced to react to problems rather than to exploit opportunities. Planning is a continuous process, in which case short-term and long-term plans must be prepared to ensure the continuity and certainty of goal accomplishments (Miller, 1988). Because the future is uncertain, the plan and its implementation should be reviewed regularly to compare the actual results against the plan. Adjustments are necessary if the anticipated conditions on which we based our action plan do not materialize. Major revisions can be undertaken every few years, unless the organization is experiencing dramatic changes, in which case revisions should be made more frequently.

A well-conceived plan should:

(a) indicate the philosophy and desired image of the organization;

(b) record the direction the organization should take;

(c) provide guides for the goals and results of each work unit or person;

(d) allow appraisal of the results contributed by each work unit or person;

(e) contribute to a successful overall organizational performance.

Aimlessness produces unpredictable results. It is possible to succeed without planning, but such success is likely to be the result of luck. Responsible leaders do not risk their organization's future by relying on luck when they can prepare for change. Thus, companies and many other organizations prepare and use planning consciously. In today's dynamic business world, planning is a necessity for achieving success; planning has become a way of business life.

While the basic process is the same for all planning activities, the specifics of the process can vary significantly, depending on the nature of the issues we are trying to address. For example, planning to build a new plant where the company will produce an output using a well-established process requires relatively little creativity. A highly structured planning process will work well for such problems. By contrast, creativity is a requirement when it starts the planning process that should lead to new products to be added to the company's line. At least in the first phases of the process, an unstructured process that encourages creative ideas is paramount for success. Ideas should not be dismissed quickly just because they sound unrealistic. That is, the first steps of the planning process are exploratory in nature and the eventual outcome is uncertain. This is in contrast with the previous example, where the general terms of the outcome were known in advance and only the details had to be planned.

Example 7.1

Swiss watches are famous. Until the 1970s Swiss watches dominated the market. When Swiss watchmakers developed the first electronic watch, management dismissed them. The first digital watches were bulky and not as elegant as the traditional watches. The American and Japanese watch industries were of a different opinion and developed the electronic watch further, with great success. The pre-emptory dismissal of the electronic watch during the early stages cost the Swiss watch industry its dominant position and forced it to play catch-up in a technology that it had pioneered.

Organizing

Once the organization has made its plans, it is necessary to develop the means to implement them. This requires development of an organizational scheme that is appropriate and helps the organization reach its goals in an efficient manner. The organizational scheme assigns responsibilities, co-ordinates tasks, and assigns human and material resources to transform plans into reality. That is, it establishes an internal structure of roles and activities required for meeting the organization's goals. It assigns functions of positions and, at the more detailed level, establishes the work routines and standard operating procedures for each unit. The organizational structure must strive for compatibility between the goals of the organization and those of its constituent parts. The organization must also be concerned with the flow of work through the system and with the people involved and their interrelationships. People have different skills and interests and it is important that they are matched to jobs that use their skills and appeal to their interests, otherwise motivation and productivity are likely to suffer. The well being of the employees is important; they are the most valuable assets of the organization. Sensitivity to the needs of employees is, therefore, important for the long-term success of an organization.

There is no one best way to organize, but there are some criteria that are helpful. Work that is stable and involves many routine tasks can be organized down to the details. The same is not the case, however, for work that is changing, complex, and requires judgement case by case. Predictability of the work is an indicator of how much of the job is routine. For tasks that are relatively stable and routine, procedures, policies, and plans can be written down in manuals for employees to follow. Much of the decision making is removed from the employees. Skill requirements for such tasks are usually lower than for tasks that require judgement and decision making. For complex tasks, it is usually not possible to write down procedures and processes in detail. Many individual decisions need to be left to the discretion of employees. It is important that the organizational scheme reflects their responsibilities and gives them the authority and resources to carry them out.

Poor organization results in poor management. Efficient organization of tasks and responsibilities is the foundation of effective management. Therefore, we should not neglect organizing but dedicate sufficient resources to it. Effective managers go through a planning process to develop an effective organizational scheme (Miller, 1988).

1. *Set clear goals*. Formulate an action plan to accomplish the goals. The action plan should incorporate the organization of tasks and assignment of resources, responsibilities and authority. Planning and organizing combined result in successful work groups.

2. *Once work groups are established, build efficient teams*. Matching people to the right tasks is an important part of this step.

3. *The whole process of organizing, establishment of work groups, and team building provides useful information for human resource planning and development*. By identifying tasks and achieving the best matches of employees to tasks, human capital needs are identified and can be translated in development and/or recruitment programmes.

4. *The organizational structure is also important because of its impact on leadership*. Different organizational forms and structures require different leadership styles. A highly structured organization that is engaged in routine tasks can lead in top-down fashion. By contrast, an organization in a quickly changing environment needs flexible structures so that it can change and adjust quickly. In such an organization power and authority must be distributed more evenly so that individuals can act without a lengthy approval process.

5. *The clear organization and assignment of tasks and responsibilities provides direction and guidance to employees*. Employees who understand their roles need less direct guidance and supervision. Clear expectations

also reduce friction and other sources of frustration and dissent that lower the employees' well being and the organization's productivity.

6. *Another benefit of clear organization is that it facilitates delegation.* Without a clear understanding of who is responsible for what tasks, it is difficult to delegate. In addition, the manager may be called upon to decide disputes about assignments and authority. With well-defined goals and an action plan, many such decisions are already made and communicated to those concerned. This frees up the manager's time for activities that will yield larger returns. It will also make the work of the manager easier, more interesting, and more satisfying.

7. *Finally, good organization improves morale.* Few things destroy morale quicker than uncertainty about responsibilities and disputes over assignments. Good organization clarifies roles and expectations. Frustration is a much smaller problem in a well-organized workplace.

If management is a body of knowledge, then organizing is the skeleton or framework on which management is built. The connection between planning and organizing is the key relationship in management. Organization has a plan as its point of reference. The goals and objectives of a plan indicate what organizing must occur. The following steps to effective organizing are based on the work of Miller (1988).

1. Set up the organizational structure that shows the various departments and divisions.

2. Determine what jobs are to be done to accomplish the objectives of the plan.

3. Decide how the jobs will be grouped into viable work units.

4. Decide how the jobs and/or work units must be co-ordinated within your department and between other departments; establish relationships to organize teamwork.

5. Decide on formal relationships and staffing of employees. Who reports to whom?

6. Decide how much authority must go with a job or work unit; define lines of activity.

7. Determine who will make decisions and what their authority will be.

8. Delegate jobs or tasks to the appropriate employees.

9. Select, allocate, and train personnel in needed skills and technologies.

10. Monitor results to accomplish the goals and objectives of the organization.

Controlling

The word control when used in management does not mean restriction or application of power over fellow employees. The relationship of power over or restriction on followers falls under the function of directing. Control in management describes an information system that monitors plans and processes to ensure that they are effective and that the organization is meeting predetermined goals. Thus, an effective control system contributes to accomplishing objectives by monitoring progress and sounding a warning when remedial action becomes necessary. The process associated with control shares some similarity with a score card at a basketball game or with a thermostat. Control is a series of methods used to track the results of planning, organizing and leading. In the body of managerial knowledge, control is the nervous system that reports the function of the parts of the body to the whole system (Miller, 1988).

The control function is the process of monitoring performance, recording information, and taking corrective action to keep work on track. Thus, decisions related to the control function focus on how well things are being done. Are the organization's goals and objectives being achieved? If they are not being achieved, is it because of problems that can be corrected or because the goals and objectives turned out to be unrealistic in practice? Without management assessing progress toward the goals defined in the planning process, there will be no feedback to departments, divisions, or employees. Controlling is part of implementing the plan. Without the application of control the plan will be ineffective and the organization will encounter many of the problems that are likely to occur when there is no planning.

Controls are found at all levels and include measures of an individual employee's performance, of the contributions of individual departments to goal achievement, and of the progress of the whole organization. Managers should set high standards for the organization; their vision should be ambitious and the organization's goals challenging. The control system and process need to be fair. Managers should develop a philosophy of how to assess employees and departments. From this philosophy they should derive criteria about how to assess progress. Progress should always be measured against the standards established by the goals developed in the planning stage. That is, actual performances should be compared with planned objectives and established standards. If there is severe deviation of the actual performance from the established standards, managers need to investigate if fault rests in the setting of the standards or if there is a problem in the performance of the organization. Proper control offers an organization the time and information to correct programmes and plans that have gone astray. Below are some criteria for a fair evaluation process.

1. *Hold employees and departments accountable only for actions that are within their control.* This means that the evaluation should focus on ac-

tions and performance, not just results. Sometimes poor results are obtained not because of poor performance, but because of events outside your control. Sometimes good results are obtained by luck.

2. *The assessment process should focus on weaknesses, problems, and on strengths and accomplishments.* Performances and other related data should be recorded, as this becomes a source of new and often improved information to use when making adjustments and for improving future plans.

3. *A good evaluation does not engage in fault finding but in problem solving.* Evaluation is used to make changes and improve the performance, to reinforce success and correct shortcomings.

4. *Assessment should be positive, not punitive.* An important purpose of assessment is to identify excellent performance and accomplishments so that they can be rewarded. Recognizing excellence is itself a reward. Rewards, which do not have to be financial, encourage excellent performance. Few things are more discouraging than excellent work that is not recognized. If assessment is seen as something positive, those who are being assessed will co-operate in the assessment process. If the assessment is viewed as punitive, they may tend to hide negative information, making the evaluation process less effective.

The assessment process may reveal the need for corrective actions. The specific actions should not be decided in haste but determined after careful consideration of the situation. Drastic actions should be avoided if possible. They send a dramatic signal to employees and, sometimes, customers, who may interpret a hasty action as a sign that the organization is in a crisis. It could lower the confidence of these important stakeholders in the organization. The age-old advice, recognize accomplishments and give compliments in public, but critique and correct people in private, is still excellent advice. The key to correcting a problem is the proper identification of its causes. Controlling is most effective if it recognizes problems early. Problems are more likely to occur when an organization takes new initiatives, e.g. develops a new product. Management should, therefore, spend more efforts on controlling new initiatives than on well-established activities. The organization has had time to gain experience and correct problems with established activities. The system of controls should reflect the risks of engaging in new activities.

Directing

The simple act of directing and influencing another person is the fundamental building block of management (McLean and Weitzel, 1992). Directing is the fourth function of management. This function brings together planning, organizing, and controlling to transform the plan into reality. Directing is the proper implementation of the other three functions of management. Directing involves carrying out decisions based on the plan. To this end management assigns duties and responsibilities, and communicates objectives to be reached. An important part of directing is communicating the organization's goals, implementing the system of controls, carrying out the human development programmes or hiring the new employees needed, and taking other actions that were planned earlier. In addition, management will analyze the feedback received through the system of controls and determine appropriate responses.

Directing is one of the functions of leadership. It includes supervision, evaluation, motivation, guidance, communication, delegation and personnel development. When done well, directing contributes to the success of an organization by providing proper direction and guidance, and by co-ordinating the activities of groups of people and departments. Directing accelerates the movement of an organization by providing a proper direction and guidance to its constituents. Directing is the ability to co-ordinate a diverse group of people over various tasks to accomplish goals and objectives of the organization. The manager meshes the plan, the physical resources of the organization, and the controls with the human resources in such a manner as to accomplish the desired objectives efficiently. The success of directing often is largely dependent on the amount of enthusiasm and commitment the manager can generate among those who actually do the work. Wise managers pay particular attention to their human resources because, if properly managed, employees can make even a poor plan relatively successful and a weak organization stronger. Skilful managers are vital to every dynamic and successful organization. Capital and technical knowledge are also needed, but without competent managers no organization can long hold a place of efficient management and effective leadership.

CHAPTER EIGHT

INTERPERSONAL COMMUNICATION

The man is only half himself; the other half is his expression.

Ralph Waldo Emerson

Communication has long been recognized as an essential organizational skill. Effective communication in an organization depends on the communication skills of individuals and on the organizational structure that is in place. No organizational structure is better than the people of whom it is composed. People's understanding of the structure and their willingness to work within it are essential to its effectiveness. Yet even when people are trying to work efficiently, problems arise. People have emotions, misunderstandings, and ego needs that sometimes get in the way. Effective organizations recognize the need for interpreting the formal structure in terms of the human element by adjusting and working through misunderstandings when they occur. No organizational structure can be successful without concern about the flow of information and the networks of communication.

The key to the success of any of the management functions is communication. Communications must flow effectively not only downward from management to followers, but also upward from followers to management and laterally at the same level. Too often managers depend almost exclusively on downward communications and then wonder why policies and procedures are misunderstood, and why goals are not accomplished. Communication channels should be open if new ideas are to flow into the organization and leaders must be open to ideas and willing to listen to others. The result of an effective communication system is feedback. The communication cycle is incomplete without giving and receiving feedback. Feedback allows the manager to determine whether understanding has indeed occurred. It also allows the good ideas and potential contributions of employees to become part of the collective success, wisdom and knowledge of the organization. The manager must create a conducive environment and provide the opportunity for feedback and involvement through deliberately designed communication processes and networks (Stenmark, 1994; Miller, 1988; Downey and Erickson, 1987).

Learning the Art of Communicating

To communicate means to learn, impart, transmit, share and understand information (and feelings). Creative communication enhances our natural ability to understand the needs and motives of others. It also builds trust and removes unwanted barriers. Communication is a shared responsibility and the final outcome is creating understanding. Good relationships depend on good communication. Communication is not a thing, but a process, which begins with the care and attention one brings to individual communications. Although we have been communicating all our lives, we have probably not given the process much thought. Sadly, much of the hostility and lack of co-operation in organizations is caused by clumsy and careless communication. Ineffective communication often creates or inflates problems and is sometimes more detrimental than no communication at all. Communication can create and escalate problems, or help solve them. Communication is neither a good thing nor a bad thing, but a tool. Like any other tool, communication can be used for good or bad purposes. Abusive language is hurtful and undermines morale. Acknowledging good work, answering questions, or discussing ideas are examples of positive and constructive use of communication. When people feel listened to, and when they listen to others, i.e., when the communicate, they come to better understand each other. This fosters mutual appreciation, respect, and contributes to a positive work environment (McCroskey and Richmond, 1996).

To create an effective communication system and to promote mutual understanding, it is necessary to first determine the purposes of communication, consider the perceptions of the audience, and then obtain feedback to check if mutual understanding has been achieved. Since successful communication involves the process of sharing information, we need to consider what to say, when to say it, to whom to say it, how to say it, and anticipate the effect the communications have on the receiver. In addition, leaders often feel that the communication skills they employ in the workplace – the office, hospital, or factory – differ from the skills they use at home with family and friends. The communication skills they use are not different at all, however, except that they are used in different ways and to different ends. Many business managers and leaders are successful at the office or at home because of the manner in which they communicate. Communication does not have one set of rules for work and another for family and friends (Stenmark, 1994).

The ability to communicate well is ranked as the number one key to success by leaders in business, industry and politics. Since communication is such an integral part of everyday life, we take our ability to communicate for granted. After all, our communication skills are, and have always been, a function of our instincts. Communication is a skill and like most skills, it is not inborn. We learn and acquire our culture's communication skills, just as we learn and acquire our culture's social skills and manners. Most of our early training comes from our parents, siblings and friends. The art of communication does not come naturally; it is an acquired skill. Communication skills can be enhanced mostly through self-training and practice. The most gifted and talented person is not always the best communicator, but it is the best-trained mind that will often triumph over pure natural ability. Many great writers, thinkers and achievers have believed that education and communication skills are not just preparing us for life, but are, in fact, what life is all about (Stenmark, 1994). The key to mastering communication skills so necessary in the workplace, and in our social lives, is practice. Even though those who think that they have a natural ability or born gift or talent for communication, have to work to develop it further. Singers with wonderful voices still take singing lessons and sport broadcasters with outstanding talents practice to improve their skills and talents. To communicate effectively is to communicate consistently. Alvin Toffler (author of *Future Shock*), wrote decades ago: "The illiterate of the future are not those who cannot read nor write, but those who cannot learn and relearn" (Stenmark, 1994).

Different leadership styles require different levels of communication. Authoritarian leaders who rely on their own judgement and that of their peers will be less concerned about feedback (though even they need some feedback to make better informed decisions) than about efficient channels through which they can communicate plans and decisions to their employees. By contrast, leaders who encourage participation and who delegate authority can do so effectively only if communications flow easily and freely between all who are working together. They need to be concerned that important information is shared; they cannot afford an important contributor to the joint effort who is 'left out of the loop'. Feedback in the form of verbal or non-verbal communication is critical so that leaders can assess how the effort is progressing. As is true for all management functions, there is no single communications system that fits all needs, but there are a few criteria that must be met.

1. Regardless of leadership style and the nature of the organization and/or project, the communications system must encourage, not just permit, timely and accurate feedback.

2. The communications system must ensure that all stakeholders – in a firm these include suppliers, employees, and customers – receive the information they need to function properly.

3. Organizations that do not become aware of emergencies as soon as possible after they occur have little chance for long-term success. Therefore, there must be a channel for communicating emergencies. There must be no penalty for someone who in good faith alerts management to an apparent emergency, even if it later turns out to have been a false alarm.

Providing and sharing information is an important aspect of communicating. Leaders communicate and share their vision, they represent the organization to those on the outside, and they negotiate on behalf of the organization. The ability to express oneself well, both orally and in writing, is a valuable asset. Information is the key ingredient of communication. The listener receives, evaluates, and reacts to the information and may respond with new or additional information. In this process, all those who are part of this exchange may gain additional and/or more reliable information. From the interpersonal perspective, communication has a dual function: on the one hand, people make their thoughts and wishes known to one another by conveying information. On the other hand, communication serves to shape and maintain relationships that already exist between individuals or within a group setting. Thus, the art of communication is essential in leadership because it creates a professional image, confidence and understanding. The personal attributes that leaders display when interacting with employees are important factors related to their credibility as leaders as well as followers. Leaders cannot aspire to communicate persuasively until they have critically and objectively examined just how they routinely present themselves to others (Gebremedhin, 1994; King, 1994).

It is evident that leaders who communicate effectively advance further and faster in their careers than those who do not communicate. Since so much of the success of leaders depends on their ability to communicate, we should raise our awareness of verbal and non-verbal communication. Each of us has a unique style of communicating with others. We tend to prefer our own style of communication and, in general, feel less comfortable with the communication styles of others. This somewhat rigid attitude can get in the way of effective communications. Successful leaders tend to match their styles of communicating, as well as their vocabulary, to the person(s) with whom they are interacting. This means paying special attention to how the other party speaks – how quickly they speak, their rhythm, volume, and tone, the gestures they use. They adjust their own speech to that of the other person (McLean and Weitzel 1992). The following example illustrates the value of matching our communication style to that of our partners.

Example 8.1

Bill worked as a packaging salesman. He was visiting with a new company. A young entrepreneur, who had founded the company, liked an informal environment and gave his employees considerably more leeway than was common in other firms. Bill liked the young entrepreneur and was impressed by his ideas. He thought that the firm had excellent growth potential and therefore decided to work with him to develop attractive packages for the firm's product. To work with the founder and the firm's staff, he adopted the same informal forms of communication as they did. He soon was a trusted advisor and received the order for the firm's packaging materials. Bill's assessment turned out to be correct. The firm grew quickly and developed into Bill's most important and profitable client.

Spoken Words

Probably the most common and important form of communication is verbal communication. Communicating with groups is different from one on one communications. Some people are soft-spoken and are afraid of speaking in front of others, particularly a large audience. Others have poor speaking habits. Some people are verbose; others lack confidence in their ideas. Inexperienced leaders, maybe because they are nervous, often undermine the credibility of what they say and their authority by starting with an apology. The foreign-born, in particular, may be more difficult to understand because of an unfamiliar accent or pronunciation. No matter how much you already know about the art of communication, you can improve your skills and gain more confidence and develop more powerful speaking skills. In a formal presentation you should appear poised and confident, even when you are nervous, in order to persuade others that your ideas deserve their support. Learn compelling communication skills that make you more effective with people at all levels and in a variety of situations, including meetings, presentations, and relating to associates and employees on a one on one basis (Miller, 1988; King, 1994).

In verbal communication we need to focus on the words you use. Choose your words carefully and avoid imprecise language. As Rudyard Kipling insisted: "Words are the most powerful drug used by mankind." We need to select what we say and say it well. It is commonly said, 'Kind words are keys that fit all locks.' The analogy here is that you can catch more flies with honey than with vinegar. Mother Teresa gives us good advice: "Kind words can be short and easy to speak, but their echoes are truly endless." This is because kind words always create confidence and love. It is then important to say it with a sparkle, say it with sincerity, say it with substance or all three of those things, but if you are going to say it at all, say it with style.

Your voice tells the listener much about you. Your voice often gives you away. Make sure your tone of voice communicates the message you want. A low voice conveys a sense of insecurity, while an overly loud voice is annoying and the speaker may be perceived as aggressive. It is not only what to say, but also how to say it. The way you speak reflects the way you feel and think. When you have to respond to a request or a problem, you often say the first thing that comes to your mind. This can cause problems or misunderstandings. Do not address controversial issues unprepared. Silence is usually better than ineffective verbal communication. To speak well is to think well. When you have time to think, you will usually come up with a better statement, and express your thought more elegantly, than if you have to respond immediately. In addition, it is not how much people say but what they say that matters. Quality is more important than quantity. A common mistake made by inexperienced presenters is that of providing more information than is necessary to make their point. Redundant information may distract your audience from the core message you wanted to communicate. Although electronic means are replacing some face to face communication, verbal communication still remains a critical skill for all leaders (King, 1994; Stenmark, 1994).

Written Words

Although verbal communication is used much more often, the written word is powerful because of its permanence. You may forget something that you heard but you can always re-read something that is in writing. This makes writing the appropriate means of communicating important announcements. There can be disagreement over what has been said, while the written word is more certain. That is why important commitments, such as contracts, are usually confirmed in writing. Samuel Johnson once said, "Words once they are written in black and white as it is for all who care to read, have a life of their own." This is both good advice and a warning. As we said above, a careless statement made in a conversation may be forgotten. The same statement in writing may come back to haunt us.

Robert Louis Stevenson noted, "All speech, written or spoken, is a dead language until it finds a willing and prepared hearer." Stevenson's advice points to the importance of considering the audience for our communication. This is equally important in spoken and written communications. The power of the written word cannot be underestimated, but it is a verbal exchange which produces mutual understanding (Stenmark, 1994). That is, the purpose of the communication should determine its form. Since the primary goal of communication is to transmit information, communication in written or spoken words in any situation should use the simplest and most open and direct technique, for getting your message across. Leaders must find a way to communicate the vision in a way that attracts and excites members of the organization (Miller, 1988; Conger, 1992).

Listening

Communication consists of much more than spoken and written words. Although the spoken and written words are important forms of communication, they are not nearly as important as listening. According to Bolton (1979), listening is the primary communication activity. Listening accounts for 45 per cent of all communication activities, compared to 30 per cent for speaking, 16 per cent for reading and 9 per cent for writing. Listening is the foundation of good communications. Good listening is not demonstrated by being able to repeat what has been said, but by understanding what has been said. Good listeners are active participants in the communication. Listening is a critical skill in leadership and management. When you wish to learn something, you need to listen because learning to listen and listening to learn is an art. You listen with your ears for meaning, but you also 'listen' with your eyes for behaviour and with your heart for feelings. To listen, per se, is the single best tool for empowering people. To listen to someone is a sign of respect and interest in that person. Listening helps leaders discover strengths and needs, and it motivates followers.

Too often you hear but may not listen. One of the most common obstacles to good listening is the tendency to formulate a response in your head while the other person is still speaking. This habit prevents you from listening with an understanding for the speaker's perspective. To overcome it takes deliberate effort. Practice by trying to understand not only what is being said but also why the speaker is saying it. Maybe the speaker has a different perspective or values. Unless you make an effort to understand, you may never learn what is really meant.

We want to stress that communication is a two-way street. Listen so you can hear what is really being said because people listen more attentively to those who listen to them. If you do not listen to your followers, you can not expect them to listen to you. A simple rule of thumb works here: talk and listen to those who work for you the same way you want your boss to talk and listen to you. Listening to what the followers have to say and appreciating their particular viewpoints demonstrates respect for them and their ideas. Listening to others means giving them your full attention. This increases their sense of being appreciated and needed. By listening, leaders inspire confidence in their followers, learn when something is wrong, and meet an important human need, that of being taken seriously. Leaders have to start to listen carefully and take measures to communicate with their employees. The chief executive of government organizations and businesses must come out of their offices and start walking the floor and talking and listening to the people with whom they work. The top men and women need to pause in their shuffling of papers and stop saying 'my door is always open', especially when it is not, and 'I am only a phone call away' when you know the line is permanently engaged or when the secretary does not give the line at all because she is told to say that the boss is busy. Listening correlates positively with high intelligence. Someone who does not listen well will probably not become a successful leader (Fairholm, 1994; King, 1994; McLean and Weitzel, 1992).

Listening is 'taking in', storing, analyzing and evaluating the content of what we hear. While we may be hearing what is said, we are only listening for some of the time. We are capable of listening intently for a short period, followed by periods when we work or process the information we receive. Listening involves this continual process of making sense of what we have heard. It is only after we have tuned in and thought critically about what has been said that the listening process becomes effective and understanding is developed. Effective listening increases clarity of understanding, enhances communication, supports co-operation, improves morale, increases job commitment and focuses on productivity (Stenmark, 1994).

In verbal communication, 'seek first to understand'. Research shows that most people listen with the intent to reply (Bolton, 1979). They are either speaking or preparing to speak. According to the National Seminars Group (1997), studies show that up to 75 per cent of our interpersonal communication is ignored, misunderstood or forgotten because we do not listen carefully or pay full attention to what is said. On average, in a face to face discussion people absorb only about 30 per cent of what is said. In other words, employees of an organization may hear less than a third of what their supervisors tell them directly. Thus, the first rule and initial step of effective interpersonal communication is listening. Listening is more than hearing what is being said. Bolton (1979) summarizes a discussion of what listening is as follows: "Listening, then, is the *combination* of hearing what the other person says *and* a suspenseful waiting, an intense psychological involvement with the other" (Bolton, 1979).

Listening is not a skill that comes naturally to most of us, but it is a skill that can be learned. It requires hearing and understanding what is being said. There are situations when effective listening can be very difficult. Any time strong feelings are involved in an issue, communicating about it tends to be difficult. Let us look at a hypothetical case.

Example 8.2

After ten years of service as a regular employee, Ann was appointed supervisor of her department. Prior to her appointment she was one of the best team players in the department. Ann enjoyed the company of her colleagues and occasionally met with them socially. John is one of those colleagues. As his supervisor she is satisfied with his work in general, but there are some aspects of his performance Ann would like him to improve. John also likes Ann but he still feels some disappointment that she won the promotion and he didn't. Ann is aware of this. During the annual performance evaluation she was trying to address those areas that she would like for John to work on. Because of her previous status as John's colleague, and because she knew that he was disappointed about not being promoted, she did not want to hurt his feelings. In her discussion with John she did not state her concerns directly and clearly, but only alluded to them. John who had some concerns of his own, also did not address them clearly, because he was worried that Ann would interpret any comments on her leadership as 'sour grapes' on his part. Because they did not express their concerns clearly, nothing changed after the performance evaluation, and both were frustrated with the lack of progress.

This is a fairly typical situation. Many of us are uncomfortable critiquing someone and few of us welcome critiques of our actions. These are among the leading reasons for failures to communicate. Thus, to communicate well we need to learn to critique the actions of others; we also need to learn to deal with others' critique of our actions. Let us first look at how to evaluate the performance of others.

Critiquing

Leaders have to evaluate the performance of their employees. To communicate such an evaluation is not an easy task. We refer to this task as a critique. A critique is not the same as criticism; to critique is not the same as to criticize. A critique is an assessment of actions, behaviours or outcomes. It includes positive and negative aspects. Most importantly, it does not criticize the person. This is the key to a good and supportive evaluation: focus on issues, not on people and personalities. The following is an example of what not to do.

Example 8.3

The supervisor has just called Robert to his office. He is concerned with interpersonal frictions among some of the employees that are affecting morale in the office. To start the discussion he asks Robert, 'Why do you always have difficulties working co-operatively with others?' Robert reacts very defensively and blames his co-workers for most of the conflict. The discussion is not going anywhere. The supervisor is frustrated because he has not learned the source of the conflict. Robert is furious because he feels unfairly singled out and blamed.

The supervisor started the discussion with a statement that accused Robert of being the cause of the interpersonal conflict in the department. It did not allow Robert to offer his views on what was going on. From the very beginning he was put on the defensive and given no incentive to share his opinion and tell his side of the story. The supervisor, therefore, learned absolutely nothing, but appeared to be taking the side of those with whom Robert was in conflict without first listening to all involved. It made Robert feel like he was treated unfairly. It is unlikely that in the future Robert will go on his own to see his supervisor for advice. Here are some guidelines for fair and constructive evaluation.

1. *Stress the positive.* Do not devalue a positive assessment with statements such as, 'You did your work really well *but* you are capable of doing even better.' Instead, if you would like to suggest how a good performance could be further improved, say something like, 'You did your work really well *and* I think you can build on that success to make the following future improvements.'

2. *Focus on specific actions and behaviours, not on personalities.* It is helpful if you can state why a behaviour is undesirable. Use statements that explain how the behaviour affected you. For example: 'When you were late to the team meeting yesterday, I was frustrated because the team project is very important to me.'

3. *Be honest.* Do not give praise or appreciation if none is earned. Explain

why you think something is good or bad. Give positive and constructive feedback to employees that do not demoralize them.

4. *Allow the person who is being evaluated to respond.* Encourage responses that focus on actions and behaviours, not personalities. Encourage self-assessment. Reward honesty in self-assessment; it builds trust and the confidence necessary to openly address problems.

Managers must be able to communicate with their employees. This includes listening to their concerns. The task of listening to the concerns of employees can be very difficult because some of these concerns may be threatening to the manager.

Example 8.4

The department recently announced the pay raises for the next year. Jane found out that her raise was less than that of other employees with similar responsibilities. She has made an appointment to see her supervisor. Jane is disappointed and feels treated unfairly. Recommendations for pay raises are made by the supervisor and are usually approved by management.

In this case Mary, the manager, needs to be aware not only of Jane's emotions, but also her own. Mary should be careful not to react defensively to having her recommendation questioned. If emotions take over, the meeting will not yield positive results. Mary must explain her evaluation criteria and how she arrived at the recommendation for a pay raise for Jane. If Jane's raise is smaller than those of other employees because her performance is not as strong, then the manager's comments should make this clear and explain what Jane must do to earn a higher performance rating. Failure to explain the pay raise will only confirm to Jane that she is being treated unfairly and does not identify weaknesses that she can address to improve her future performance. In addition, we all know from experience that *how a person is told often is as important as what the person is told* (Miller, 1988). That is why it is helpful to separate issues from personalities. Discussions about issues are less threatening because they do not deal with who we are or our self-worth, as do discussions about personalities.

Employees may hide their real feelings because they worry that expressing their feelings may offend their supervisor or manager. They may be reluctant to complain about the behaviour of a co-worker because they fear that word will get back to them. Instead of addressing the issues that concern them directly, they may only allude to them. If the manager does not realize what is truly bothering an employee, frustrations may accumulate over a period of time and result in an outburst over a trivial issue that has nothing at all to do with the real issues. Good listening, therefore, is more than hearing what is being said. It is also trying to understand why it is being said. Bolton (1979) distinguishes between three types of skills that can help us improve our ability to listen effectively. The following descriptions are a summary based on his work.

1. *Attending skills.* These include a "posture of involvement", i.e. body language that communicates that you are listening. Keeping an open posture is usually perceived positively while tightly crossed arms are often taken as a sign of closeness and defensiveness (Bolton, 1979). Eye contact also tells the speaker that you are engaged and interested in what the other person has to say. Finally, attending skills include holding important conversations in a non-distracting environment. If the meeting is held in your office, hold calls and other interruptions. Keep a distance that is close but still comfortable for both speaker and listener.

2. *Following skills.* Bolton (1979) refers to some of these as "door opener" skills. To illustrate what he means, consider the following example. You may notice that an employee looks very frustrated and encourage him to talk by saying, 'You seem to be really frustrated with something. Would you like to talk about it?' It is an invitation to talk, not a command. Once the employee is talking, use "minimal encouragers" (Bolton 1979). These are very short statements, such as 'tell me more', 'I see', 'go on', or simply 'oh?' and other short statements that encourage the speaker and signal that you are an interested listener. Questions should be infrequent. Open-ended questions that leave it to the speaker to determine the direction he wants to go are preferred over closed questions. "Attentive silence" is a sign of good listening.

3. *Reflecting skills.* To make sure you understand, it is often useful to paraphrase what has been said, i.e. you reflect back what has been said and let the speaker correct you if you misunderstood. This works not only for facts, but we can also reflect back feelings. Words that reveal feelings (enjoy, anger, fun, frustration, etc.) can help the listener understand the speaker's feelings.

Example 8.5

Elizabeth had called John into her office. She had noticed that he seemed unhappy and frustrated. She asked him if something was bothering him. John was a bit reluctant at first. He said 'Well, George and I just cannot work together.' Elizabeth replied only 'I see.' 'Yes,' continued John, 'he does not pull his weight. And when I confronted him, he got mad at me. I just don't like working with him.' Then John stopped. Elizabeth waited awhile. When John did not continue, she encouraged him, saying, 'It sounds like you are angry with George.' With this encouragement, John continued to tell her more.

Dealing with feelings is not easy and we often try to hide or ignore them. While it is important that we control feelings, it can be dangerous to ignore them in us or in others. Acknowledge them and if they are potentially destructive, find out their causes and try to address them. This can often be accomplished through listening. People with good listening skills are more likely to become successful leaders (Fairholm, 1994; King, 1994; McLean and Weitzel, 1992). One of the reasons for their success might be that leaders who listen gain a better understanding of their followers. A good understanding of the followers helps to effectively communicate to them the leader's vision in a way that attracts and excites them (Miller, 1988; Conger, 1992).

When dealing with problems, timing is important. It is best if we deal with difficult issues when we are not distracted; without our full attention, we are not likely to solve such problems. If a discussion becomes emotionally charged, as could happen, for example, in a discussion about employee performance, we should try to calm emotions. Objectivity decreases as emotions increase. Therefore, it is wise to stop a discussion if one of the participants has become overly emotional and provide time to calm down. Sometimes this may require that the discussion be rescheduled for another date.

Just as the use of appropriate skills improves communication, poor skills erect barriers to communication. One of the greatest barriers to communication is judging. Judging consists of criticizing, name-calling, diagnosing what is wrong with the other person and praising evaluatively (Bolton, 1979). Insincere praise is a roadblock to communication. To praise well is to praise honestly. Insincere praise is often used to manipulate someone. A statement such as 'you are so skilled at doing this task, it is best if you take over here', may be less a compliment than an excuse by a colleague to avoid an assignment.

Sending solutions is another roadblock (Bolton, 1979). We sometimes became impatient with someone when we think we know how to tackle a problem. Unless the other person asks for our suggestions, however, we should listen instead of offering solutions. Sometimes the other person needs to talk about an issue to come to terms with it. The need of the other person is not met when we cut the person short by offering a solution. When we focus on getting a problem solved in a manner that we think is efficient, we may encounter another obstacle to communication: avoiding the concerns of others (Bolton, 1979). When we offer solutions we take over the discussion and determine where it will end up. The solutions we offer will most likely reflect *our* interpretation of what the problems are, *our* problem solving skills, and *our* values, and not those of the other person. Thus, our solution may not meet the need of the other person. In addition, we may also send the (non-verbal) message that we do not trust the other person's ability to solve the problem without our assistance (Bolton, 1979).

Imagine the previous example. How would John have reacted if Elizabeth had not encouraged him to tell her why he was angry with George? Would he have continued talking with her if she had said, 'I see that you and George have had a difference of opinion. I think you should go and tell him that you want him to pull his weight.' Most likely, John would have left, no closer to a solution than when he entered Elizabeth's office, and probably even more frustrated.

Cultural Differences

Communication can be difficult even when people share a common culture. When individuals from different cultural backgrounds communicate with each other, misunderstandings are more likely to happen. Since today's business world is increasingly international and global, awareness of other cultures is becoming more important. Such awareness prevents misunderstandings when dealing with members from other cultures. The following example illustrates a difference in how individuals interact in the United States and Germany, respectively.

Example 8.6

In the United States interactions between individuals who meet for the first time are often quite informal. It is not unusual for people to be addressed by their first names. When Americans call another organization and leave their name, staff members answering the phone will often respond by using the first name, even though they never have met the person they are calling. In many other cultures this kind of informality would be considered rude, or at least unprofessional. In German culture, for example, adults address each other by their second name and the title 'Herr' or 'Frau' (Mr, Mrs). They use first names only by mutual agreement. The offer to switch to first names indicates that a certain level of familiarity has been reached and is usually made by the more senior person.

The more different a culture is from our own, the more likely it is that social and cultural norms of verbal (and non-verbal) interactions differ from our own. Therefore, it is to our benefit to learn about such norms if we enter into discussions with members from other cultures. We should avoid parochialism and try to view the world through the eyes of someone else. This does not mean that we relinquish our beliefs and values, only that we are trying to understand those of others. Such understanding will help us better understand their actions and judge situations more correctly. The following example illustrates how expectations may differ between cultures (based on an example in Adler, 1991)

> **Example 8.7**
>
> A leading Canadian bank invited a Chinese delegation for dinner. Two executives of the Canadian bank shared the responsibility of hosting the event. There was no welcoming speech or exchange of toasts. At the end of the meal the Chinese delegation departed quite abruptly. Both the Canadians and the Chinese were dissatisfied with the event. Having two hosts was confusing to the Chinese, who tend to be more hierarchy-minded than North Americans. Also, because age is a sign of seniority in China, the two hosts' relative youth was interpreted as disrespect. Finally, in China the host offers a toast of welcome to the guests, who then propose a toast in return. The Chinese thought the Canadians, who were not aware of this tradition, were being rude. The Canadians were upset by the Chinese delegation's abrupt departure. It is not unusual, however, for Chinese to retire relatively early.

To avoid problems and misunderstandings, it is wise to learn about the cultures of employees and customers. The benefits from such knowledge can be great. When people are treated with disrespect, they become less co-operative. Even the way we present our qualifications can make a difference. For example, in many cultures, personal relationships are more important than the college where we earned our degree. Stressing the reputation of one's alma mater might be considered bragging. There is no universal solution, but there are some simple guidelines.

1. *Always be courteous.* If in doubt about how to behave, use formal rather than informal forms of communication. Be careful when using jokes; humour also knows ethnic differences.

2. *Prepare ahead of time.* Read about the other culture and seek the advice of people who are knowledgeable about it.

3. *Be sensitive to your guests.* Ask them, 'Are you comfortable?', 'Is there something you need?' Enquire before a dinner meeting, 'Do you have any dietary restrictions?' If your guest seems uncomfortable, try to discreetly find out the reason. If you are the guest, following the example of your host is a good solution whenever you are not sure how to act.

Body Language

We communicate in various ways and forms: verbal communication is expressed by listening, written and spoken words through laughter and through design, music and the arts. One of the reasons that communication can be difficult is because it is not limited to verbal interactions. We interpret actions and behaviours, facial expressions (a frown or a smile), body language, tone of voice and appearance. Non-verbal communication is also expressed by silence, gestures, moving hands or crossed arms, appropriate physical speaking distance, posture, even positions of the body, clothing (dressing patterns and styles), and an unmistakable and calm projection of complete self-confidence and integrity. We can lower the chances of misunderstandings by being aware of how others might view our actions and personal behaviours and by becoming familiar with the cultural background and expectations of the organization.

Communications experts estimate that only 10 per cent of our communication is represented by verbal communication. Another 30 per cent is represented by sounds and 60 per cent by body language. That is, the literature (Richmond and McCroskey, 1998) suggests that anywhere from 65 per cent to 90 per cent of the meaning in the communication process is produced by some nonverbal component. In other words, body language speaks volumes. Non-verbal communication is most often associated with effect or emotion, whereas verbal communication is associated with ideational context (Richmond and McCroskey, 1998). Nonverbal communication also embraces silence. Powerful written or spoken words are often misleading; they get in the way and we have to rely on the unspoken words of silence and body language for deeper communication. Effective verbal communications have the ability to distinguish between communication that will solve problems and that which creates problems. People disagree on values and issues, and verbal communication can sometimes do more harm than good. Ineffective verbal communication can create new problems or make problems worse than if no communication had been attempted.

- *Silence*, to some, is the essence of non-communication. Those who listen realize that, in some circumstances, silence can speak volumes. Silence at the right time is artful conversation; there is eloquence in it. As Dorothy Nevill insists, "The real art of conversation is not only to say the right thing in the right place but to leave unsaid the wrong thing at the tempting moment" (Stenmark, 1994). Popular culture is also aware of the value of silence as expressed in the Simon and Garfunkel song *The Sound of Silence*: "People talking without speaking, people hearing without listening."

- *Facial expressions* are another important type of non-verbal communication. The face provides information related to race, gender, emotional state, age and even the type of person you are. As McCroskey and Richmond (1996) indicated: "Our faces are our windows to the world." People make judgements about our attitudes and feelings based on facial expressions. A smile is a universal expression of happiness and friendliness.

- *Touching* is another form of non-verbal behaviour. It is related to the concept of 'personal space'. By personal space we refer to the comfortable distance between two people. Touching and personal spaces vary from culture to culture. People from the Middle East and Latin America tend to maintain close distance when talking to each other. By contrast, people from the United States, Japan, and China generally prefer greater distances when talking to each other. Northern Europeans and Americans tend to be non-touch-oriented, whereas Arabs and Latin Americans tend to be more touch-oriented. This is not to suggest that the North Americans do not like to touch or be touched, they simply do not employ touch as a form of communication as much as some other cultures do, but reserve it for those they feel very close to (McCroskey and Richmond, 1996). In general, interpersonal distances are shorter and touching is more frequent when we talk with people we know well. When in doubt about what is appropriate, maintain a respectful distance and do not touch. It is always essential to understand and respect cultural difference, when communicating with people of different culture and tradition.

• *Smell* can be a part of non-verbal communication. Pleasant smells evoke pleasant feelings. Maybe this is one of the reasons why so many business meetings are held in conjunction with a meal. The smell of good food is pleasing to most people. Our sense of smell helps us to perceive the world around us and determines what communication is appropriate. The sense of smell is a pervasive, unconscious determinant of how we feel about others. It affects our mood, attitude about others, perceptions of others, and communication orientation toward others (McCroskey and Richmond, 1996). The following is a simple illustration about how smell is used to influence a potential customer.

Example 8.8

A few years ago one of the authors hired a real estate agent to help him sell his home. The agent advised him to buy ready to bake cookie dough and bake a few cookies just before the time when a potential buyer is scheduled to view the house.

The interpretation of non-verbal expressions is not error-free and is influenced by the interpreter's own feelings, mood and culture. People in different cultures use different gestures, postures, speaking distance, and other non-verbal signals to communicate their feelings, social values and status. People who would feel uncomfortable putting some information or messages into words may use body language to send and receive information. Body language is usually a part of, and contributes to, verbal communication. There is one rule of body language that everyone should follow in conversations: maintain eye contact (but without staring at the other person). Maintaining eye contact shows interest in the other person; it does not mean patronizing or talking down to others. If you are really trying to listen to what is being said, you will find that it is much easier if you look at the other person. If you are listening closely, most of the appropriate body language will follow automatically (King, 1994).

Body language reflects cultural norms and practices. For example, traditionally women were expected to be supportive, emotional, timid, modest and passive. They were assigned lower status and less power than men. Their role in society was communicated through body language. Non-verbal communication included a tendency to lower the eyes and tilt the head slightly downward to avoid direct eye contact, rounding shoulders and batting eyelashes, smiling and nodding more than is necessary, yielding space and talking time to the males, and generally exhibiting less dominant non-verbal behaviours. These are expressions of body language that we should avoid if we want to be treated as equals. To be accepted as equals we must show confidence. Otherwise, our conversation partners will subconsciously 'read' the body language as signaling a lack of confidence and they will discount an otherwise persuasive presentation.

Dramatic changes are taking place in how communication must be made to reach today's audience. Verbal communication alone is not enough to get the message through today's demanding audience. The value of communication skills is diminished if the body language does not support the verbal message. This information is intended to illustrate the dual nature of verbal and non-verbal communication.

Dressing

You are judged on the basis of many factors, and one of them is how you dress. Clothing communicates status, attitudes, purpose, and significance of an occasion, values, and professional goals, cultural background, occupation, gender and age. The way you dress influences how others communicate with you. Along with the dress, artifacts, such as jewellry, make-up, briefcase, hat, and eyeglasses contribute to how others judge you. For example, people who wear eyeglasses are perceived as more intelligent, industrious and dependable. In general, the type of clothing and the kinds of artifacts you use give others cues to your socio-economic status, your attitudes, and even your job. These enhancements of physical appearance impact your interpersonal communication and the kind of professional image and confidence you want to project (McCroskey and Richmond, 1996). It is evident that first impressions are important. Appearance counts heavily in preliminary judgements of you by professionals or others who do not know you. It effects how people listen to you, since it effects how they perceive your attitude about your work. When others observe you, they tend to make many judgements about you, such as your economic level, educational level, social position, sophistication level, credibility, management potential and other leadership measures.

What is considered appropriate dress varies between organizations, type of business, job responsibilities, places and countries and events. For example, employees of financial institutions tend to dress more conservatively than employees of educational institutions. Within educational institutions, top administrators dress more formally than regular faculty members. In most other organizations, formal attire also indicates high rank. Dress also expresses function. This is particularly obvious in the case of specialized work clothing, such as the heavy shoes or boots and sturdy clothes of a construction worker. Formal dress is out of place on the construction site. Even the architect will wear less formal and sturdier clothing when she visits the construction site than when she is working in the office.

Because there are so many differences in what is appropriate attire depending on place, culture, function, etc., there is no standard dress code that projects an acceptable professional image. There is also no one rule that one can learn. The best advice is to determine what is appropriate within the organization, to observe what those who are respected within the organization do, and to ask for advice from admired and respected persons as to what is a proper dress code in the organization.

Institutional Communication

We usually think of communication as an individual activity. We need to be reminded that organizations communicate, too. Firms issue announcements that represent the view of the whole organization. They communicate their policies to their employees. Organizations communicate to the public through their logos, letterhead and printed materials. A leader's statement is often taken as representing the view of the whole organization. This is true even if the leader speaks as a private person. It is therefore important that leaders clearly state whether they are expressing their private opinion or whether they are representing the organization.

Clients often base their view of a company on the behaviour of a few employees. Thus, the secretary who answers the phone, the executive who talks to a reporter, and the driver of the company truck all shape the company's public image. It is important that managers provide leadership that ensures that the messages sent by different people and media are consistent with the values of the organization. The following example illustrates this point.

Example 8.9

Ruth owned a large bookstore. She found it increasingly difficult to compete with some of the large stores that are part of a chain. Those stores could offer prices that were too low to even cover the costs of operating her store. She decided that she could not compete in price but that she held an edge in customer service. To enhance this advantage she remodeled the store, adding some comfortable chairs and a coffee bar. She also trained her employees to provide a better service. For example, she trained them how to use a new computerized system that allowed her store to keep track of inventory and of customer purchases. Over time, the data that accumulated about customer purchases allowed her to shift her stock so that it better reflected her customers' tastes. At first, Ruth's employees were skeptical. They were swayed, however, by Ruth's own efforts at providing outstanding and personal service to customers, the investments into the store, and the training they received.

Managers set the tone. If their interactions with their staff are rude, curt, unfriendly, and unprofessional, their staff will probably not be persuaded that the firm really values good manners and friendliness. This is one area where leading by example is particularly important.

CHAPTER NINE

DELEGATION AND EMPOWERMENT

If you want one year of prosperity, grow grain;
If you want ten years of prosperity, grow trees;
If you want one hundred years of prosperity, grow people.

Chinese Proverb

We feel stress most acutely when we have no control over the situation that causes it. This insight alone suggests that delegation and empowerment are important. People want to achieve control over their environment. Receiving responsibility and the authority to make decisions can make a job more enjoyable. Fairholm (1994) even suggests that the survival of an organization in the future will depend on having empowered, self-directed workers. The ability to increase the self-control and self-direction of employees has become a valued leadership skill. It is accomplished when leaders discover and make use of the full potential of their employees. People are encouraged to go beyond an average performance if their talents are recognized, enhanced, utilized, and if they are given the necessary authority to decide how to carry out their tasks. It motivates them to keep learning, become more involved in teamwork, and makes work more interesting for them. Empowered employees respond with more commitment than employees who are treated as subordinates. Employees who have no authority to make decisions will demonstrate little initiative and commitment to the goals of the organization. They will limit their efforts to the tasks that are assigned to them. By contrast, empowerment encourages employees to develop their talents. By allowing them to judge situations and make decisions, empowered employees reap intrinsic rewards from taking initiatives that help improve processes and products of the organization. Such employees will truly feel part of the organization through the contributions that they can make. In developing, rewarding, and recognizing their employees and others working with them, leaders promote their development. When leaders empower their followers, they make them more aware of their abilities and encourage them to develop their full potential (Fairholm, 1994).

Benefits of Empowerment

In the preceding paragraph we argued that empowerment enhances employee motivation and the performance of the leader/manager. Conventional wisdom suggests that managers with empowered people on their staff are more effective – they achieve more of the goals and objectives at the organization and they achieve them more easily. Empowerment embodies the concept of intrinsic motivation, internal justification for decision making, shared responsibilities and integration for problem solving. By delegating decision making power about specific issues to those who are best qualified, the organization will make better, more informed decisions. Leaders will gain time and energy to dedicate to other issues, including issues that have less immediate urgency but that may determine the direction and future of the organization. Empowered employees can be allies in shaping the future. They are more likely to produce new ways to do their work and challenge the status quo. They are more open to change, more supportive of change, and more involved in determining the direction of changes made in the organization (Fairholm, 1994).

A person who tries to do everything and who does not delegate demonstrates a lack of realistic self-assessment. No person has unlimited energy or knows everything. It is unrealistic to expect one person to be the fount of all wisdom and to know how to address every situation in the organization. An unenlightened leader who does not delegate or bestow responsibilities and motivate the potential of the employees is like the honeybee that tries to pollinate all the flowers alone. To be effective, managers must delegate tasks and authority. The strongest case for leadership is you do not have to do it all yourself. The responsibility of managers and leaders is not to do all the work themselves, but to see that it is done. Delegating the tasks and authority to capable employees builds trust between individual employees who work together and between managers and employees. Delegation provides employees the opportunity to develop leadership skills of their own and allows them to spend time on matters that truly demand their attention. Delegation can lead to the building of multi-skilled and cross-disciplinary teams. Such effective leaders who share responsibilities ultimately reap the human harvest of their efforts by the simple action of empowerment. It endows employees with the authority required to perform a given task and the autonomy to take initiatives related to the assigned responsibilities. Leaders who delegate authority do not give away power, but add to their power by developing the talents of their employees (Fairholm, 1994; McLean and Weitzel, 1992).

Empowered people are more self-confident and motivated. Self-confidence contributes to the feelings of self-worth and self-acceptance. These feelings contribute to self-control and the ability to contribute to team efforts. Working with others can be threatening. People who are insecure and lack self-confidence are more likely to react to disagreement over an issue by being defensive or confrontational, behaviours that are not conducive to cooperation. People who are empowered can develop their talents more fully. Accomplishments that are the results of our own efforts and creativity appeal to the innate values of independence, self-reliance and individualism. Thus, empowerment allows people to self-actualize on the job. It allows employees to take risks. Employees who feel responsible for their work are more likely to seek help and advice when they encounter a problem with which they have little experience. They seek such advice not to avoid responsibility, but because they feel pride in the quality of their work. In an organization that empowers its employees, collaboration and teamwork are more likely to develop spontaneously and work successfully. Teamwork can only flourish if each team member has a share in the decision making process. That is, teamwork and other forms of collaboration are based on the delegation of power from manager to employees, from leaders to followers. When they are empowered they can make the best use of their talents to further the goals of the organization (Fairholm, 1994).

Leaders who believe that their followers are talented, motivated, and willing to accept responsibility will provide them with opportunities to use their capabilities. Such leadership behaviour is empowering. Several ideas underlie empowerment (Fairholm, 1994; Bradford and Cohen, 1984).

1. People achieve more when they see value in their work, when their work is in tune with their own values, and when it is challenging enough to arouse and keep their interests.

2. People get more satisfaction from their work if they see how they contribute to the success of the organization.

3. People work harder, more consistently, and more creatively if they feel that their work contributes to goals that are moral and worthwhile.

4. Employee performance is higher if employees share responsibility and see themselves as vital to the organization's survival and progress.

5. People are more strongly motivated if there is mutual trust, respect, integrity, and concern for each other as group members and human beings.

Leaders who do not trust their employees and therefore do not delegate authority and responsibility can achieve more only by working harder. This strategy may succeed for a while, but is likely to eventually lead to burnout. To sustain a higher level of accomplishments, they will need to work with and through the efforts of others. They have to learn to trust their employees.

Letting go of authority and depending on others is difficult. Some leaders fail because they are reluctant to delegate authority with responsibility. Without the authority to carry out their responsibilities, employees will either learn to 'get around' the leader to complete their work or frequently go back to the leader for permission. The first 'solution' ends up undermining the authority the leader is trying to project; the second 'solution' is inefficient and discourages employees from developing initiative. Recently appointed managers who have not yet fully made the transition into their new role may feel responsibility to contribute and try to become 'working managers'. Managers who contribute to the work of the employees when there is a temporary shortage of staff can have a very positive impact on their staff's morale. The message sent by such managers is that the work is important enough for the manager to personally help, making sure it gets done. To do so on a regular basis, however, would take away time and energy from leadership activities that benefit the organization. Junior managers who do not delegate because they fear being disliked by their employees will only lose respect when their leadership suffers from being overextended. Most employees respect leaders who assign them responsibility and authority. Such delegation shows trust in, and respect for, employees. When leaders share responsibility and delegate authority, they increase the confidence of their followers and create a relationship that is characterized by mutuality. In such a relationship, the effective (nominal) power of the leader often increases. Employees are more likely to consider a manager's new ideas because, in a mutual relationship, they know that they can influence them and that their suggestions will be heard. The possession of influence and responsibilities increases employee satisfaction, co-operation with management, and commitment to the goals of the organization (Bennis and Nanus, 1985; Miller, 1988; Bradford and Cohen, 1984).

Delegating authority is perhaps the most difficult task because leaders remain responsible for the actions of their followers. Fear of failure and the sense of diminished authority and power are obstacles encountered by all leaders. Such fear and worries should not immobilize leaders from delegating, but should encourage them to think carefully about what tasks can be delegated, to whom they should be delegated, and what resources and authority should be delegated along with the responsibilities. Successful leaders distinguish themselves more by what they enable their followers to accomplish than by what they accomplish on their own. To accomplish great things on your own is the mark of talent, commitment, and perseverance, but not of leadership. To lead means to be a leader of others and to make a team or organization more successful, not to work alone. Leaders should often remind themselves that they are not judged by the work they do but by what others accomplish because of their leadership.

Example 9.1

Frederick is Director of the Department of Marketing and Distribution of Koltex Oil and Petroleum Company. The success of this company depends upon the organization, promotion, and distribution of goods and services of the department. Frederick thinks that the productivity and efficiency of his department depends upon his own performance. When he first became a manager he believed that he had more detailed expertise than any employee and was confident that he could solve almost any problem that might arise in the department. He viewed a leader as the person responsible for providing all direction and making all decisions. The department's action plan was therefore developed with minimal consultation of the employees. Frederick also assumed sole responsibility for its implementation. He wanted to be kept informed of every detail and did not trust others or share responsibility. Having authority and power was important to Frederick because he associated them with leadership. Because he feared loss of power, he was unwilling to consider delegating authority. He was also worried that his employees might fail to properly carry out their responsibilities without his supervision. After Frederick had been department manager for more than a year, two of his most skilled and reliable employees requested a transfer to another department. Frederick hated to lose these employees. Because he had established a good rapport with Luciana, one of the two employees, when they both worked in the same position, Frederick felt comfortable asking Luciana why she wanted to leave the department. After some initial hesitation and encouragement from Frederick, the employee finally told him that she was frustrated with Frederick's apparent lack of confidence in her abilities and professionalism. This came as a shock to Frederick. He had never considered that his employees might interpret his behaviour and actions in this way. He talked about his conversation with a senior manager he admired and trusted. With the help of this mentor, Frederick started the process of adjusting his management style.

Effective Delegation

Leaders cannot be everywhere. They have to delegate some of their responsibilities. Delegation empowers employees and gives them an opportunity to exercise and develop their own leadership skills, starting with relatively easy tasks. Delegation thereby serves not only to increase overall performance, it also provides training opportunities for the next generation of leaders.

1. Delegation is the process of *assigning* certain tasks to employees who can accept responsibility. The less skilled and experienced the employee, the more important it is that the job assignment be made very specific. For highly skilled employees it is often more appropriate to give open-ended assignments. Leaders, therefore, need to assess the capabilities of their employees. This assessment should go beyond skills but also take into consideration maturity, reliability, and other personal characteristics that affect performance.

Example 9.2

George joined the Oil Company only recently. He quickly demonstrated great technical talent working with computers and computer networks. When the department's computer co-ordinator requested a two month leave of absence, the supervisor granted the request and appointed George as the acting computer co-ordinator. George, however, had no previous experience responding to requests for assistance from many different individuals. He found it very difficult to prioritize how to spend his time, at least in part because he had not yet had enough time to learn about all aspects of the department. On a few occasions he misjudged the importance of requests. Although he possessed the necessary technical skills, he had not yet developed the organizational skills and the knowledge of the department to perform his new assignment well. A more gradual introduction to more responsibilities for the computing system would have been less frustrating for George and the department.

2. Delegation without the *granting of authority* does not work. If you do not trust that an employee can carry out a task well without supervision, do not delegate. If you wish that the task be completed exactly as you would have done it, do not delegate but do it yourself. If you delegate you must be willing to accept that others might take a somewhat different approach. This does not mean that you give 'carte blanche' control. It is advisable to set boundaries and to give minimum specifications that must be met. Within those boundaries, however, you must accept the results of the independent judgement of your employees, provided that they meet the minimum requirements as specified by you.

Example 9.3

John came to his supervisor and asked for permission to replace a piece of equipment in his work area. Florence, his supervisor, approved the request. Without asking him any specific questions she told him to order the equipment John thought he needed. When her office received the invoice she was surprised at the cost. She had assumed that John would order the cheaper of two available models. John, however, had decided to order the better and more expensive one. John was fortunate that his supervisor realized that she had failed to set the financial boundaries that she considered appropriate for the purchase and therefore did not hold him responsible for spending more than she thought appropriate. However, it was a mistake that she never repeated.

---

3. Delegation creates a *sense of responsibility* in the employee to perform assigned tasks well. By delegating responsibility we appeal to the professional pride of employees. If a task is not completed in a timely fashion and to appropriate standards, the employee who was assigned the task will often feel responsible, even if nothing is said. On the other hand, if the task is done well, they will take pride in *their* work. Thus, delegation can contribute to the motivation of employees more than relying exclusively on the intelligence and skills of a few leaders 'at the top of the pyramid'. It is a particularly effective motivator when combined with recognition and rewards for superior performance. Thus, it is important to

seek ways to engage the mind of every single employee and make everyone valuable to and responsible in the organization.

4. Delegation requires *planning*. To delegate effectively you need to think ahead and assign priorities so that you know what task will need to be completed, and by what date. This is possible only if you have clear goals. Once you know what you want, we you determine how to get it done. You can estimate personnel requirements and other resources needed. This kind of information must be available to delegate. Without a plan and without good information, you react to events as they occur. When you are forced to 'put out fires' you cannot delegate because you have no time to plan and you do not know what problem will be next.

5. *Accountability and ultimate responsibility cannot be delegated*. Managers, therefore, face a very real conflict: how can they risk the possibility of their employees' failure when they are the ones who will be held accountable? New managers in particular must work to overcome a tendency to hold on to special assignments or projects because of the fear that employees might not do a good job. If the 'pleasing others', 'trying harder' or the 'being perfect' trap is operating, the manager is likely to become overextended, overwhelmed and overstressed. A related danger is the tendency to check and recheck all delegated tasks. It can be destructive to the manager's effectiveness, the department's productivity, and the employees' morale and motivation. As a leader, avoid 'over-supervising' your employees. If you are concerned with your employees' skills and fear that they may not be able to properly carry out some of their responsibilities, then either restructure the work to match their skills, provide training, or add personnel who already have the necessary skills.

6. If you only delegate routine tasks, you will become overwhelmed and fail to meet the responsibility of leaders to *develop and motivate employees*. How leaders contribute to the development and growth of the next generation of leaders has a big impact on the future of the organization. A leader should recognize that nearly every employee has a potential for leadership and management.

7. *When should you do a task yourself?* This is a key question. Unfortunately, there is no unambiguous answer. For example, some experts suggest that a line supervisor is not supposed to or expected to do the work of the employees of the department at any time. But there are times when a supervisor may wish to work side by side with the employees, such as when (a) trying out a new procedure or equipment, (b) instructing or training employees or (c) assisting during temporary overload situations. We believe that getting involved in such a situation is almost always appropriate.

Delegation is empowering and contributes to the formation of leadership capacity among employees and builds constructive relationships between employees and managers. It is not often an easy matter for leaders to share responsibilities with and delegate authority to their fellow employees. In the process of delegation, it is essential to decide whom to delegate to, what to delegate, and what resources need to be provided. However, to empower employees effectively, four critical conditions need to be met.

1. Adopt a leadership style that is appropriate and encouraging to sharing responsibilities and decision making with employees. An authoritarian leadership style tends to discourage sharing authority while a democratic leadership style accommodates it.

2. The organizational structure also needs to support sharing of authority. Hierarchical decision making processes (e.g. chain-of-command in the military) do not work well.

3. Make a realistic assessment of the capabilities of your employees. Do they have the skills required to complete the assigned tasks? Are they experienced enough to handle significant authority with minimal supervision?

4. Use planning procedures to decide what to delegate, to whom to delegate and what resources need to be provided. The following steps describe a typical planning process:
   (a) analyze the project that needs to be accomplished, and establish standards for results and control;
   (b) divide the project into units that can be delegated;
   (c) consider qualifications and expertise of available employees and match them to the tasks to be completed;
   (d) analyze resource needs, including equipment, facilities, materials, etc.;
   (e) if appropriate, form teams to work on tasks;
   (f) prepare an explanation of each task and present it to the employee (or team);
   (g) explain your standards of performance and other expectations, including time lines, limits of authority, etc.;
   (h) establish priorities, set goals and timelines and motivate the employees (team);
   (i) establish guidelines for the supervision and control that you will provide. Be prepared to coach and mentor the employees (team) if necessary. It is preferable that you are asked to help, or intervene only to address significant problems;
   (j) deal promptly with performance problems due to lack of effort;
   (k) do not delegate additional authority or responsibility without repeating the steps described here;
   (l) reject requests that you judge to be unreasonable or if you have not had sufficient time to consider the implications of granting a request.

Successful delegation will free-up time to engage in important leadership activities rather than day to day management. You will gain time to think about and plan for the future. You will also have more time to continue the development of your leadership skills. By delegating you can afford to focus on the most important issues, that is, those issues with the highest long-term impact. These issues may be about product development, expanding the customer base, employee development, or building relationships with other organizations. Leadership is forward-looking and goal-oriented. It is the vision of leaders that motivates others to work together to make the vision a reality. The performance of leaders is determined by how well they succeed in this fundamental function, not by how well they can do the day to day work themselves. To succeed as a leader therefore *requires* that you free yourself from routine work and spend your time planning for the future. Table 9.1 provides a brief summary of the advantages and disadvantages of delegation.

Trust in Delegation

Leaders have power. However, leadership has much less to do with the exercise of that power than with the empowerment of others. Only in totalitarian societies do leaders even attempt to use their authority and power to control every aspect of the lives of their followers. Judging by the poor record of totalitarian regimes, we conclude that it is not an effective leadership style for long-term success.

A more promising approach to leadership is to work in partnership with followers. This requires that we trust them with responsibilities and authority, and it requires that we empower them to use and further develop their talents and skills. As we have repeatedly stressed, leaders are judged by what their followers accomplish. The failure to empower followers is a form of betrayal by the leaders. The employees cannot trust a leader they cannot follow, nor can they follow a leader they cannot trust. Lack of trust in a leader and consequently feelings of betrayal can easily cause followers to betray the leader. The leader must know and understand the strengths and weaknesses of those who follow. Without responsibility and authority followers are prevented from reaching their fullest potential. It is no coincidence that the long-term economic performance of totalitarian societies has historically always fallen short of that in democratic societies. Delegation is powerful because it results in greater creativity as more minds tackle problems. It encourages co-operation between individuals and organizations. Thus, although delegation increases risk in the short-term, it enhances opportunities in the long-term (Fairholm, 1994).

Working together builds trust. Without trust effective teamwork does not exist. Without trust followers will not follow their leaders.Therefore, leader in totalitarian societies must use coercion. We know from our own experience that coercion does not result in strong motivation. It is therefore not an effec-

Table 9.1. Advantages and Disadvantages of Delegation

Activities	Advantages	Disadvantages
Responsibility and authority	Sharing responsibility and authority with employees allows organizations to assume more responsibility than would otherwise be possible.	Sharing responsibility reduces management's control over day to day operations.
Employee performance	Delegation appeals to employees' intrinsic motivation such as pride in work, creativity and sense of accomplishment.	It may take longer to identify poor performers because of less formal supervision.
Co-ordination of efforts	Allows for informal co-operation and co-ordination	May undermine formal processes and organizational structures.
Customer interaction	Customer concerns can be addressed quickly. Employees can make binding decisions.	Management may not receive systematic feedback when employees do not have to check with supervisors before they can make a commitment.
Dealing with problems	Employees can decide how to address problems. This allows quick action.	Management may not receive systematic feedback if problems are dealt with in a decentralized fashion.

tive approach to accomplishing an organization's goals, even if we ignore its other disadvantages. Thus, trust is a prerequisite for effective leadership. Trust, however, is based on mutuality. Followers trust their leaders only if their leaders trust them, and vice versa.

It takes time to establish trust, and mutual trust is enhanced by effective communication between leaders and followers (Fairholm, 1994). The ability to trust others is an important quality of leaders. Withholding trust may sometimes be necessary for self-protection, but the price of always being on guard is high. The trust followers have in their leaders is a measure of the legitimacy of leadership. It cannot be mandated or purchased, but must be earned. Trust is the basic ingredient of all organizations. It is the lubricant that maintains organizations and makes leaders and followers work together effectively.

Delegation and sharing are based on trust. Trust is central to leadership in organization because followers are people who choose to follow leaders. The trust of followers allows leaders to lead. Trust is the emotional glue or bond that binds followers and leaders together. Leaders establish trust through their actions. Leaders build trust, or tear it down, by the cumulative actions they take, the words they speak and the environment they create for their followers. The total character of an organization determines in large part the kind of leadership that is exercised. The goals, vision, and behaviours provide clues about how an organization functions. Interpersonal trust is founded on shared values and creating such an environment is a hallmark of effective leadership. Trust can be lost through carelessness, as the following example illustrates.

Example 9.4

Susan is shy and does not speak up in front of a group. When confronted with a divisive issue, she tends to withdraw, either by finding something else to do, or by giving evasive answers. When pushed hard she tends to give in rather than fight for her point of view. She is, however, a good employee. Monica is Susan's supervisor. She has become aware that something is bothering Susan and she has talked with her about it. Susan has begun to trust her and confided that Eric, one of the other employees, has been bullying her. Monica talked with her supervisor about this and asked for her advice. Without consulting with Monica, at the next team meeting, her supervisor told Susan, 'What you are saying is that Eric is mean to you.' When confronted with this statement, Susan blushed and answered hesitatingly, 'Well, maybe not really.' She was clearly uncomfortable. Monica was disappointed. She had finally gained Susan's confidence and had planned to talk with Eric about the problem between him and Susan. The supervisor had just made Monica's job more difficult.

Trust is easily lost; it sometimes takes only one action. We encourage leaders to build an environment that values trust. Such an environment is based on honesty, respect for the law and the organization's rules and policy, and respect for others. The kind of environment that is conducive to effective leadership is one based on high levels of interpersonal trust (Fairholm, 1994).

CHAPTER TEN

TEAMWORK MANAGEMENT

Give a man a fish and you feed him for a day;
teach him how to fish and you feed him for a lifetime.

Chinese Proverb

Global markets, multinational corporations, and changes in social behaviours
and needs have created new circumstances for management. Leadership styles
that were appropriate in the past may not serve current needs well (Wellins,
Byham and Wilson, 1991). To meet the challenges of the present and the
needs of an ever-changing organization and its evolving constituents, contemporary management theory emphasizes the importance of shared management. Group efforts and team activities are recommended and implemented at
all levels of modern organizations, regardless of whether they are in the private or the public sector. In this age of co-operation and group interaction,
leaders do not direct by some fixed set of rules, but manage through relationships. Teamwork is an excellent approach to reach well-defined priority objectives of a technical nature and helps to bring groups together around specific objectives. Teamwork leads to dynamic synergies within the group. Intellectual and professional democracy is broadened and the scope of the work
is better distributed are more diffused in a team environment.

Working within a team means a bigger challenge, with more debates but
also more inspiration, and better quality control. Teamwork also provides employees with opportunities to develop and test their managerial and leadership skills. Teams break down psychological or hierarchical status barriers
and replace them with a liberal and participatory approach and more open
exchange of information. The ability to freely express ideas requires interactive, not hierarchical, communication. Creativity requires personal relationships among team members that are based on mutual respect. If these ingredients are present, teams are very effective. Successful teams are characterized
by improved sharing. Members share information and co-operate in solving
problems. Interactions among team members are characterized by mutual acceptance, recognition of the good work of others, and constructive feedback
(Rogers, 1991).

All cultures practice teamwork to some degree. For example, the extended
family in traditional societies has many of the characteristics of a team. The
extended family system reflects the cultural norms of working together, encouraging family solidarity, developing co-operation and helping one another.
In developing countries the extended family system is also a risk-sharing

mechanism that provides a safety net for family members who have fallen on hard times. In industrialized countries, these cultural norms are not equally strong, possibly because the state has replaced many of the functions formerly fulfilled by the extended family. It may therefore be more difficult to persuade employees of the value of teams. Although most people like the idea of working together, they are concerned that poor performance by other team members may negatively affect their rewards. This is a difficult issue to resolve. If each team member is paid according to her individual performance, we undermine the incentive to assist other team members who may be experiencing a problem, i.e. such a reward system would undermine the co-operative behaviours that make teams effective. If we reward all team members equally, then we may create incentives for some team members to shirk their responsibilities. To reduce shirking to tolerable levels, individual performance problems must be addressed promptly. Appropriate steps include a verbal rebuke, peer pressure, and dismissal, depending on the severity of the problem.

How Teams are Perceived

Some organizations and individual leaders view teams as a management panacea. They form teams even when the work does not require it. Other organizations and individual leaders create teams without really supporting the fundamental concept of a team and without providing the training programmes and operational structures necessary to make the teams effective. If a team is needed to take on issues such as improving productivity and efficiency, addressing conflicts among members of work groups, and creating a more participatory work climate, then it is necessary to create one.

Teams are not appropriate for all tasks. Some tasks are still best left to be done by individual effort. Teams work well when co-operation is critical, and when we need creative problem solving skills. One reason for the appeal of teams is not directly related to work efficiency, but to the development of cohesion and solidarity. More generally, teams embody a culture of co-operation and an environment of working together with a unified commitment and willingness.

A team is a group of individuals who work together to achieve a common set of goals and purpose. Work teams and sports teams share several similarities. In both cases, there may be outstanding individual efforts. Unless the other members perform their tasks well, however, even the most talented individual will perform at a lesser level. Therefore, it is appropriate to credit the whole team. The organized interdependency of members of a team results in better outcomes than would be the case if one simply added up the outcomes of non-co-ordinated individual efforts. The common purpose, when combined with effective leadership, makes teams into unified, cohesive, and interactive groups, and such teams can help deliver better products to customers. When teams are successful they also establish high employee morale.

Sports teams provide excellent illustrations of the characteristics of the best teams. The best teams are characterized by high participation, shared responsibility, common purpose, high and broad communication, task orientation and co-ordination, utilization of the talents of members, commitment and trust and rapid response to opportunities. A group is therefore not automatically a team, but a group can be organized to work together as a team. To make a group a team, individual members must agree on a common purpose, a shared set of values and co-ordination of efforts.

Teams are more powerful and more permanent if they are recognized by and embedded in the culture and life of the organization. The success of Japanese companies has motivated more research into teams. While American culture is individualistic, Japanese culture expects a strong commitment to and concern for the group and common good. Therefore, many important events in Japanese life are the result of collective action. For the Japanese, little of value occurs as a result of individual effort. The foundations of the Japanese culture are the ideas of trust, intimacy and friendship. Japanese are more likely to give up self-interest to preserve the harmony of the group than we would normally expect to occur in the United States. Although this behaviour, based on cultural values has many benefits, we should not ignore its potential costs. One of the strengths of a culture that values individual expression and accomplishment is the possibility of doing things of which the group disapproves. Often such behaviour is disruptive, but this same behaviour of non-conformance is also one of the mechanisms by which innovation is introduced. As we try to adopt the lessons taught by the successful uses of teams in Japan, it is worthwhile to consider how we could blend the best of both cultures to build highly effective teams. This is particularly essential in a society where diversity is an increasingly important factor in leadership as organizations become more diverse in terms of gender, race, ethnicity, age, national origin and other personal characteristics.

In a democratic society the real power of leaders comes more from their ability to persuade and motivate than from their position and formal power. Leaders enhance their legitimacy, and thus their power, if they organize work in such a fashion that allows employees more control over their work and the end product. Leaders plan and guide teams to discover their purpose, establish goals, assign responsibilities, obtain resources, maintain action, co-ordinate programs, and evaluate progress (Wishart, 1965). Managers facilitate the team-building process by clarifying the roles of employees and building trust and confidence. They recognize the emotional needs of team members, share the recognition of goal accomplishment, enhance employee decision making and problem solving skills, and create co-operation and interaction among individuals, groups, and departments (Bennis, Parikh and Lessem, 1994; Mallory, 1984).

Teamwork flourishes and grows in situations where leaders and followers share unifying values, ideas and goals. It does not just happen by decree. It takes a careful planning and design process in which team members can learn to visualize their goals, prioritize issues, acknowledge individual and group personalities, develop problem solving styles, define the role played by each team member, and acquire communication skills that enable them to unite together. The development of high performance teams takes the combined effort of visionary leaders with expertise in team building and competent team members. A team leader is responsible for creating a supportive structure and establishing a collaborative environment that will foster the development and growth of an effective team.

Team Building and Maintenance

Team member selection is important for the team's success. However, an effective team must first have an elevated goal, a clear mission (purpose), vision (picture of success), action plan and success measures. Group goals must take precedence over individual goals. Team members must have clearly defined expectations of one another to give each other feedback effectively and reinforce individual progress. Candid communication and a collaborative climate must be established. Team members must have a unified commitment and established standards for excellence. Members must value their diversity and deal with differences in a healthy and productive way. Members must keep an open mind in teamwork. Team members must be willing to share their ideas with other members and to listen to the ideas of others. The following are criteria to be considered in making the selection.

1. All necessary skills should be represented on the team.

2. It is often desirable to put experienced employees on the same team with less experienced employees.

3. Consider gender balance and ensure that ethnic minorities are given equal consideration for team membership as other employees.

4. Team members must be able to get along with each other.

5. Teams work better if complementary learning and problem solving styles are present among their members. For example, if one member is strongly task oriented ('let's do it'), it may be useful to have another member who checks and double checks everything to make sure there is no problem.

6. Select a team leader. If you want to leave the selection of the leader to the team, make sure that there are several members on the team who have leadership abilities and who can facilitate when there are conflicts.

In addition to job competencies and skills, prospective team members must display personal behaviours and characteristics which indicate that they work well with others. For the efficient workings of the team, the following characteristics are particularly desirable (Fairholm, 1994; Wellins, Byham and Wilson, 1991). Look for employees who:

(a) notice work that needs to be done and do it without being asked;

(b) ask for help or advice when encountering a problem that they cannot solve;

(c) offer to help others who seem to have a problem;

(d) volunteer ideas and listen to, respect and consider the ideas of others;

(e) accept constructive suggestions without displaying hurt feelings.

Good team members demonstrate initiative and concern for other members. When a new team is to be formed, management assumes responsibility for member selection. However, when a new member is to be added to an existing team, it may be desirable to involve team members in the evaluation of applicants (Wellins, Byham and Wilson, 1991). To make the process work well, evaluation criteria should be determined beforehand. It may be necessary to provide at least a short orientation and training session to team members in the recruitment process. Inexperienced evaluators often misinterpret information or allow too great a role for their personal preferences.

Although views on how to treat employees have changed over time, it was not so very long ago that workers were described simply as 'hands' and managers as 'bosses' who commanded employees much as an officer commands the troops. This very strict hierarchical approach has undergone significant change. The modern manager is regarded much more as a leader than a commander. 'Let us work together to get the results' is more in tune with present-day management philosophy. The most successful organizations today are those that can create synergies and a sense of purpose among their members. Managers and scholars who study management have come to realize that employees should not be treated as if they operated in isolation, but that much can be gained in efficiency and employee well being if we deal with them as members of a group. Because of the emphasis on groups, the functions of managers have changed to include responsibilities as team organizers and leaders. Emphasis on the use of authority has decreased and more emphasis is being put on legitimizing authority. Authority is legitimized if it is recognized and accepted voluntarily. This happens when leaders persuade their followers.

Teams are not structured in a hierarchical fashion. In fact, the very nature of teams requires that hierarchies and chains of command can change quickly and easily. Only if there are no potentially intimidating supervisor-subordinate relationships can the full talent of all team members be developed and utilized. Each member of a team must feel that it is safe to challenge or offer a dissenting opinion. They must feel able to show initiative and assume a leadership role. All team members must have equal opportunity to provide input into decisions. This does not mean that all have equal status, though teams are egalitarian. To function properly, teams need a leader. The team leader has several functions. They are a facilitator of team discussion and have the main responsibility for enforcing the team's norms of behaviour. The leader is also the representative of the team to the rest of the organization.

Because the egalitarian nature of teams runs counter to the traditional structure of most organizations, introducing teams is difficult. Blanchard, Carlos and Randolph (1996) express the difficulties of establishing teams in the title of their book: *Empowerment Takes More than a Minute*. Teams must be empowered to be successful. To do so, leaders and managers must change some of their practices. One of the changes recommended by Blanchard *et al.* (1996) is that leaders and managers freely share information with employees. This means that leaders and managers must change traditional information practices. Team members cannot develop initiative if they do not understand how their actions affect the goals and objectives of the organization. As Blanchard *et al.* (1996) pointed out, employees who are excluded from acquiring important information also do not feel trusted. Without trust, teams cannot function.

When a new team is formed it goes through several phases. Regardless of how careful the preparation and team member selection, teams need time before they reach peak performance. At the beginning, the team must rely on its leader to give it purpose and direction. As members become familiar with the team's purpose and develop norms of behaviour, the role of the team leader should change. The team leader should assume the role of facilitator and play a less visible role. Team members should be encouraged to assume a greater voice in determining their roles. As the team matures, the team leader becomes even less important in day to day decision making, as members deal with one another to settle conflicts and work out assignments. The team's focus also begins to shift from just doing the job to doing the job better. Finally, when the team is fully established and experienced, the leader's role becomes that of challenging the team to strive for even better performance and innovation. The process described here is not linear. It is possible for a team to jump over one of the phases or to revert back. This may happen because of members leaving or new members joining, or because the initial team purpose has changed. When this situation arises, the team leader has to judge whether the team should stay together or be dissolved.

There will be times when stress or interpersonal differences threaten teams. To survive such challenges, teams need to be maintained. Managers and employees both play roles in maintaining team spirit. Some team building should occur on a regular basis, such as in monthly meetings of the members. At these meetings the distribution of work and responsibilities can be discussed, problems identified, and plans for the week or month can be agreed on. Regular team maintenance reduces the likelihood that small problems will grow into big ones. There will be times when holding regular meetings may appear unimportant. Once we start cancelling meetings because none of the agenda items are important, we break the good habit of meeting regularly and tackling problems when they are so small that they can usually be resolved with little effort. If a problem has become so big that it cannot be resolved with reasonable effort, management leaders must intervene. They may have to dissolve the team and build a new one.

Teams are established for a specific purpose. When this purpose is no longer important the team should be dissolved. Why can we not simply give the team a new purpose? A new purpose usually requires new roles, new knowledge, and new skills. A team that worked well together in the past may not have the appropriate mix of skills and experience when its purpose has changed. Rather than trying to adjust membership, it is best to start the process of building a new team.

Benefits of Team Building

Developing a successful team is one of the most effective ways leaders can produce outstanding results. Team building is an ongoing process that has many benefits. In addition to creating a group of employees who work together and accomplish goals more effectively, the following are other benefits of team building.

1. The co-operative and collaborative spirit of teams spills over into other areas and activities and contributes to the organization's overall success.

2. Employees assume more responsibility and become partners with management in planning and decision making.

3. Teams contribute to the creation of an atmosphere of trust that tends to reduce friction between labour and management. Labour issues are more likely to be resolved internally and constructively rather than externally and with the use of threats.

4. Because teams require open and regular communication, communication skills are improved. In particular, teams provide employees with an opportunity to communicate their concerns to management, and they provide management with opportunities to hear such concerns. In more traditional hierarchies, most communication is from the top down.

5. Teams provide a training ground for future managers and leaders as employees learn and practice interpersonal skills, participate and gain experience in problem solving and decision making, and are encouraged to take on leadership responsibilities for specific tasks.

6. Job assignments are flexible and responsibilities are defined and clarified to achieve co-ordination between team members.

7. Teamwork encourages mutual assistance. Employees feel comfortable asking for assistance from another team member.

8. Employees share responsibility and feel valued and challenged. Teams prepare skilled junior managers and competent supervisors.

9. Teams provide opportunities for cross training and the development of generalists as opposed to narrow-minded specialists. This gives teams greater flexibility in adapting to change.

10. Leader intervention is needed less often because individuals have team assistance.

11. Teams facilitate delegation.

Not all individuals are equally comfortable working in teams. There are differences in personalities, learning and working styles, and social values. Such differences may be particularly pronounced between members of different cultural and/or ethnic backgrounds and between male and female team members. Differences need not be a problem and can enrich the group. It is important, however, that the team be inclusive of all members and not make some of them feel isolated and discounted. To achieve inclusiveness, it is important that the group not be dominated by a few individuals. If some members feel left out, the advantages of working as a team will eventually be lost. The following are five strategies for increasing group credibility and performance (Miller, 1988).

1. *Effective communication goes a long way toward reducing misunderstandings and hurt feelings.* Although cultural and gender differences can be important, most problems result from poor communication or lack of communication.

2. *Be prepared.* Do not go to a team meeting without having done your homework. Preparation reduces the chance that the team may act on incomplete or incorrect information (i.e. it improves communication), and increases self-confidence and the confidence of other team members in the speaker/contributor relationship. When team members are confident that your contribution is well considered, they will value what you have to say and gain and keep trust in you. By being prepared you exercise the power that comes from expertise.

3. *Practice good interpersonal skills.* These include listening skills (refer to Chapter 8) and a general sensitivity to the needs and concerns of others, as well as respect for their opinions. If the other team members like and enjoy your personality, you gain power and influence. The power that comes from a likeable personality reinforces the power that comes from position or expertise.

4. *Serve as a role model and be sensitive to prejudice and stereotypes.* Seek out mentors among more experienced members of the organization or in other organizations who have greater experience and suggestions on how to deal with such problems.

5. *Build confidence among employees.* Collaboration, confidence and trust do not happen by accident. These are essential characteristics that a team leader must plant, nurture and grow. Employees' confidence and skills must be constantly rejuvenated and built if they are to continue to be productive and co-operative in the teamwork.

In addition, since not all employees will have prior experience working in a team, the initial function and fundamental principles of an organization should stress co-operation over competition as the key value of team building. In a team, employees learn and develop the norms and culture of co-operation instead of competition. The difference between co-operation and competition is illustrated by the following example.

Example 10.1

When Tesfa (co-author of this book) and Kiflay, his brother, were growing up in Eritrea, they used to compete at home and in school for their father's attention and recognition by the community. They worked hard to obtain high grades in all courses they took and tried to impress their parents and teachers. They were highly successful in school and admired by their peers and the community, but not very much by their father. Even though it was a·healthy competition, their father did not like it. One day he called them and made them sit in front of him for some fatherly advice. He brought some dry sticks and gave each a single one and asked them to break it. Both of them broke each stick without any problem. Then, he put ten single sticks together and added glue to make the union tight. After a while he asked them to break the united sticks. Each of his sons tried to break the sticks, but both of them were unsuccessful. He illustrated to them the lesson to be learned from the demonstration. He explained to them that if they worked independently or as competitors they had less chance to succeed than if they co-operated and joined in working together. He concluded his advice by indicating that co-operation is always better than competition. (This story is also told in one of Aesop's fables).

Competition is one way in which society organizes and co-ordinates efforts. It works extraordinarily well for many activities. As Ronald Coase (1937) successfully argues, however, competition has its limitations. Firms and other organizations exist because of the limitations of competition as the most effective mechanism for co-ordinating efforts. Markets are human institutions; they are not free. When the costs of maintaining markets, or the costs of making market transactions, are high, non-market solutions are often preferable. Most non-market solutions are co-operative rather then competitive.

Competition is effective when there are conflicting goals. Members of organizations are characterized by their pursuit of common goals. To accomplish these common goals they engage in co-operative behaviours. All members of the organization gain if the common goals are reached. By contrast, competitive behaviour results in winners and losers. Competitive sports provide a particularly striking illustration of this characteristic. Competition does not mix well with co-operation. The losers in a competition may harbour resentment against the winners. Competition is largely a self-regulating process. Each participant is responsible for his or her own success. By contrast, co-operation works best with leaders who co-ordinate collaborative efforts. That is why leaders who foster collaboration enjoy more credibility than leaders who promote competition among members of the same organization (Kouzes and Posner, 1995).

We have reinforced the discussion of teams with a comparison of the advantages and disadvantages of using teams versus assigning work to individual employees. The following table highlights strengths and weaknesses.

Table 10.1. Teamwork versus Individual Effort

Abilities	Teamwork	Individual Effort
Ability to carry out complex tasks	Very good.	Limited by knowledge of individual employee.
supervision required.	Little supervision required.	More supervision required.
Risk of temporary performance problems.	Fairly high.	Low.
Time before peak performance is reached.	Medium to long.	Short to medium.
Individual accountability.	Low to medium.	High.
Reward system.	Conflict between desire to reward individual merit vs encouraging co-operation between team members.	Based on individual merit and responsibility.

Employee Orientation and Training

The orientation of an employee into a new position is important, since it shapes attitudes and values. Many organizations, therefore, spend time and effort on orientation sessions, training and other development activities. While these are appropriate activities, the returns on this investment will be increased if there are follow-up activities at a later date. When employees get a very large amount of information in a short time, they will retain only a portion of it. By reinforcing the information and skills later, more will be retained and new employees will contribute sooner and more effectively. The way new employees are socialized and trained into becoming team members is particularly important because teams rely on good interpersonal relationships, co-ordination between members and a co-operative attitude.

Lack of initial training and introduction to the values of the team can be frustrating to new members. While some employees find it easy to fit in, others need some initial assistance. New employees are receptive to learning about the organization. They usually realize that they have to make some adjustments. If we do not guide them in their efforts, they may acquire attitudes that are not in the organization's best interests. Attempts to get them to change later may lead to resentment and resistance. Areas that need particular attention in the orientation process are the formal and informal rules that guide how the organization works, information about training and future development opportunities, and personal characteristics that reflect organizational values (trust and trustworthiness, communication, mutual assistance, respect for others).

The first days in a new job can be frustrating and stressful. An orientation should recognize that new employees may experience anxiety and should, therefore, include information that addresses the causes of their anxiety. Specifically, an orientation of new employees or new team members should include the following.

1. *An explanation of the workplace.* New employees should learn about their job and the scope, nature and history of the organization. The organizational chart and physical layout of the building should also be explained in the orientation.

2. *Job responsibilities should be outlined and the new employee should be introduced to the immediate supervisor and fellow employees.* This can be done in a group meeting, but is often more effective when done individually. In the latter case, the new employee has to absorb less information all at once and can meet other employees where they work. The immediate supervisor should review work-related matters and job expectations.

3. *A tour of the facilities will help the new employees to become oriented more quickly and contribute to the understanding of the organization.*

4. *An explanation of rules and restrictions, policies and regulations, telephone system, working hours, emergency procedures and how to report absences.* The orientation should also provide information about standards of performance, job evaluations, and performance management.

5. *Guidance with filling out necessary employment papers.*

6.   *Help new employees to begin the job*. Make sure that they have the necessary supplies and equipment, are familiar with how the equipment operates, and know where to find work accessories and whom to contact if they experience problems. These steps should be taken even if a new employee has relevant previous job experience.

The orientation process should make new employees comfortable with their work environment and be a pleasant learning experience. The orientation should proceed in reasonable steps. It is tempting to save time by 'cramming' as much information into an orientation session as possible. This is not an effective strategy. What seems obvious to experienced employees is new to the most recently hired people; they need to be given sufficient time to absorb the information. In the initial orientation, focus on the few points that matter most. In additional orientation sessions, these points can be elaborated and additional aspects of the job, organization and others can be covered. The orientation format should be sensitive to different learning styles. Some individuals prefer written materials that they can study at their own pace, others like hands-on experience, and some may benefit from demonstrations. Orientation sessions should, therefore, utilize different formats to convey information and train new employees.

New employees may appreciate being assigned an experienced employee as their mentor during the first few months on the job. Mentors can be particularly valuable in organizations where employees have significant independence in how they carry out their work, must exercise judgement often, and where assignments are complex. However, the positive role of mentors is not limited to such organizations. Support during the first few weeks and months alleviates stress for new employees and contributes to their being socialized into the organization. By viewing orientation as a process rather than as a one-time event, the supervisor has opportunities to watch, guide, and correct the new employee during the critical first few months on the job, and to reinforce information about required work habits and other expectations (Miller, 1988; Downey and Erickson, 1987).

In addition to providing new employees with information about their job and the values and expectations of the organizations, new employees usually need training to do their job well. How this is accomplished depends on the capabilities of the organization. On-the-job training is the most widely used approach. An experienced co-worker trains the new employee at the workplace. Even while training, the new employee is already carrying out real work. On-the-job training is an effective method to teach practical skills. A form of on-the-job training is also used to prepare teachers when they engage in supervised student teaching. On-the-job training is limited to jobs where the cost of making a mistake is not very high. It would not be an appropriate method to train pilots or surgeons. Members of these professions start their training in simulated work environments. On-the-job training is also an inefficient method for teaching abstract concepts; this is better done in a classroom and through study.

Even when there is no formal on-the-job training programme, new employees will learn much about how to perform their jobs and about work habits and attitudes, from fellow workers. When managers assign an experienced employee to serve as mentor to a new employee, they formalize and take advantage of a process that usually occurs informally.

The supervisor may assist in the training process by making periodic follow-up visits to see how the employee is doing. Good managers do not assume that things are going well, they make sure that they are. The manager should determine how the new employee is getting along on the job with fellow workers and supervisors. If there are problems, the manager should help solve them. Routine follow-ups are not only useful in making sure that things are going as they should and allowing for corrective action, it also affords an opportunity to encourage new employees and assure them of management's continuing interest. Some managers tell new employees to come and see them if they need help. This approach ignores the common reluctance of new employees to admit that they are experiencing difficulties. In this case, follow-up visits are a much more effective tool.

On-the-job training and mentoring are cost-effective, but they are not free. Senior employees who assist new hires take time away from other activities. While this usually involves no cash outlays, management should include this opportunity cost when they assess advantages and disadvantages of different training methods.

In off-the-job training, employees are sent to participate in special training sessions away from their job. Such sessions could be in the form of a traditional class or training workshop. Training may be full-time or part-time. In the latter case, the employee will spend part of the time working on-the-job and part of the time in training. The duration of training varies greatly. The employee's department may choose to organize short training sessions itself. When a short training session is sufficient, it is often advantageous to have the new employee's team (if teams are used) take responsibility for providing the training. This enhances the socialization of new employees into the team by ensuring that the training conforms to the norms and values of the team. Personnel development involves costs. The return is a more dynamic and more highly skilled labour force. Training of employees should be regarded as an investment in the future of the organization. By providing training, the organization makes a commitment to the new employee. If employees leave after only a short time, the organization will not earn a positive return on the investment made in developing their skills. Thus, to make sure that the investment is worth making, the organization must foster labour relations that encourage a labour turnover rate that is low enough to make training a worthwhile investment.

CHAPTER ELEVEN

CONFLICT MANAGEMENT

Nature desires eagerly opposites and, out of them,
it completes its harmony, not out of similars.

Heraclitus

Conflict is inevitable in any situation or relationship and it is conflict, not
harmony, that binds people together. Each culture has a unique understanding
of conflict. Some cultures encourage open and emotional disputes; others value
strict politeness and very cautious disagreement. Conflict can lead to positive
changes. If conflict is not properly managed or ignored, however, it can become destructive. Most of us already have some conflict management skills.
The purpose of this chapter is to list conflict management strategies and styles
to raise our awareness of how we tend to deal with conflict.

Leaders are exposed to conflict in two ways. First, they may themselves
be involved in a conflict. Leadership is a relationship between at least two
persons, and conflicts between individuals occur over goals, means to achieve
them, rewards, responsibilities, etc. Second, leaders are often called upon to
mediate in conflicts between followers. In either case, defining and understanding the nature of conflict and conflict resolution techniques is a fundamental step to understanding conflict management and relating it to other key
concepts such as teamwork and co-operation, delegation and empowerment,
performance evaluation and management, and communication and networking. Conflict management is central to understanding individuals, groups, families, politics, social structures, economic systems, organizations, and history,
as well as international relations (Tjosvold, 1996; Rogers, 1991).

The Essence of Conflict Management

Conflict per se is neither good nor bad. How we use and resolve conflicts
determines their nature. Conflict is always present. It can be internal to one
person, such as when someone is trying to decide between the conflicting
desires of tasting a wonderful dessert and not gaining weight. Internal conflicts can be important to an organization, such as when employees agonise
between commitment to the organization and private needs that conflict with
that commitment. Such conflict can result in employee theft, work of low
quality, absenteeism and other problems. This is a major reason why leaders
must be sensitive to the values and needs of their followers.

Conflicts arise over various issues. They can be interpersonal, maybe as a result of different values or miscommunications. Another type of conflict arises when expectations are not met. A particularly common example is supervisor-employee conflict as a result of unsatisfactory employee performance. Finally, a third type of conflict is between groups. At our university, teaching co-operation between different departments is difficult to achieve because the university's rules set them up as competitors for students. Of course, intergroup conflict can also arise because of different values and cultures, as in the case of inter-racial conflict.

Conflict situations among people are often characterized by expressions of strong feelings and emotions. Our society does not encourage the free and open expression of sentiments and differences; we expect people to be in control of themselves. This is not always positive, as the following example will show.

Example 11.1

Janet is an excellent employee. She is well educated and has significant professional experience. Other employees often consult her when they have a technical problem. Because she is ambitious and hopes to advance within the firm, she has taken some college courses in management and accounting; she already holds a master's degree in a technical field. Janet has also been reading books on leadership and has made efforts to prepare herself to assume more responsibility. Janet is well liked by supervisors and fellow employees. A few months ago, the supervisor of Janet's department retired. Because of her excellent performance, documented by positive annual evaluations, Janet had thought she would have an excellent chance to be promoted into the supervisor's position. There was only one other candidate. He had less education, less experience, and there were some employees who did not like him very well. Janet was therefore devastated when it was announced that the other candidate was given the position. She did not want to show her disappointment for fear that she would be considered too emotional. Starting that day, however, she began looking for advancement opportunities elsewhere. Based on her strong qualifications, she quickly found a challenging new job and left the firm less than a month after her application for the position of supervisor was turned down. The manager was surprised by her sudden departure. He had hoped to make her supervisor of a new department that he was establishing. Her experience, people skills, and strong technical training were just what he needed. Too bad he failed to talk to Janet about his plans for her.

This example shows that latent conflict is often the result of poor communications. Had Janet expressed her disappointment, management could have explained to her that she would soon receive a promotion that was more interesting and where her skills would be even more valuable. Of course, had management told her in a timely fashion of plans for her promotion, there would have been no problem to begin with.

The example holds a second lesson. To deal with conflict, to bring it out in the open and resolve it, prevents harm. If relationships turn to resentment or bitterness, they will adversely affect the organization. Anger is only one expression of conflict. Because of its extreme nature, it is easily recognized (although even then it is not always taken seriously). The example shows that conflict does not need to be violent, but can be very subtle. The listening skills that we discussed earlier are helpful tools for detecting conflicts. Conflicts are rooted in issues and can be personal, interpersonal, inter-group or inter-organizational in nature. Few human relationships are immune to conflict. Causes of conflicts within a group, between individuals, and among groups or departments are plentiful. Many seem to be rooted in personality differences or interaction, organizational structure differences or interdependence, and substantive differences in the points of view or incompatible individual goals. Leaders need not be intimidated by conflict, because most breaks and strains are not fatal. Indeed, a carefully nurtured fracture can become a point of strength for the future by promoting change. Thus, leaders should pay attention to signs of conflict. Leaders need not deal with every conflict because many conflicts will be resolved without the help of management. This strategy is often appropriate for dealing with conflicts between equals. When the conflict is between individuals of different rank, the situation is complicated because of the unequal power of those involved. In such cases leaders should observe and intervene constructively, if necessary (McLean and Weitzel, 1992; Barge, 1994).

Fear of conflict is common, and most people will go to some length to avoid it. It may be that they worry that the conflict could get out of hand. All too often, however, avoidance does not lead to resolution. On the contrary, conflicts which are not dealt with properly gradually grow into resistance and resentment; that is, they become personal and ultimately difficult to deal with. Instead of avoiding conflict, it is essential to recognize the potential benefits of dealing with conflicts. Many conflicts arise because of poor communications. Misunderstandings or feelings of not being heard are frequent sources of conflict. Thus, the first rule in dealing with conflict is to listen and try to understand the true concerns. As we discussed earlier, this is not always easy and becomes more difficult the more personal feelings become involved in the conflict. If we succeed, however, the information gained will help us address the source or sources of conflict. The following example illustrates how this may benefit the organization.

Example 11.2

Monica joined the department less than a year ago. She had considerable prior experience in another industry. Her supervisor had been in her current position for over ten years and had developed clear ideas on how the various tasks should be carried out, although she has always been willing to listen to ideas about how the work process could be changed. Lately, however, she has been impatient with employees, and she brushed off Monica when she came to her with an idea she had seen implemented in her former job. Monica, who does not yet know her supervisor very well, took the incident personally. She, and most other employees, did not know that her supervisor's husband was seriously ill and that she was under a lot of stress. Thus, the incident affected Monica's relationship with the supervisor. She talked to some of the other employees to air her frustration. Another supervisor overheard one of these conversations and alerted management to this beginning conflict. The manager first met with Monica's supervisor and then with Monica. She encouraged the supervisor to discuss Monica's idea. Recognizing her stressful home situation, the manager also discussed the possibility of temporarily appointing an employee to assist the supervisor with her responsibilities. In her discussion with Monica the manager stressed the supervisor's excellent track record and good relationship with her employees. She also told Monica that the supervisor's husband was very ill and asked for her understanding. These discussions and the recommended actions defused what could have developed into a disruptive interpersonal conflict.

The Styles of Conflict Resolution

Leaders confront a variety of conflicts. A conflict is a perceived divergence of interests or beliefs between two parties. Skilled mediators note that many perceived conflicts are not real. Seemingly divergent interests can often be reconciled and turned into compatible interests. This may take creativity and always requires skill. Conflict resolution, therefore, becomes a significant leadership task. As a step toward developing conflict resolution skills, we will discuss five basic conflict management styles that are commonly distinguished by some prominent writers (Barge, 1994; Bennis, Parikh and Lessem, 1994; Miller, 1988):

Avoidance

Avoidance describes behaviours that ignore conflict. This may also include behaviours that are unassertive and unco-operative. Some leaders use this style to stay out of conflicts, ignore disagreements or to remain neutral. This style is often used in the hope that the conflict will go away. Although it may sound like a poor strategy, it has its proper uses. It can be a reasonable strategy to 'buy time' to think more carefully about the problem underlying the conflict. It is also a proper approach to find out if a situation that looks like a conflict really is one. In general, however, avoidance offers only a temporary solution.

Avoidance is a useful strategy if a problem will go away on its own. The following example illustrates why direct intervention by management may be of little use in some situations.

Example 11.3

A business firm had developed a new product. Its success in the marketplace surpassed expectations. Employees were therefore working overtime to keep up with demand. The exposure to stress caused by long working days resulted in friction among some employees over issues that normally caused no problems. Management decided not to intervene because they were ready to advertise for additional employees, so the problem would soon resolve itself. While management did not formally address the various interpersonal conflicts, they did announce their decision to seek additional employees. Their hope was that the prospect of having regular hours back soon would help employees deal with stress.

In this example, the management did not address the conflict among employees. In that sense it avoided the conflict. Instead, it addressed what it perceived as the underlying cause and took steps that encouraged others to address and deal with the problem. It is often useful to address conflicts without becoming directly involved in solving the problem. Even trained facilitators who directly intervene in conflicts sometimes become party to the conflict itself and lose their neutrality. If that happens, the conflict is made worse rather than better.

Do not use avoidance because of an aversion to tension and frustration. Although you may fear dealing with a conflict because of the risks involved, ignoring a real conflict can be much more costly than trying to tackle it. Employees may gain an unfavourable impression and come to regard you as indecisive, even weak. Avoidance is a passive style and should not be used excessively.

Example 11.4

One of the authors once had a supervisor who refused to deal with a personnel problem because it "would affect his personal relationship with a member of the staff". This is not a valid reason for avoiding dealing with conflict. First, the supervisor did not fulfill his professional obligations to the department. Second, by not addressing the conflict that was the result

---

of poor performance, he signaled to the staff member that "it was not that bad". Finally, the supervisor's behaviour made the task of the department leader more difficult. When the leader talked with the staff members, about insufficient performance, she was able to downplay his assessment by using the more positive assessment that was implied by the silence of her immediate supervisor.

Avoidance is not possible if one of the parties involved is not willing to ignore the conflict. Weak leaders may then use flattery or try doing favours as a means to defuse the conflict. This strategy rarely works. Unearned compliments and flattery devalue compliments given for real accomplishments. Some people, sensing the weakness of the leader and the desire to avoid conflict, may be encouraged to make unreasonable demands in return for non-confrontational behaviour. The morale of other employees will usually suffer when they see unco-operative behaviour rewarded while they obtain no rewards for behaviours that serve the interest of the organization. In the worst case, the result will be an escalation of conflict.

Withdrawal

Withdrawal is related to avoidance. Whereas avoidance may include denial that a conflict even exists, withdrawal acknowledges the conflict. In withdrawal, some of the parties to the conflict remove themselves from the conflict situation. The following example illustrates how this strategy might be useful.

Example 11.5

Norman is the manager of a large department. Two of his supervisors recently became engaged in a 'turf battle'. Norman tried to mediate between the two but was unsuccessful. Rather than try again right away, he told the two supervisors that he expected them to work the problem out on their own. He made several suggestions and offered them the assistance of a trained mediator. The supervisors received one month to develop a plan for resolving their conflict. Norman mentioned that if there should still be a problem after a month, he would take steps to address the problem himself.

This is an example of temporary withdrawal. Norman tried to mediate but was not successful. There was a chance that he had become a party to the conflict. The failure of mediation may have left some of the parties to the conflict frustrated, even angry. Trying a different approach to resolving the conflict is difficult when emotions run high. Norman therefore withdrew from the conflict situation. Note that he did not avoid the conflict. Even in withdrawing he dealt with it. He put the two supervisors on notice and announced steps he would take if they did not resolve the conflict themselves.

Conflict resolution styles can sometimes be combined for better results. If there are only minor problems, the reluctance to deal with conflict, particularly interpersonal conflict, may reduce the willingness of those involved to address the underlying issues. Avoidance may be the best strategy until the cumulative effects of the conflict make it easier for management to persuade the parties to the conflict that they need to work together to resolve it. At that point an assertive strategy replaces the passive one.

Domination

Domination is assertive but unco-operative behaviour. It is the easiest conflict management strategy but will not usually resolve conflict unless the parties to the conflict can be separated. There will be winners and losers. It is a rare loser who does not feel at least some resentment in a situation where domination is being used. Leaders have the authority to order certain behaviours, but co-operation cannot be ensured. Ordering employees to 'drop it and get on' may be incompatible with delegation and teamwork. Delegation relies on the employee's voluntary compliance. If compliance can be obtained only with constant supervision, the benefits of delegation are lost. People will voluntarily comply only if they feel treated fairly.

The domination strategy resolves conflict with little concern for interpersonal relationships among the conflicting parties. When conflicts are made to be resolved by using force, it involves some elements of abusing authority. It reflects a 'win-lose' approach to settling a conflict. Because the losers may try to change the outcome at a later point, this strategy may require ongoing monitoring and use of management authority. The conflict may re-emerge into the open if the authority who dictated the solution loses interest.

There are situations when domination is a useful strategy. When an organization is in a crisis, it cannot afford to be distracted by conflict. In such a situation, leaders may use their power to at least postpone the conflict. They may threaten those who are unco-operative with punishment. Ordering and domination are particularly widely used resolution management styles in the military and other strictly hierarchical organizations. In modern business management, however, domination has lost favour. Domination has in it the seeds of its own destruction in the form of mistrust and resentment. These often grow out of it and the conflict comes back at a larger scale.

Compromise

Compromise represents behaviour that is co-operative and assertive. Compromise is characterized by concessions and negotiations rather than aiming for the ideal solution to a conflict. Unfortunately, compromise is often little more than each side giving up on some of their initial demands. Compromise without collaboration can be described as a strategy where all parties give up some of their demands. In practice it does not work in the long-term because the conflicts are not truly resolved. If those involved in non-collaborative compromise have unequal power, compromise may give way to domination. Without collaboration, compromise will rarely result in the best possible outcome and often leaves all parties dissatisfied. When this happens, the conflict may not really be resolved but will re-emerge at a later date.

Collaborative Problem Solving

Collaborative problem solving is behaviour that is collaborative and assertive. The difference between compromise and this approach is in the collaboration. Collaborative problem solving means literally working together to find solutions that are mutually agreeable and that can result in a win-win outcome. The parties to the conflict work together, try to understand the needs of each other, and seek solutions that come as close to meeting those needs as possible. By collaborating, the nature of the conflict can be changed. The following is a simple example of how this could be done.

Example 11.6

Bill and Tom were both planning to take their summer vacation at the same time. However, the department could not afford to have both of them absent at the same time. Their supervisor suggested that they compromise. He suggested that Bill move his vacation and leave one week earlier and Tom one week later, than originally planned. This would meet the department's need that at least one of them would be working. Bill and Tom were not really pleased with the solution, however, and asked for permission to try to work it out themselves. The supervisor agreed. In talking about their plans, Tom learned that while Bill really was looking forward to a nice summer vacation, he was even more eager to have time off later in the year to visit his parents on the occasion of their 50th wedding anniversary. He also learned that Bill had not yet made any reservations for his summer vacation and therefore would suffer no financial loss from changing its date. By contrast, Tom would have to change the plane tickets for himself and his family and probably end up paying more. Tom and Bill agreed that Bill would move his summer vacation and that Tom would commit to cover his responsibilities later in the year so that he could leave to visit his parents. Both were pleased with their solution that also met the needs of their department.

In many cases a good solution can be found by adding a new dimension to the problem. While this adds complexity, it also adds options for making trade-offs.

Example 11.7

Tom and Patricia had a fight. She wanted to spend her vacations at the beach, he wanted to visit the mountains. They could not agree where to go. Patricia had hoped to go to the beach in South Carolina. As she was thinking how to resolve her conflict with Tom, she remembered that he had recently mentioned how much he would like to see an old family friend living in San Diego. She therefore suggested that they use their vacations to make this visit. By changing the destination they could visit with their friend, spend some time at the beach, and also take a couple of day to travel to the mountains of Southern California. Both felt that the opportunity to see their friend justified the added cost of traveling to the West Coast.

Conflict can be productive if its resolution addresses problems and recognizes the needs of those involved. In such cases conflict resolution may lead to new ideas and new ways of doing things. The mutual respect that is generated by learning of each other's needs and the trust that is gained from the parties working together to meet their needs can establish a foundation for future co-operation and collaboration, including the resolution of even more difficult conflicts. Trust and collaboration both enhance effective implementation of conflict management. An unwillingness to bring up dissenting opinions and avoiding confrontation of problems impedes it. Thus, conflicts can be a test and training ground for team building, delegation, motivation, communication skills, and practical problem confrontation and resolution.

If collaborative problem solving is such a superior approach to conflict resolution, why is there any need for the other approaches? Each of the approaches we discussed is a tool, and each fits some situations or some conflicts better than the others. Conflict management styles also differ from person to person and should be compatible with leadership style. Collaborative problem solving is a very effective conflict resolution method, but it is also time consuming. When time is pressing, it may not be the best solution. It is almost never a reasonable method in crisis situations. Its costs may also be too high when the stakes are low. Compromise may be the more cost-effective approach. In other words, there is not one method that is always the best, but which method should be used depends on the specific situation, the leader's personality, and the skills in the practice of different methods. In general, the leader's attitude toward conflict determines the way the leader deals with it. As a leader, what is your attitude toward conflict? Do you perceive it as a positive or a negative force in your organization? Your answer will probably depend on the nature and causes of conflict. Just remember that whether or not conflict is a positive or a negative force will often depend on how you approach and deal with it.

Procedures for Conflict Management

Conflict management is as old as history and as new as today's problem looking for a better solution. In today's changing business environment, conflict management is an important leadership task. Our social norms also have changed and put more emphasis on conflict prevention and conflict management. A first step in conflict management requires the ability to distinguish between 'productive' and 'unproductive' conflict. For example, conflicts over production methods or administrative processes have the potential to lead to improved efficiencies. It is therefore important to manage such conflicts to maximize the likelihood of positive outcomes. Good conflicts are those that help to understand difficult problems and choose among alternative solutions. 'Bad' conflicts are those that have deteriorated into personality conflicts. This means that every conflict has the potential to become a 'bad' conflict. 'Bad' conflicts are destructive and hold no potential for beneficial change. They cause confusion, poor decisions, hurt feelings, anger and can lead to the break-up of teams and groups. Such conflicts need to be addressed immediately before they harm the organization. Conflicts left unattended often get worse and spread. The best approach to unproductive conflict is to prevent it from happening in the first place (Rogers, 1991).

There is no realistic alternative to confronting problems and managing conflicts. Confronting problems that underlie conflicts is the key to conflict resolution. Learning to manage conflicts is potentially a common goal that people everywhere can share. Initially, confronting problems that underlie conflicts is the key to conflict resolution. The emphasis in the conflict resolution process is on confronting problems, not people and personalities. The process should focus on the behaviours to be changed and the actions that cause the conflict. It should not focus on the personalities of the parties to the conflict. Do not allow the conflict to become one about personalities. It is best to deal with conflict when you have time and feel positive. Do not tackle conflicts when you are emotional; too often emotions override reason.

Example 11.8

John was arguing with Michael. He was unhappy because Michael had damaged the new company car. Why did this have to happen? John had ridden in a car with Michael a few times and thought then that he was an aggressive driver. However, Michael's driving record up to this time had been clean. In ten years of driving, he had never had an accident or received a ticket. By contrast, John had recently received a speeding ticket. But John was angry and asked: 'Why do you always have to drive so aggressively?' Up to that point, Michael had felt contrite. When John attacked him, however, he shot back, 'Look who is talking, Speedy John!'

When we make a conflict personal, emotions take over, eliminating any chance to solve the problem. To prevent this from happening, be specific and focus on behaviours, not personalities. Was Michael speeding when the accident happened? Is there anything that could be done to reduce the chance of another accident in the future? Such questions lead the way to solutions. Statements that attack the person distract us from the real cause of the conflict and therefore stand in the way of finding a solution.

Conflict management and resolution require sensitivity to other people and their needs. It is often possible to make significant progress and defuse a potentially explosive situation simply by acknowledging the concerns of others involved in conflict. Acknowledgment does not imply agreement. All it does is tell the other person that you are open to listening to them, that you have heard them. This is important because it can be difficult to find out the true underlying causes of conflicts. We discussed in the chapter on communication that people are sometimes reluctant or embarrassed to admit their real concerns. Instead, they give reasons for the conflict that they judge to be more acceptable to others. Personal attacks just confirm their fears that others will not take their real concerns seriously. Unless people feel safe, they will not reveal what is really bothering them.

Example 11.9

Elaine was the secretary for a small department. She was responsible for typing, keeping department files and answering the phone. She liked her work. Recently the department had received a new supervisor. On several occasions he had asked Elaine to run personal errands for him. Although Elaine felt that these requests were inappropriate, she did not dare to refuse them. After all, he was her boss and would be responsible for her performance evaluation. Elaine became frustrated because she felt powerless. Her frustration began to affect her mood at work. When other members of the department asked her if something was the matter, she replied, 'There is just too much to do, I am stressed out.'

Conflict resolution shares similarities with negotiating, and it often involves negotiation. As Fisher and Ury (1981) in their book on negotiating explain so well, it is essential to (1) focus on issues, not on personalities, and (2) be tough on problems and issues, not on people. Although their advice is for the negotiation process, it is also applicable to conflict resolution. In this chapter, we use Holton's (1996/97) model for conflict management: (1) to identify the conflict, (2) to identify the solution and (3) to implement the solution.

1. Identification of the conflict involves six steps, all of which are necessary to understand the nature of the conflict.

    (a) *Identification of the parties involved.* While this step sounds obvious, it can be difficult in practice. Those who are directly involved in the conflict and those who are most outspoken about it are easily identified. Sometimes there are actors who stay in the background but whose co-operation may be critical if we wish to resolve the conflict. For example, one of the parties to the conflict may listen to the advice of a trusted colleague about how to deal with the conflict. In such a case it may be very helpful to involve this colleague in the conflict resolution process. This example also demonstrates that knowledge about the relationship between those involved, and each person's role, is important to understanding the conflict and developing solutions. In addition, identification of the position within the organization may also be important information. If one of the parties involved holds more power than others, this is almost certain to shape the nature of the conflict.

(b) *Identification of the nature of the conflict.* This step should include identification of emotions, not just the objective nature of the conflict. It is quite possible that the objective problems that are the initial cause of a conflict have, over time, diminished in importance relative to emotions such as hurt pride and hurt feelings. Successful conflict resolution must address such emotions.

(c) *Identification of the start of the conflict.* The beginning of a conflict may be difficult to pinpoint, often because it started as a small annoyance. The importance of this step is to identify the root causes of the conflict and to determine whether it is an ongoing or cyclical conflict. Perhaps the conflict occurs whenever a specific assignment is given, or maybe it occurs every year around the time when performance appraisals take place.

(d) *Location of the conflict.* The physical location of the conflict may or may not be of importance if the conflict is located within the organizational structure. Opportunities for conflict management are almost certain to be different if a conflict is between peers than if it is between a staff member and a senior administrator.

(e) *Prior attempts to resolve conflict.* If past attempts have been unsuccessful, we may learn something from the experience. It is possible that past failure has made the parties more or less amenable to conflict resolutions.

(f) *Possible consequences of the conflict.* What will happen if the conflict is not resolved? A thorough evaluation and understanding of the consequences of the conflict would be needed to determine its impact upon the performance of the unit or department if it is not resolved. Likewise, it is necessary to analyze the impact if the conflict is resolved. This information may be helpful in designing a conflict resolution strategy. For example, if there has been a recent unsuccessful attempt to resolve the conflict, and if the conflict has no serious consequences for overall performance, it may be helpful to use conflict avoidance before trying again to resolve it.

2. The next major step is the identification of solutions. Those directly involved must work together. The services of a neutral third party as moderator of discussions and as mediator can be very helpful. It is indispensable when there is lack of trust between the parties. Setting the stage and getting the parties involved in conflict to communicate and work together are necessary parts of this phase of the process. The steps are as follows.

   (a) *Be positive about the chances that the conflict can be resolved.* If there are reasons to believe that resolution is not possible, additional time and effort should be spent to get ready. Those who believe that resolution efforts are doomed to fail should not attempt to intervene in a conflict. If the parties are not ready to work and sit down together, an order (dominance) may be appropriate to at least control the conflict until such time when resolution can be attempted. Before an order is issued, however, leaders should make sure that they have the means to enforce it.

   (b) *Establish ground rules.* Conflict produces a feeling of chaos; the purpose of ground rules is to reduce chaos. Ground rules should cover the following aspect of the conflict resolution process: (i) structure – frequency and place of meetings; (ii) communication – agreement on the use of feedback and confidentiality; and (iii) the membership of the group which is involved in resolving the conflict.

   (c) *Identify the interests of the parties.* Parties must understand their own priorities and desired outcome(s). As both parties identify interests rather than positions, the answer to the conflict often becomes obvious. Sometimes it helps to explain to those involved what will happen if they do not manage the conflict. Sometimes the threat of an externally imposed solution is enough to get parties to agree to work together.

   (d) *Develop alternatives.* The parties to a conflict often find it difficult to see options for resolving their conflict. By focusing on interests, we take the first step to break the gridlock. Once interests (needs) are properly understood, brainstorming is an excellent process to identify possible solutions. In an environment of trust, disputants can develop multiple alternatives by working together. It may be helpful to identify solutions to similar issues in other organizations. It is not the purpose of this step to determine the feasability of proposed solutions, only to develop as large a set of alternative solutions as possible. A large number of alternatives will later provide opportunities for negotiating a solution.

(e) *Identify criteria.* Not all of the ideas generated during the previous stage will be feasible. It is important to identify criteria before negotiating agreement. What are the cost constraints? Is the solution acceptable to the organization? Are there time constraints? Criteria will generally be both objective and subjective. Emotions are important in conflict; sometimes the conflict is about nothing else. A solution generally should allow parties to 'save face'. If someone feels humiliated, the conflict may well resurface again at a later date. Thus, one criterion may be that all parties feel good about the solution.

(f) *Weigh solutions against criteria.* The alternatives generated earlier should be judged against the prioritized criteria. Some alternatives will be dismissed on the basis of this analysis. This must be done by mutual consent. Discussion can then focus on a smaller subset of possible solutions. For example, during these discussions the solutions may be modified by combining features from different alternatives. A solution will emerge that is accepted as the best feasible solution. It is important to determine whether that solution is, in fact, felt to be the best one by all parties. Too often, after a solution has been determined, parties realize that they left out some important criteria. This will usually happen if the parties include only rational, logical criteria and ignore emotional aspects of the decision.

3. The solution implementation phase needs to be done with as much care and time as the identification of both the conflict and the solution. It consists of the following steps:

(a) *Develop a plan of action.* Many proposed solutions fail because of poor implementation. A plan of action must include the following: (i) Who will be involved in the implementation of the solutions? Participants need not be restricted to parties to the conflict. For example, if trust among the parties is very low, it may be helpful to involve an outside mediator in the implementation. Consideration must be given to the development of a mechanism that assures all parties to the conflict will keep their part of the agreement, or implementation of the solution could easily break down. Management should check that the solution is properly implemented. (ii) What exactly is to be done? It is important to itemize all actions that need to be taken, whether they are major or minor. (iii) When will the parties act? Without deadlines when actions have to be taken and when they have to be completed, one of the parties could hold up implementation of the solution through delay tactics.

(b) *Determine how to handle future conflict between the parties.* Although a conflict has been resolved, we should not regard the solution as final, at least not until it has withstood the test of time. Therefore, as a part of the conflict management process, the parties should agree on a way to deal with conflict in the future. For example, the parties may agree to work with a mediator if the same or a new conflict breaks out between them. The agreement may state that they will continue to work together professionally while negotiations to end the conflict go on, etc.

Benefits of Conflict Management

Conflicts arise when people or organizations have serious differences regarding their goals and aspirations in working together. Conflict, either help to adapt to change or makes change fearsome. Conflict by itself is neither positive nor negative. It can produce mutual destruction and despair or lead to an honest exchange of views and the finding of common ground (Tjosvold, 1996). The impacts of conflicts depend on how we deal with competing goals and interests. Conflict resolution requires excellent communication skills. When little is at stake, the cost of miscommunication is low. In conflict situations, the cost of poor communication is high. Lack of communication or unclear communication can create misunderstandings that fuel conflicts.

We would be ignoring human nature if we believed that we could avoid conflict. Regardless of how well we communicate and regardless of how pure our intentions are, there will be instances of conflict. If we handle conflicts well, they may actually help rather than hurt the organization. Here are examples of how conflict may benefit the organization.

1. Conflicts bring problems out in the open. They are the symptoms that allow us to diagnose the 'illness' in an organization.

2. A constructive conflict resolution process may enhance communications in the future.

3. Conflicts may initiate positive change as they are addressed and resolved.

4. The search for a solution provides opportunities for creativity and innovation. The very nature of conflict implies that different people are looking at an issue from different perspectives, a prerequisite for innovation.

5. Successful conflict resolution builds trust and confidence. People who can resolve a difficult conflict will work well together under easier circumstances. The experience also prepares those who were involved in a conflict and its resolution to deal more constructively with future conflicts.

6. Conflict provides an opportunity to examine interests and goals and revise them, if necessary. This process leads to a better understanding of self and others.

7. The outcome of successful conflict resolution is problems solved, with commitment to the organization and common goals reaffirmed and strengthened.

Although conflict can be beneficial, if handled poorly, it damages the organization. One of the most important rules of conflict resolution is to separate issues and problems from people. It is essential to realize that it is not possible to please all members of the organization all the time. Members must be willing to compromise on minor issues, as long as the general direction and goals of the organization are compatible with their own. Difference of opinions over small issues should not lead to conflict.

One of today's most significant management challenges is dealing with the demographic realities of a changing labour force. Organizations with a diverse workforce are becoming more multi-cultural. In a diverse society, the potential for creative conflict resolution is higher as individuals from different backgrounds and cultures bring different experiences, values, customs, and beliefs to the workplace. This makes the workplace more challenging, but also potentially more rewarding. Whether or not diversity results in increased creativity for conflict resolution or in more negative conflict depends at least in part on the leadership of management. One of the roles of leaders is to first understand the differences between themselves and their followers, and second, to educate their followers so that they will work well together. An organization with a diverse labour force may need diversity training that will educate members of the organization about other members.

With training, diversity produces ideas and encourages people to clarify their views. The resultant tension stimulates interest and creativity. It can also produce frustration and cause waste of human energy and other resources. Potentially, diversity results in more complex interpersonal relationships, fosters long-standing but implicit problems and causes people to suppress their differences (Fairholm, 1994). The attitudes of leaders toward conflict help determine whether diversity is a positive force or a cause of stress. They determine whether employees will be comfortable with the differences between them, or whether there will be pressure on minorities to conform (superficially) to the values and attitudes of the majority.

CHAPTER TWELVE

PERFORMANCE MANAGEMENT

A good leader must be tough enough to have power and influence, but not tough enough to use force and kick an employee when s/he is down.

Douglas McGregor

The ability of an organization to function, progress, and develop excellence depends on both the individual performance of each employee and the performance of teams and departments. The overall performance of the organization also depends on how well the performances of individual departments are co-ordinated. Thus, the efficiency and productivity of the organization depend on the skills and talents of its employees and managers, and on how effectively those skills and talents are marshalled. The establishment of a performance management system assists in the achievement and maintenance of high quality performance and achievement. A comprehensive performance management system should encourage professional growth and retain and develop employees who have demonstrated a high level of performance. It should recognize achievement, promote continuing productivity and efficiency in the workplace, and ensure the welfare of the organization.

Performance evaluation has become standard practice in many private and public organizations. It is quite common for organizations to have an annual performance review, usually to provide input into the determination of salary adjustments. We discourage such an approach. Instead, we recommend that performance evaluation be a continuous process. We also recommend that the evaluation process not be linked to rewards. This does not mean that we oppose merit-based reward systems, but when we link the performance evaluation process to rewards, employees have an incentive to hide problems and highlight strengths and achievements. This prevents management from addressing problems efficiently. Thus, we believe that an employee should not be penalized when we identify a performance problem during the evaluation process but should be given the opportunity to address and correct the problem. Only if the employee fails to address the problem should there be negative consequences.

When a continuous performance management system is designed and integrated into the daily work programme as a communication process, not as a measurement process, it can improve job understanding and competency, motivate employees and increase their ambition, establish mutual expectations of standards, and improve communications between management and employees. Effective performance management is an important aspect of personnel development at all levels and for all functions. Managing employees and reviewing performance is part of the control process. It serves as a reference point for evaluating and improving employee performance. Employee performance should be evaluated against the organization's goals and objectives, i.e. the performance of an employee is measured in terms of the degree to which the individual employee contributes to the accomplishment of the organizational goals (Barge, 1994; Miller, 1988). Continuous performance management accomplishes its purpose of promoting productivity and communication in the organization and enhancing employee development and training.

Reasons for Poor Employee Performance

Employees reach their best performance when they are motivated and working in an appropriate environment. When they perform poorly, they are often the first to realize it and are quite willing to make changes to improve their performance. For this to occur, however, they must feel supported by management, agree with the organizational goals and objectives, feel part of the organization, and believe that their contribution matters and is appreciated. Their motivation to improve their performance comes from different sources. The psychological need for approval by others (recognition) is a powerful motivating factor. Job security, promotion, or pay raises are other rewards for excellent performance. While our culture seems to assume that the causes for poor performance can usually be found within the individual, surprisingly often the causes are not specifically related to the employee. The following are reasons for poor employee performance.

1. *Inappropriate reward systems can lead to loss of efficiency.* For example, if teamwork is valued but rewards are based on individual performance alone, the willingness of team members to spend time on efforts that cannot be clearly attributed to one person may suffer. As a result, team efficiency would be undermined.

2. *Attitude and behaviour.* Some employees may have a negative attitude toward work or display inappropriate behaviours. Even if their own performance is good, they may have a negative impact on the performance of others.

3. *Inappropriate supervision.* Employees can receive too little or too much supervision. Under-supervising is most likely in the case of new employees. What seems easy or obvious to experienced staff members may be puzzling and intimidating to new staff members, even after some initial training. Lack of supervision may lead to stress and frustration that affects job performance. Over-supervision is often a sign of lack of confi-

dence of the manager in staff members. If an employee does not deserve the manager's confidence, the reason for the lack of confidence should be addressed. Regardless of whether the lack of confidence is justified or not, over-supervision will rarely address the manager's concerns, but is likely to lower the morale and self-confidence of employees.

4. *The match between employee skills and job requirements is poor.* This can be the result of a lack of skill/need for additional training. Assigning a highly skilled employee to a job that makes poor use of those skills is also a mismatch. While under-qualified employees should never be assigned to a job, over-qualified employees can be assigned to a job that does not use all of their skills, but such an assignment should be of a short duration. A longer term assignment would likely lower the employee's morale. Mismatch often occurs as a result of vague or otherwise poor job descriptions or poor employee selection (hiring process).

5. *Lack of communication.* If employees do not understand what is expected of them, their performance will reflect their own expectations and possibly those of their fellow workers. These expectations may not be fully compatible with those of management and the organization. Lack of communication results if no standards of performance and/or standards of conduct are established, or if existing standards are inappropriate or poorly articulated.

6. *Poor correlation between performance and rewards.* Good performance should be rewarded. Rewards can take many forms: public recognition, certificates, bonuses, pay raises, promotions, gifts, an extra day off, etc. Unearned rewards are worse than no rewards. When undeserving employees receive rewards, it tells them that their performance is very good and therefore, they see no reason to change. Even worse for the organization, deserving employees are treated unfairly and may see no reason to maintain their previous excellent performance.

7. *Lack of initial orientation and job training, and lack of support and guidance for personal development and growth.*

8. *Unrealistic goals.* Goals should challenge the organization and its employees and should not be set too low. However, while organizational goals and/or objectives should be ambitious, they must also be attainable.

Benefits of Performance Management

A coherent performance management system is a blueprint for efficient performance evaluation and employee development. According to Lee (1996), a system designed for performance evaluation has to meet and integrate the following basic requirements:

(a) set the right goals and objectives for each employee;

(b) provide the right measures for assessing an employee's progress;

(c) offer regular feedback to employees on how they are doing;

(d) provide information for identifying the source of a problem;

(e) provide information for coaching and counselling employees;

(f) provide systematic information on which to base rewards such as salary adjustments, transfers, promotions and reinforcement;

(g) provide information that may also have to be used to justify demotions or terminations;

(h) provide information on how to enhance employee development and training.

A continuous performance management system evaluates employees and makes them aware of their contributions relative to team efforts and organizational goals. It is an employee-driven process that helps leaders and employees share responsibility for managing their performance and to help their organization achieve its goals. Its focus is on the results of team efforts and employee development (Weaver, 1996; McGregor, 1966). Thus, effective evaluation programmes concentrate not only on past performance but also on future opportunities. In particular, evaluation programmes contribute the following.

1. *Help managers identify the untapped potential of employees*, such as special talents or interests that can challenge and increase their job performance.

2. *Inform employees on how managers view their performance.* If the performance is judged positively, the management should explain the criteria that were used to form the evaluation. A specific assessment is more useful and has a stronger effect on employee morale than a compliment without any explanation. Similarly, a negative assessment should identify areas that are in need of improvement. The employee should be given sufficient time to correct problems. Where substandard performance is the result of insufficient skills, additional training should be offered or a job reassignment made.

3. *Help employees make career decisions.* Performance assessment assists in developing a strategy to achieve career goals.

4. *Provide information to management for making decisions regarding rewards (pay increase, promotion, recognition, etc.) and disciplinary actions (demotions, termination, etc.).*

5. *Identify personnel training and development needs for employees to gain skills.*

6. *Encourage communication between the managers or supervisors and employees.* The system should allow employees to respond to concerns and encourage them to assess their own performance realistically.

7. *Reinforce performance expectations and provide employees with benchmarks by which they can evaluate their own performance.* Employees should be asked to provide a self-assessment of their performance.

8. *Include the employee in the performance planning process.* Participation in setting goals results in more effective implementation and accomplishment of goals.

Barriers to Performance Management

Both managers and employees often view performance evaluation with apprehension. Managers say, 'Oh no, it's that time again', because they do not look forward to confronting problem employees. Many people are uncomfortable when they are put in the position of having to judge others. Having that much power over others is intimidating. Employees often feel threatened by the process and unappreciated if the outcome is less positive than they had expected.

The apprehension is probably the result of past performance evaluations that were done poorly. Evaluation is a tool to improve performance, not to punish employees. For this reason the performance evaluation and coaching meeting should not be used to determine salary raises. Salary decisions should be handled in a separate meeting. Employees should not be penalized for problems when they are first identified, but be given the opportunity (and resources, if necessary) to address them. Many problems can be prevented if managers are aware of some of the most frequent mistakes made in the performance evaluation process. The following is a list of barriers to effective performance evaluation (McGregor, 1966; Weaver, 1996).

1. *Limited review scope.* Traditional performance reviews focus only on individuals getting the job done, not on improving job performance and employee development. The focus on the individual employee and their job responsibilities also tends to ignore contributions to the organization that are not directly related to the job, such as assisting other employees or team spirit. Yet, if the evaluation is based on individual performance, employees will focus on how to please the boss rather than how to achieve organizational goals. If the evaluation is also based solely on the perception of the boss, not on the team effort, the evaluation process cannot lead employees to pursue quality and productivity improvements. Likewise, if the purpose of the evaluation process is only to judge employees against

their job responsibilities, then there is no time to help and nurture them.

2. *Performance evaluation is not criticism.* First, critique and evaluation are only one part of the process. It is normal that employees who are being evaluated are apprehensive. Unless the process also focuses on positive aspects and is not limited to identifying areas in need of improvement, managers should not be surprised if employees are reluctant participants in the process. Second, the way the performance evaluation is conducted matters. The evaluation should focus on issues, actions, outcomes, and consequences, not on personalities. Managers may be tempted to 'get personal' when dealing with a difficult employee, but this temptation is to be resisted. What we want to change are behaviours and actions. Comments about an employee's personality will not make that individual more co-operative, but could easily damage the relationship between the employee and the manager performing the evaluation. In summary, the evaluation should be as objective as possible and performance criteria should be limited to actions and behaviours and their consequences. Personal likes or dislikes should not play a role in the process.

3. *One-way communication.* Performance evaluation should be a dialogue. Employees should be invited to perform and present a self-assessment and should be given opportunities to express their concerns and ideas. The performance evaluation should be treated as a draft document to be discussed and, if appropriate, changed as a result of the dialogue.

4. *Lack of correlation between performance evaluation and rewards.* If employees come to believe that the performance evaluation is unrelated to rewards, they will stop taking the process seriously. However, discussions of performance and coaching for improvements should be held separate from a meeting to determine salary.

5. *Mistrust.* If employees do not trust management, they will not trust the performance evaluation process. That is, they will not believe that it will be conducted fairly and will therefore resist it.

6. *Inexperience with the evaluation process.* If performance evaluation is introduced for the first time, it is important that the process be explained to employees ahead of time. Explanations should cover criteria to be used and the use made of the information obtained through the evaluation process. They may also mistrust the validity of the evaluation instrument and the implications of the assessment. Without such information, employees may feel threatened by the process and participate unwillingly.

7. *Lack of performance management skills.* Good communication skills, understanding of the employee's job, and knowledge of customary job expectations are prerequisites for an effective and fair evaluation.

8. *Inability or unwillingness to make decisions that may affect an employ-*

ee's future. Some managers are uncomfortable with judging other individuals; they are afraid of the power they hold over them. Their understanding of the great responsibility that comes with that power may help make them particularly effective evaluators of employee performance, provided that they can overcome their discomfort with performing the task.

9. *Poorly defined evaluation criteria.* The evaluation criteria should be based on (a) the employee's job description, and (b) the mission of the employee's work unit. In general terms, the evaluation should determine how well the employee performs job responsibilities and how effectively they contribute to their unit's mission.

10. *Lack of follow-up.* An evaluation that gathers dust once it has been completed is not worth much. Management and employees should act on the findings to address weaknesses, develop talents, or change job responsibilities, as appropriate.

Formal performance evaluation should be conducted regularly. In most cases, a one-year cycle is sufficient. As part of the process, the supervisor and employee agree on a set of performance objectives. Informal appraisals that provide feedback, however, should be more frequent. They may occur at any meeting with an employee when nobody else is present. If the objectives are reached, more ambitious objectives may be appropriate, or maybe the employee is ready to be promoted to a position with more responsibility. If the objectives are not reached, the reasons should be identified and appropriate actions determined and implemented. In other words, each performance evaluation is based on the results of the most recent prior evaluation.

How to Conduct Performance Management

The natural response of most people to a new situation is to categorize what they see and perceive in an attempt to give it relevance and meaning. It is from these interpretations that we form our initial responses or evaluations. Responses are effective if they are based on appropriate assumptions and procedures. First reactions serve as filters for subsequent information. They therefore play an important role. If our first impression is positive, we tend to look for other positives, thus gradually building a positive view of a situation or person. Similarly, if our initial impression is negative, we tend to look for other negatives and form a negative overall impression. Unfortunately, first impressions are often incorrect. It is therefore especially important for leaders to learn to move beyond the obvious and collect specific information before coming to conclusions about a person or a situation. They should not be guided by likes and dislikes or they will undermine the assessment process to the detriment of the long-term performance of the organization (McLean and Weitzel. 1992).

Organizations should evaluate employees in terms of their individual performance and actions and their impact on the organization. The performance evaluation must be guided by principles and procedures that ensure accuracy, rationality, fairness, equity, and integrity in the application of defined standards and criteria. Managers should keep a record of significant accomplishments (or problems) of their employees. Documentation is important because it provides specific evidence of behaviours and actions and their impacts. As we have already stressed, evaluation should focus on behaviours. It should encourage desired behaviours and attempt to change undesirable behaviours. A focus on behaviours and their impacts is more likely to result in an objective evaluation than one based on vague information. The integration of performance management into everyday tasks motivates genuine co-operation and teamwork, encourages employee development, and improves quality and system output. The following are six suggestions for conducting a performance evaluation.

1. Hold the meeting in a quiet place or surroundings without interruptions.

2. Review the employee's responsibilities and record prior to the meeting.

3. Establish an agenda for the meeting and share a copy with the employee.

4. Tell the employee how to prepare for the meeting. Explain that you wish the performance evaluation to be conducted as a friendly dialogue between the employee and you.

5. Put the employee at ease before starting the evaluation. At the beginning of the evaluation meeting, go over the agenda; answer questions about the agenda. Then proceed with the following steps.

    (a) Review job responsibilities and expectations. Ask the employee if responsibilities have changed or should be changed.

    (b) Review and explain performance evaluation criteria.

    (c) Ask the employee to present a self-assessment of job performance. The assessment should cover accomplishments and strengths, and failures and weaknesses. Do not discuss or respond to the self-assessment until the employee is finished.

    (d) Agree or disagree in a professional manner. Do not personalize problems that you perceive, but focus on actions and behaviours. Explain why certain behaviours or actions need to be modified by showing that they have a negative impact on achieving organizational goals and objectives.

    (e) Summarize key points, including strengths and areas needing improvement.

    (f) Add your observations and suggestions for the employee.

    (g) Seek to reach agreement about actions to be taken. Do not ask for changes in responsibilities or behaviours without first explaining your reasons for them.

(h) Find the real causes for unsatisfactory performance. Be a good listener. Let the employee talk without asking too many questions or otherwise interrupting.

(i) Schedule follow-up activities, particularly if actions are to be taken to address unsatisfactory performance or if responsibilities are being changed.

(j) Set clear goals and objectives. If appropriate, formulate specific development plans for the employee.

(k) Be appreciative of efforts, even if outcomes are not satisfactory. Encourage employees who are struggling and reinforce good performance.

6. Make an effort to talk with your employees throughout the year. Ask them how their work is progressing and otherwise show interest in what they do. Create a relationship that makes employees feel comfortable to come to you to discuss their problems.

The success of performance evaluations depend on the skill of the leader and quality of the tool. The evaluation instrument itself should be as clear as possible. It is important to understand that evaluations cannot be objective. The word 'value' is embedded in the word 'evaluation' for good reason. The criteria to be used in any evaluation reflect organizational needs, goals and objectives, and values; therefore, they change as the organization changes. Although objectivity cannot be achieved, consistency must be achieved to prevent criteria being applied in an arbitrary fashion. To achieve consistency, managers and leaders must be trained so that they all apply the criteria in a similar fashion. Consistency is also enhanced if employees understand the criteria.

Self-assessment by employees is a useful tool. The comparison of the assessments by the manager and employee, respectively, serves to identify differences in perceptions regarding roles, responsibilities and performance expectations. The professional dialogue can then focus on those issues where there are differences. The outcome of the dialogue could be revisions of the job description, clarifications of performance standards, or design of a training programme. An open conversation where managers demonstrate that they value the opinions of their employees will enhance morale, build trust, and managers may gain more accurate information about jobs than can be gained just by reading job descriptions (Downey and Erickson, 1987).

For an evaluation to be most effective it should be performed at regular intervals. Once a year is usually frequently enough for formal meetings, although a shorter interval is recommended for dealing with employees whose performance has been judged unsatisfactory. The evaluation should fix the date by when steps to address problems must be completed. At that time, at the latest, another meeting should be scheduled. In addition to formal evaluations, managers and supervisors should regularly and informally interact with their employees. Casual conversations and visits to the employees at their place of work can reveal useful information about problems and opportunities. A presence of managers among their employees can also serve to demonstrate interest and involvement.

Personnel evaluation is a delicate matter. It can generate negative effects if it is done without sensitivity to the feelings of employees. The scope of the evaluation should be determined and explained before evaluations are conducted. Performance evaluation should be based on measures of impact and results and related to employees' assignments and responsibilities. Evaluations are to be based on both quantitative and qualitative evidence. Behaviours and personal traits are to be considered only to the extent that they are job-related and could affect job performance. The primary evidence to be weighed must be contained in the personnel file. The following are three major performance evaluation areas to focus on (Miller, 1988).

1. *Evaluate job-related behaviours, nothing else.* Do not get into personalities, biases or attitudes. Discussions of personality factors should be avoided. If an employee wishes to discuss personal characteristics, agree only if the discussion is tied to job responsibilities and performance. Personal matters generally should be dealt with in an informal way, if necessary.

2. *Evaluation must measure two things, ability (skills, knowledge) and conduct, as they relate to performance and organizational objectives.* Both positive and negative aspects of performance need to be explained, including their effects on the performance of other employees.

3. *Evaluation process should discuss how the employee contributes to work of a group or team.* Group goals and group goal accomplishment should be discussed and explained. Such a discussion helps employees understand the importance of their work to the group.

How to Reward Superior Performance

People value being genuinely appreciated for their contributions. They become suspicious, however, when they are complimented and rewarded for efforts that they themselves do not judge to be meritorious. Therefore, special credit should be given only when it has been earned, that is, when employees worked hard and went beyond customary expectations. Honest praise by itself is a powerful reward and stimulus. The personal satisfaction that we experience when we achieve something special is reinforced by praise. It costs very little to express appreciation. In fact, employees prefer sincere, immediate recognition and praise from their direct supervisor over a little cash reward for a job well done. Honest thanks enhance productivity, boost morale, build trust, and strengthen the relationships of employees with the organization and its leadership (Kouzes and Posner, 1995). The use of rewards for mediocre performance is often manipulative to get someone to do something they really do not want to do (Kohn, 1993).

Managers have no choice but to address poor performance. Unless they want to be perceived as overly critical, they should balance their critical comments with encouragement and, when appropriate, expressions of appreciation. Employees who never receive encouragement will become discouraged and disillusioned and their performance will reflect their feelings. When you highlight only the weak points in their work, the employees become depressed and feel worthless. Employees who never receive praise, compliments, gratitude or encouragement lose their confidence and enthusiasm for their work. They become cynical; they resort to gossip and turn against the system that undervalues them. Even when an employee's performance is seriously lacking, the evaluation should not focus on how poor the performance was but on what behaviours need to be changed to improve it. This approach does not dwell on the employee's failure, but tries to identify solutions. In the long-term this approach is more successful than that of fault finding.

A critical assessment can be softened and even turned into encouragement. One way to accomplish this is to focus on strengths first. Then, the supervisor can move from a discussion of strengths to a discussion of concerns by suggesting that addressing weaknesses would further enhance the employee's capabilities. Unfortunately, managers/leaders often devalue their positive comments with sentences such as:

> Your technical accounting skills are excellent *but* you seem to have troubles getting along with some of your colleagues.

The following statement will elicit more positive reactions in the employee:

> Your technical accounting skills are excellent. I would like you to make them even more valuable to the department by helping you and your colleagues interact more effectively. Can we discuss how we could accomplish this?

In the first statement, the emphasis is on the problem. The employee has hardly heard the initial compliment before the supervisor starts talking about the negative. The statement implies that the blame for interpersonal difficulties rests with the employee. By making an accusation without first having obtained information, the employee is put on the defensive from the very start. His trust in the evaluation process and his willingness to co-operate will both suffer. The second approach separates the compliment from any concerns, thereby increasing its positive impact. Secondly, the manager uses the employee's strengths to justify addressing the problem she is concerned about. This strategy allows her to discuss problems with interpersonal skills without implying a threatening accusation. Her moving on to discussing the work relationships between the employee and his colleagues is a logical continuation of the evaluation, and her statement is formulated to avoid any implicit assignment of blame.

If it is necessary to draw attention to problems and mistakes, give the employee a chance to explain what happened before drawing conclusions. It may just be that the real cause was something not within the control of the employee. More generally, performance evaluations should not make employees feel that they have to defend themselves. Instead, they should be given the opportunity to explain their behaviour and performance and participate in the search for a solution to problems. Employees often have superior knowledge of details, more so than do managers who must concentrate on the 'big picture'. The knowledge of employees should not be ignored. More generally, the process should focus on finding solutions to problems, not on assigning blame. Problems should be discussed in private. In fact, it is important that a leader should *praise loudly and blame softly*.

Leaders should recognize employees' contributions and celebrate accomplishments by thank you notes, a smile, an award or public praise. Managers should let employees know how much they mean to the organization. They should express pride in the accomplishments of their teams and inspire them in their performance. Public celebration of success that honours employees and teams instills pride, creates role models, establishes high expectations, and gives courage and hope to continue in their quest for excellence. Celebrating the recognition in public shows the process of honouring employees and sharing with them the sweet taste of success. To recognize and celebrate accomplishments, a leader can use the following strategies.

1. Develop measurable performance standards.

2. Establish a formal and systematic process for rewarding performance.

3. Be creative about rewards; involve others to help design rewards.

4. Go and find people who are doing things right.

5. Recognition should be given in public; it will bolster employees' self-esteem (Kouzes and Posner, 1995; Terry, 1993; Miller, 1988). A bank manager once said, "If you do not show your appreciation to your people, then they are going to stop caring, and then you are going to find yourself out of business" (Kouzes, 1993).

How to Undertake Disciplinary Action

How should we proceed when confronted with situations requiring disciplinary action? We often ignore relatively minor problems such as occasional absenteeism, tardiness and poor attitudes. Experience tells us that such tolerance is poorly rewarded (Miller, 1988). The problem rarely ever disappears, but usually becomes bigger unless an immediate action is undertaken. If action is delayed, the authority of the leader will be undermined and other employees will also begin to bend the rules and try to get away with violations of rules, procedures and standards of conduct. After all, we sent a clear message that there will be no negative consequences. One of the most important guidelines for disciplinary action is to enforce norms of behaviour and act promptly before a relatively minor problem turns into a major one.

The purpose of disciplinary action is not to punish but to change or eliminate the undesirable behaviour. Disciplinary actions should follow a process that is well known to employees and that gives them the opportunity to present their perspective on what the problems are. Consistency is critical; if similar situations are not judged and treated similarly, employees will lose faith in the fairness of the disciplinary process. In a typical organization, disciplinary actions proceed according to the following general guidelines.

1. *Standards of conduct and performance are explained to all employees as part of their orientation to the job.* Staff meetings or other meetings with employees will occasionally be used to repeat some of the information. Employees need to know in advance what is expected and what offenses lead to discipline.

2. *Employees should know the consequences of violating standards of conduct and behaviour.*

3. *Disciplinary actions are initiated as soon as management becomes aware of problems.*

4. *Discipline is consistent.* Every violation is followed by management action. Similar actions are used to address similar situations. The severity of disciplinary actions is proportional to the severity of the problem.

5. *Discipline is job-related.* Disciplinary action does not get involved in personal accusations.

6. *Above all, the goal of disciplinary action is to return the employee to acceptable performance levels or standards of conduct.*

In recent years there has been a trend to use positive discipline. This type of discipline stresses coaching, counselling, and problem solving; it seeks to avoid an adversarial or confrontational approach to dealing with performance problems. Particularly in the case of employees without a history of performance problems, this approach replaces warnings and suspensions with coaching sessions and reminders by the supervisor of expected standards of performance and conduct.

Sometimes the only way to solve a problem is through terminating an employee. Firing an employee is always a difficult decision. It is possible that the immediate supervisor does not have the authority to terminate an employee, but can only make a recommendation. Regardless of who makes the decision, it is important that the reasons for terminating an employee are well documented. The documentation should show that the employee was given reasonable opportunities to improve conduct and performance. This includes information on counselling sessions, training, or other support provided to the employee. Documentation of problems should not create the impression of an overly critical supervisor but should document major problems with conduct or performance and unwillingness or inability to address them in a timely fashion. It is helpful if documentation of problems shows more than one source of information to avoid the possibility, or even only the impression, that a supervisor tried 'to get' an employee. Multiple sources of information will be helpful if the employee should challenge the termination. Where multiple sources are not available, examples of unsatisfactory work serve the same purpose. Documentation should be specific, including dates and times of unacceptable behaviours. General statements without documentation will not stand up to a legal challenge.

How to Supervise Former Peers

Being promoted over your peers and then supervising and evaluating them can result in difficult and stressful situations. Some of your former peers may harbour resentment for having been passed over. Others may want to take advantage of a friendship that was established when you were working together as peers. Some colleagues, and maybe you as well, may not yet have completed the transition to your new role so that behaviours are still based on your former role.

How can you minimize problems associated with supervising employees who just a short time ago were your peers? It may not be possible to avoid all problems, but there are some guidelines that will make conflict less likely. First, be tactful and sensitive to the feelings of the people you supervise. If they include former peers and friends, demonstrate that you still value your personal relationship with them, but discuss with them how you think your professional relationship has changed with your promotion. Do this at the earliest possible time. If you won the promotion over one of your colleagues, be particularly sensitive to the feeling this employee may experience. If she, the employee, is also highly qualified, acknowledge her skills and accomplishments. Do not treat her as a rival. One of the most important qualities in leaders and managers is fairness. As a new manager you must make it clear from the beginning that personal relationships, while important to you, cannot be used to gain favours that are not earned and available to all. You should also communicate that you expect friends and former peers to interact in a professional fashion with you and that they cannot exploit your mutual relationship for favours you are not willing to also grant to others.

Many people have trouble shifting to being a supervisor over friends and former peers. If you experience difficulties establishing good working relationships, you may need help from a trusted, more experienced leader. Perhaps the beginning of a mentor relationship can evolve from asking for help. As a starting point, ask yourself these questions to evaluate your leadership qualities.

1. Do I possess the key traits of a successful leader such as initiative, flexibility, self-direction, confidence, team spirit, interpersonal influence and system knowledge?

2. Do I demonstrate good management skills? Can I plan, organize, control and lead?

3. Do others see me as credible, competent and effective? Have I gained visibility with those who make decisions?

4. Do I fit into the norms of the organization? Am I dressing appropriately, in proper attire for the position? Am I co-operative or competitive? Is my leadership style and behaviour compatible with the organization's culture?

5. Do I have the ability to leave old habits behind? Am I flexible but principled when faced with difficulties or opportunities? Do I delegate and trust others to do a good job? Am I trading being liked for being respected or perfectionism for effectiveness? Am I so detail-orientated that I often lose sight of the big picture?

For new managers, such self-assessment is a particularly valuable tool. It helps them identify weaknesses so that they may develop a strategy for addressing the problems. Self-assessment also encourages them to look at their strengths. Information about strengths may suggest strategies for dealing with difficult situations and for career planning. The first year is the most difficult period for new managers. Most businesses follow a cycle that roughly parallels the calendar year. Thus, after one year, the number of tasks or events that the manager has not encountered before will drop dramatically. Because the first year is usually typical of what the next year will bring, the end of the first year is also a particularly good time for self-assessment and, if necessary, making adjustments and corrections.

PART III

MORAL DIMENSIONS
OF LEADERSHIP

The soul believes in the power of knowledge and justice over dark ignorance; it denies the authority that supplies the swords to defend and strengthen ignorance and oppression.

Kalil Gibran

CHAPTER THIRTEEN

DISCRIMINATION IN MANAGEMENT

What is important in life is how we treat each other.
So, do unto others as you would wish them to do unto you.

Golden Rules

Diversity initiatives have been, and continue to be, one of the most prevalent trends in human resource development and in contemporary management practice. Human resource development must include both sexes. Women are a growing and increasingly important part of the economic fabric of society. Social traditions and gender-based role expectations have acted to slow the rate of human resource development of women. While most societies have been changed through the universal provision of education and the impact of technology, traditional social beliefs and cultural practices have often remained comparatively undisturbed. This is particularly true in many developing countries where traditional ways continue to be used, but it also applies to Western societies. Traditional gender roles and practices have created a separation between men and women that no longer serves a useful purpose, and imposes barriers that hold women back from succeeding, to their disadvantage and that of society.

Effects of Traditional Values

Social institutions and traditional values continue to pose obstacles to women and adversely affect their role in management and leadership. Depressingly, some of these traditions have portrayed women as less important or capable than men and perpetuate injustices against women in fundamental ways, touching on some of the most central elements of quality of life, such as health, educational and employment opportunities, political participation, self-respect and life itself. In spite of the formal recognition of women's political rights, traditional attitudes towards the role of women in society still mean that there are some people who believe a woman's place is in the home and that her primary role is to be a wife and mother. A woman is expected to be modest and passive and serve as the caregiver of the family. Traditional expectations that limit the role of women to the family have hindered their opportunity to take on leadership roles in society.

There are many in Western societies who believe that traditional role models no longer play any role. We believe, however, that these values are still influencing attitudes and behaviours, although to a far lesser extent than used to be the case. Switzerland provides an excellent example of how long-held traditional values can persist.

Example 13.1

By most appearances, Switzerland has been a very modern country for some time. It has a successful and thoroughly modern economy and one of the highest standards of living in the world. In spite of these attributes of modernity, Swiss women obtained the right to vote in federal elections only in the early-1970s. In a few regions, Swiss women were still not permitted to vote in local elections, even after that date. It required the intervention of the Swiss federal government before Swiss women everywhere were given the same political rights as men.

The small percentage of women in positions of leadership and power in industry is another indication of the persistence of traditional role models. While there are some differences from country to country, there is no country where the number of women in positions of power comes close to the number of men who hold such positions. In other words, gender influences leadership power.

Women appear to be given lesser amounts of power than men, which, in turn, directly influences their opportunity to create and maintain leadership positions. Since leadership power is correlated to personal success in organizations, women are disadvantaged. Upon entering the workplace, women tend to be channeled into positions that are lower in power, information and organizational support. They generally are given control over fewer and less valued resources, and are in positions that are less visible in the organization than positions typically assigned to men with similar initial qualifications. As a result, women receive fewer opportunities to gain influence and upward mobility, and therefore their careers do not keep pace with those of men. Women may not be afforded the opportunity to be leaders owing to their segregation into formalized, low power leadership positions. Being relegated to low power leadership positions leads not only to decreased success but also to lower motivation, optimism and satisfaction (Barge, 1994).

Some organizations have an excellent track record of promoting on the basis of merit. In such organizations, women have been successful. An ambitious young woman who is considering a career with an organization is well advised to find out how many and what type of leadership positions are held by women. The record of how well women were able to advance in the past is probably a good guide to her chances. We do not want to discourage women from applying to other organizations, but they should expect to encounter obstacles when organizational values reflect traditional role models. Women who are the first to challenge such organizations play a pioneering role. The role of pioneer entails more risks and frustrations than other roles.

The laws of the United States forbid discrimination on the basis of gender. Laws, however, can give only incomplete protection against discrimination. Some forms of discrimination are fairly subtle, and therefore difficult to prove. Most organizations try to avoid open discrimination. In spite of such efforts, there are still instances of even blatant discrimination. Discrimination, as any other unfair treatment, has a negative affect on employee morale and can be devastating for the victim. We obtained the following story from a female worker. It illustrates the impact of sexism in a workplace.

Example 13.2

When a female employee left her position in the computing office of a university, a man replaced her. Melvin was the first man ever hired in the office. He was hired for a position that paid a salary that was higher than the average pay for similar positions in the same office. There were female applicants who were more qualified and experienced than Melvin. He had obtained the baccalaureate degree that was required for the position fairly recently and had no relevant prior experience. Most of the women in the office were initially hired in entry-level positions and had to work their way up to the same level of responsibility and pay as that of Melvin's job. From the day he was hired, Melvin was treated as someone who was in charge. Whenever the supervisor was out of the office for any length of time, he left Melvin in charge although there were female employees with significantly more experience. When the women balked at this unfairness, they were treated as complainers and troublemakers.

Melvin's job performance was very good. At least part of the reason for his superior performance was that he was given fewer but more interesting assignments. By contrast, many of the women had so many assignments they could not finish them on time, even if they worked through lunch and stayed late in an attempt to catch up. Since many of the female employees had families at home and carried most of the responsibilities for the children and housekeeping, this was a real hardship for them. Occasionally some women would ask the supervisor if Melvin could share their load. They were told that Melvin was too busy, even though he was allowed to pursue a graduate degree on company time. He wrote and researched his thesis during work hours. In addition, Melvin also held an outside job and he sometimes used office hours and his employer's equipment to work on the other job. Occasionally he even took off during work hours to deal with problems at the other job. By contrast to the lax supervision of Melvin, the female employees were watched closely by the supervisors. Eventually, Melvin finished the graduate degree and, after awhile, was promoted to supervisor of the computing office. Although he had started his position with less experience, fewer skills, and less maturity than several of the women in the office, the strong support from male administrators and supervisors had helped him overcome those disadvantages.

The cost of discrimination is high in terms of morale and efficiency. The organization may also suffer legal consequences if an employee brings a law suit against it. There have been some high profile cases in the United States that have damaged the reputation of the firms involved. The greatest long-term cost, however, may be the effect of discrimination on employee development. A company that does not value and promote some of its most talented employees because of the gender, race or some other irrelevant characteristic sends a powerful signal to all employees that promotion is not based on merit. When employees come to believe this message, they will either leave or lower their ambitions. An environment where advancement is not linked to talent, promise, and performance also encourages the use of internal politics to gain promotion. Such an environment encourages the formation of internal interest groups and is not conducive to co-operation and teamwork.

Informal networks and practices may work to the disadvantage of women. Their informality makes them less susceptible to management control. Thus, even if management seeks to promote the development of women, those who control informal networks may be reluctant to change practices that served them well. Since these tend to be practices that were established before women entered the workforce in large numbers, they may be insensitive to women. When women challenge traditions that work against them, they are often perceived as aggressive, and their willingness to be team players is questioned. Therefore they may face a no-win situation: either accept traditional practices that put them at a disadvantage, or challenge them and lose support among male colleagues (and often supervisors, too). Women, therefore, often find it difficult to gain leadership positions in networks. Without being part of informal networks of colleagues and superiors, it is difficult to gain access to leadership opportunities. Informal networks and groups are important *because* they are not part of the formal structure of the organization. They often serve social needs and allow people to meet in a non-threatening environment since little is at stake. In formal work settings it is more difficult to relax and establish friendships. Sexism exists in all organizations to some degree (Barge, 1994). Even where management is working to change attitudes, success is slow because management influence does not reach all layers of an organization equally well.

Women Supervising Men

In many cultures, women are excluded from leadership and management roles. They may not even be allowed to fully participate in the decision making processes at the household level. The representation of women in political parties, government, and leadership positions in industry is still quite small. Issues that are of special concern to women are therefore often given low priority. As a result, women often feel compelled to limit their participation in activities, to their disadvantage and that of society. Fortunately, society has begun to recognize the importance of including women. Even societies that still have very traditional divisions of labour along gender lines are beginning to recognize the costs of excluding women in leadership and management (FAO, 1990).

Although much progress has been made, old habits, attitudes and values do not disappear quickly. Many men, and also some women, react negatively to women in leadership positions. This is most likely to cause stress and conflict when a woman is in charge of supervising men. Below are some typical scenarios that may arise when women supervise men and advice on how to deal with them (Miller, 1988):

1. *Men may not treat women as equals.* A female supervisor may need to take the initiative in working toward an equal relationship. Inappropriate conduct should not be tolerated, but the female supervisor should avoid appearing overly sensitive. Even when employees hold sexist attitudes, not all of their negative responses to a female supervisor will be based on sexism. In other words, a supervisor should take negative reactions and attitudes of employees seriously and try to find out what causes them. If the cause turns out to be a sexist attitude, the supervisor should avoid making it a personal issue. Instead, the supervisor should state that the resulting conduct is contrary to the policies of the organization and harmful to its success. In other words, there should be no personal attack or effort to change the values of the employee. Instead, the focus should be on behaviours and performance, and how they affect the organization. Conduct is a legitimate issue to be addressed by supervisors. Thus, the supervisor does not have to accept rude or otherwise inappropriate behaviours, even if they have no direct negative effect on performance. If inappropriate conduct or poor performance persist, disciplinary action should be considered.

2. *Male employees may be concerned with the female supervisor's ability to represent their interests within the organization.* There is no immediate solution to this problem except to establish credibility. The record will eventually speak for itself. In the meantime, the employees' concerns can be alleviated by keeping them appraised of important issues and by explaining how the supervisor will deal with them.

3. *Some men may treat a woman like a mother figure.* Do not allow this to happen by insisting on a professional relationship. If you feel comfortable nurturing your employees like a mother, then that is your leadership style and it may work for you. Otherwise, it is better to be a leader than a mother. It does not mean that the supervisor should be impersonal and distant. Be courteous and friendly. Good leaders take an interest in the well being of their employees and mentor them. However, their relationship is limited to their professional responsibilities and interests. Close personal relationships usually complicate professional interactions.

4. *Men may treat a female with disrespect or condescension.* Confront such behaviour immediately. Do not ignore it. Be careful, however, to talk to the offending employee in private. Also recognize that some men do not know that they are being disrespectful to women. If you encounter such behaviours, call the employee to your office and directly indicate the unacceptable behaviour. Focus on conduct, behaviour and impact. Insist on professional behaviour and respect, if not for you, then for your position. If you do a good job, personal respect will follow. When inappropriate behaviour occurs, do not make 'a big deal' of it right then but simply say something such as 'this is not appropriate'. If disrespectful behaviour is widespread, consult with the organization's personnel office, affirmative action director or a supportive senior leader. Maybe the problem is beyond your ability or power to address. If the problems reflect the underlying organizational culture, then the senior managers and leaders must work to change that culture.

5. *Learn to ignore some complaints.* Supervisors, male or female, get their fair share of complaints. Ignore complaints that are muttered in a moment of frustration, unless there is also inappropriate behaviour. Not all complaints are justified and you will not succeed by trying to please everybody. Although a female supervisor may receive more complaints than a male supervisor, it is important not to take unjustified complaints personally. Do not 'take the bait' and respond every time someone makes a sexist remark. Respond if there is a pattern or if the remark clearly violates the limits of good behaviour. When you respond, do so in private in a way that fits the offense. Find a style of interacting that you are comfortable with and that puts most of your employees at ease. Be consistent in your demands and treat all employees with respect, even those whose behaviour is lacking.

In principle, national legislation guarantees equal opportunity and treatment of women and men. In practice, however, socio-cultural norms, customary laws and traditional practices, especially in developing countries, still restrict women from exercising their rights, and at times even contradict national legislation (ILO, 1995). Overt prejudice is relatively rare, and most prejudice is subconscious. Individuals who make prejudiced statements or whose behaviours express bias are often surprised when they are made aware of their prejudice. This makes education and training an effective tool in the fight against prejudice. Individual supervisors, however, should not try to change their employees' values, but should focus on conduct that affects the organization. This obviously includes conduct and behaviours that violate organizational policies, let alone those that violate the law. Female supervisors and leaders help change attitudes by example through their performance, actions and attitudes. Their performance and success demonstrate that women are highly effective leaders and proves that sexism is wrong (Miller, 1988).

Supervisors and managers have a special responsibility toward the organization. They must protect its legitimate interests. Sexism and other prejudice can harm the organization. The failure of managers to act against sexism can be costly.

Example 13.3

Diamond-Star, a joint venture of Chrysler and Mitsubishi, recently agreed to settle a lawsuit by female employees against this car manufacturer for a considerable sum of money. The real cost is even higher, however, because the case received a lot of publicity that created a negative corporate image.

Sexism in the workplace must be taken seriously, not only because failing to do so would be unfair to women and violate the law, but also because of its potential negative impact on the well being of the organization and welfare of its employees.

Sexual Harassment

Sexual harassment is any unwanted personal attention that interferes with the ability to work in an atmosphere free of intimidation. It includes unwelcome sexual advances, requests for sexual favours, and other verbal or physical conduct of a sexual nature. Sexual harassment can occur between employees of equal rank, or between supervisors and employees. It may or may not be tied to job performance or advancement. However, the request for sexual favours in return for positive employment decisions is one of the most serious offenses because it abuses a position of power over others. Supervisors should avoid behaviours that can be easily misunderstood. They should not use sexual innuendoes. Compliments or comments on the appearance of employees that could have a sexual connotation are inappropriate. Avoid behaviours that may make a person uncomfortable, such as standing too close (violation of personal space), frequent and unnecessary touching, staring, or making personal gifts (unless they are part of a tradition and given to all employees in the same situation). Supervisors should also be sensitive and avoid situations that can make an employee feel uncomfortable. The following example illustrates such a situation.

Example 13.4

Eric is the supervisor of a small department, two months ago he hired a new employee. Lucy is having difficulties at her new job. She is young and has little prior work experience. Eric believes that she would benefit from an internal training scheme offered by the personnel department, and he wishes to talk to her about the scheme. His schedule for the next few weeks is really busy, and therefore he requests that she meet with him in his office after business hours. He is not aware that Lucy is worried about the meeting. First, she is not sure what the meeting is all about and second she feels uncomfortable because she knows that the other employees will leave at the end of the work day and that she and Eric will be the only ones left in the department. She is not sure how to deal with Eric's request. She is aware that her performance has not been very good so far and worries what might happen if she refuses to meet after hours. At the same time she is afraid that the meeting might not be just about her performance.

In a case like this, a short explanation when the request is made will alleviate the employee's apprehension. By stating the reasons for the meeting and the unusual meeting time, Eric would have communicated that the meeting really was to be about professional issues only. In general, it is good practice to avoid meetings when no other employees are around. If a late meeting is unavoidable, the supervisor should ask someone else, in this case may be a female secretary, to stay late, too. This would add to Lucy's comfort level with the meeting and also serve to protect the supervisor from the possibility of being falsely accused.

Sexual harassment occurs when unwelcome sexual conduct unreasonably interferes with an individual's job performance or creates an intimidating, hostile, or offensive working environment. Examples of such conduct are sexual-oriented kidding, comments or innuendoes, display of sexually provocative materials, or whistling and catcalls. It is not required that such actions be directed at a particular individual. It is sufficient that they create an atmosphere that is intimidating and hostile. Management has the responsibility to establish values that discourage such behaviours. The following statement is a good example of how this can be done.

All employees want and deserve a workplace where they feel respected, satisfied and appreciated. Harassment or discrimination of any kind and especially involving race, colour, religion, gender, age, national origin, disability, and veteran or marital status is unacceptable in our workplace environment. Providing an environment that supports the honesty, integrity, respect, trust, responsibility, and citizenship of every employee permits us the opportunity to achieve excellence in our workplace. While everyone who works for the company must contribute to the creation and maintenance of such an environment, our executives and management personnel assume special responsibility for fostering a context for work that will bring out the best in all of us.

Lockheed Martin Corporation (1997)

The above statement accomplishes two things. First, it states a value; the statement is clear and strong. It says that behaviours contrary to that value are unacceptable. Second, the leadership accepts special responsibility for creating and maintaining a work environment that is compatible with the company's values and expectations.

Language communicates more than objective information, but also conveys attitudes. While terms such as 'honey', 'baby', 'sugar', 'darling', or 'doll' are terms of endearment among family members or friends, they are inappropriate in a professional setting where they communicate condescension and lack of respect. They contribute to a hostile work environment. Other behaviours that may constitute sexual harassment are comments or jokes that are stereotypical of, or derogatory to, members of the opposite sex, another race or ethnic group. Repeated comments about a person's anatomy, flirtation, excessive use of obscene language, inappropriate body language (such as leering or standing too close), invitations to meet socially after previous invitations have been rebuked, unwanted physical contact, and unwanted and unsolicited telephone calls are all examples of inappropriate behaviours. It should be obvious that physical advances such as kissing, hugging, patting, pinching, provocative touching, and suggestive body movements, let alone explicit sexual advances (such as invitations to a sexual encounter) cannot be tolerated at the workplace. That is, unwelcome advances and other inappropriate behaviours constitute sexual harassment whether or not they are tied to threats or promises regarding job rewards and advancement.

Homosexuals (gay men or lesbians) may face special difficulties and encounter physical or verbal abuse, ridicule and other demeaning behaviours. Repeated incidents establish a hostile work environment that must be corrected.

Although men can also be sexually harassed, most of the time the victims are women. Sexual harassment is about power. The perpetrator is trying to establish and/or exercise power over the victim. This can be very frightening and demeaning. The following are step by step strategies for dealing with sexual harassment at the workplace (Miller, 1988; McIntosh, 1996).

1. *Inform the harasser that sexual advances are unwelcome and must cease.* This should be done privately and at the earliest possible time. This step should be omitted, however, if the victim has reason to fear physical abuse. In that case, the intervention of a supervisor or a law officer should be requested.

2. *Do not keep it to yourself.* Inform your supervisor or the supervisor of the harasser. Management should know if an employee engages in inappropriate behaviours. A harasser may leave an individual alone who fights back but seek a new victim. Unless you tell your supervisor, patterns of harassing behaviour may go undetected for a long time. You may also find it helpful to talk with a trusted friend or senior employee. In very serious cases, you may wish to consult a counselor. Being harassed is

always unpleasant and can be traumatic. Having support from people you trust will help you better deal with your emotions.

3. *Keep a detailed log of what is said, when, where, and under what circumstances.* Include the names of witnesses, if applicable, and approximate times, dates, and location that the incidents occurred.

4. *Write a letter to be placed in your personnel file to be used for future reference, if needed.*

5. *If harassment continues, report all incident(s) to your immediate supervisor.* Immediately contact your supervisor or, if the person harassing you is your supervisor, contact your supervisor's superior and explain what is occurring. Be prepared to document dates, times, locations, and provide name(s) of witnesses, if possible. If you do not receive support from the organization, try to contact or inform an organization that fights against sexual harassment. In extreme cases, or if the company refuses to act, you may need to consult a lawyer.

6. *Work to overcome fear and a sense that you are helpless.* The leadership of most organizations will not tolerate harassment. You may also find help from one of the organizations that support victims of harassment.

7. *Avoid behaviours that could later be construed as encouraging sexual advances.* Maintain professional, job-related behaviours and dress in a way considered appropriate in your field. This advice is not limited to women. Men sometimes also dress inappropriately.

In general, in the United States, the employer is responsible for acts of sexual harassment in the workplace if the employer knew (or should have known) of the conduct, unless the employer can show that immediate and appropriate corrective action was taken. The employer may also be responsible for acts of sexual harassment initiated by non-employees if the employer knew (or should have known) of the incident(s) and did nothing to prevent or correct such incident(s). It is the responsibility of the employer to reassure the individual who indicates that they may be a target of sexual harassment. Leaders represent the commitment of the organization and they are responsible to provide a healthy work environment for the investigation into complaints.

Harassment occurs more often when inhibitions are lowered. Maintaining a professional and somewhat formal work environment establishes distance that makes inappropriate behaviours of any kind less likely. Office parties, on the other hand, are events when we interact more informally. Such events can be valuable for building team spirit. Managers should be aware, however, that they do provide an environment where harassment is more likely, and should, therefore, take steps to minimize the risk. For example, we discourage serving alcohol at office parties, particularly hard liquor, since one of the affects of alcohol is that of lowering inhibitions. More generally, management should also look at other events where formality is low and, if necessary, take steps to reduce the chance that inappropriate behaviours occur.

Responsibilities of Managers and Leaders

Harassment is about establishing and using power over others. Because managers and leaders, by virtue of their positions, have power over others, they have a particularly strong obligation to use their power properly. Our advice to managers and supervisors is to avoid making advances to their employees. Although a manager invites an employee he finds attractive for dinner, the employee may worry about negative consequences if the invitation is rejected. Work is a good place to meet other people and it is therefore natural that many couples first meet at work. However, those who hold positions of power should take great care to make sure that they do not, even inadvertently, use their power to establish personal relationships with employees.

In addition to the responsibility for their own conduct, managers are responsible for the atmosphere in their department, i.e. they must address incidents of sexual harassment and inappropriate behaviours that create a hostile environment. Sexually explicit materials do not belong at work. Even employees who have an office by themselves cannot treat it as if it were their private space. Other members of the organization, in the course of their work, may have to come to the office. This makes it a public space. With the increased use of computers, inappropriate materials can also enter via the Internet. Many organizations have specific policy prohibiting the use of company computers to view sexually explicit materials.

If a manager learns of a case of sexual harassment, swift action should be taken. If the perpetrator has no previous record and if the incident is relatively minor, a discussion with the employee may be sufficient. However, the supervisor should not accept the word of the harasser that a similar incident has not happened before, but should check with the personnel office or the affirmative action officer. The incident must be reported. While a minor first incident should not be entered into an employee's personnel file, a record should be kept in a central file. Without such a record, in a large organization a harasser could transfer every time he or she is confronted by a supervisor without the organization being aware of the pattern of harassment.

Managers and leaders play important roles in maintaining a work environment free from sexual harassment and in investigating any alleged incident of sexual harassment in their organizations. Investigating an alleged incident of sexual harassment is a sensitive matter. The process must protect the rights of the victim and the individual accused of harassment. The victim will often be emotional and traumatized. Interviewing the victim, therefore, requires patience, understanding and an appropriate approach to the situation. If possible, besides the managers and leaders, it should be done by someone with experience in such situations. The accused may also be distraught, either at being caught or at being unjustly accused. Innocence should be presumed until there is evidence that establishes guilt. The following are some guidelines that could be used in investigating sexual harassment of an employee. Most of the ideas have been obtained from a workshop offered by the Director of the Office of Affirmative Action at West Virginia University (McIntosh, 1996).

1. *Victims of sexual harassment often fear that they will not be believed and that management will not respond to their complaint.* It is important for the investigator to recognize those emotions when they are there and to reassure the victim about the investigator's role and the employer's commitment to establishing and maintaining a positive work environment.

2. *It is not unusual that the victim has denied their feelings about what has happened.* If the harassing behaviour is relatively mild, for example, a sexually explicit comment made in a low voice, victims will often initially assume that they misunderstood or that it was meant for someone else. The investigation should focus on validating facts while avoiding premature judgements. Be sensitive to the complainant's mental state. A complainant may be incoherent when first trying to talk about the incident(s).

3. *Be a good listener.* Give the complainant an opportunity to just talk without interrupting with frequent questions. If there are questions, make a mental note of them and ask them later. Let them know that you are concerned and that they are in the right office. Assure them of confidentiality about what is being said. Explain what sexual harassment is if they are not sure. Victims are often reluctant to talk about sexual harassment because they fear that they have done something to encourage it.

4. *Again, listening is most important.* Be objective and do not make judgements about the allegation, the victim or the alleged harasser until after you have had time to collect information from both of them, and from witnesses, if there are any. Stress that although you are very concerned about the victim's rights and well being, you are not an advocate for the victim. You have a duty to be impartial. Avoid behaviours that communicate belief or disbelief in what is being said. You may find it necessary to refer the victim to professional counselling because they need assistance in coping with what has happened or is happening to them.

5. *Introduce yourself and explain your role and the process of investigation.* State that you are interested in the facts so you can understand what happened in order to fit the pieces of the puzzle together. Do not let 'pencil and paper' get between you and the person you are interviewing. Do not double-team the victim of harassment. Avoid statements that judge the situation, such as 'that sounds very serious' or 'that could not have been too bad'.

6. *Do not press the victim for information during the initial call*. Schedule an appointment within one day. Have a packet of information for a victim and the alleged harasser that contains the employer's sexual harassment policy, complaint procedure, and rights. When interviewing the victim, the investigator should keep in mind that the victim might feel powerless and traumatized by the sexual harassment. If possible, have an experienced specialist conduct the interview.

In general, women are often exposed to occupational hazards in the workplace. Sexual harassment can generate emotional and physical stress including anxiety, depression and ulcers, reducing work efficiency for women, and imposing costs for the organization. Legal and institutional protection for workplace safety should be adopted. Relevant positions and guidelines can be adopted not only by governments, but also by employers, workers and women's organizations. In addition, awareness-raising programmes and training and advisory services should be undertaken to combat sexual harassment at work. Women's safety at the workplace will not occur unless employers and governments deliberate on policies and practical measures to promote and defend it.

Supporting Women for Advancement

Because of the tremendous transformation of society, a majority of women are entering the workforce. The importance of traditional attitudes is decreasing, but role expectations on the basis of gender are still widespread and often work to hinder the advancement of women at the workplace. The talents of women should be viewed in the same light as those of their male colleagues, however, and they should be given similar opportunities to succeed.

Affirmative action to ensure women's representation in decision making bodies is increasingly seen as crucial to fostering women's access to a wide range of employment opportunities (United Nations, 1995). However, affirmative action in the form of quotas has come under attack. Women who are put into positions of authority without the necessary preparation because the organization felt that it 'needed' more female managers will find it difficult to succeed. Their male colleagues may resent them and discount their qualifications. If poor preparation leads the newly appointed female manager to make mistakes, those colleagues will be confirmed in their belief that they have been treated unfairly. Therefore, the organization's leaders should make sure that female appointees are held to the same standards as their male counterparts.

In fields that until recently had been closed to women, there may be a shortage of experienced female candidates for advanced management and leadership positions. It may therefore be in the interest of an organization to identify talented female junior managers early in their careers and provide them with training, access to informal networks, senior executives who serve as mentors and other support that will help them advance in the organization. It is not necessary, and probably not even desirable, that such support be limited to women. It is sufficient that women are well represented among those who are selected; otherwise the status quo will persist for a very long time.

Stereotypes disappear if they are repeatedly proven wrong. Giving women leadership opportunities is the most effective strategy to disprove the stereotype that they cannot be effective leaders. Discriminatory practices are easier to change if they are publicized. The government and interest groups and associations can document cases of flagrant discrimination against women. Recognizing businesses that have made strides in promoting equal opportunities and career development for women provides positive reinforcement. Networking facilitates the creation of role models and mentoring systems among women (United Nations, 1995).

Other Forms of Discrimination

We have focussed our attention on gender discrimination because of its prevalence and the great and increasing importance of women in the workforce. Yet there are other forms of discrimination which are similarly destructive of interpersonal relations and organizational success. Discrimination on the basis of race or national origin has effects similar to gender discrimination. The roots of racial discrimination, however, are different. All of us know women and we have had many opportunities to interact with female family members, friends and colleagues. Racial discrimination is at least in part the result of ignorance, through many children growing up without getting to know children from other races. The children from both races grow up hating each other because they fear each other because they do not know each other; and they do not know each other because they are separated. Thus, some of the conflicts between races may be the result of lack of knowledge about each other.

Working in an unfamiliar environment is stressful. We know that from personal experiences such as the first day in a new job, or the first meeting with our future in-laws. These events were stressful even though we knew that we would be welcome and find support. When members of racial minority groups first enter an organization, they often cannot be equally certain that they will be welcome.

In the United States it has been decided that discrimination on the basis of race, gender, national origin, religion, age, or disability is not acceptable. Its history provides many examples of the high cost of racial prejudice and discrimination. It is the responsibility of an organization's leadership to ensure that members of all ethnic groups and of all ages feel welcome. The steps to deal with specific instances of discrimination are basically the same as those used to deal with gender discrimination. Educational and training programmes are helpful. The emphasis of multi-cultural education in many Western countries seems to be on teaching white students about other cultures. It is our impression that there is a shortage of good material introducing members of minority groups to the culture of the white majority. In the absence of personal exposure to that culture, members of minority groups learn about the majority group in a haphazard fashion.

Although knowledge about another culture is helpful, we should not judge individuals as if they represent an average member of their racial or ethnic group. Each individual should be judged on her or his merit. This is why we find most discussions of interracial intelligence differences not only distasteful, but also useless. Even if the average intelligence of a member of group A is lower than that of group B, this information would be useless in making hiring and promotion decisions. Within each group there is significant diversity. Rural residents differ from urban residents. Hispanics from Puerto Rico are different from the children of Mexican immigrants. Descendents of Italian immigrants in Boston hold different values than the descendents of German immigrants in rural Missouri. An African-American born and raised in Chicago is different from one born and raised in rural Louisiana. If we want to treat people in a respectful and fair fashion, we should look at them as individuals and not judge them based on their membership of a particular racial or ethnic group.

The most significant management challenge in the contemporary business environment is dealing with the demographic realities of a changing labour force. Businesses with diverse workforces are becoming more multicultural. There are many advantages to fostering a diverse labour force. Businesses and other organizations should be reasonable reflections of the ethnic and cultural make-up of their region. The same leadership strategy as that recommended for the advancement of women in organizations could be used to promote diversity in our society.

CHAPTER FOURTEEN

PROFESSIONAL ETHICS IN MANAGEMENT

The time is always right to do what is right.

Martin Luther King, Jr

Actions and behaviours are remembered and admired if they reflect important values or beliefs, such as courage, compassion, perseverance, honesty, integrity and sincerity. Ethics is the study of the standards of conduct and moral behaviour. The term also refers to the system or code of morals of a particular philosopher, group, religion, profession or organization. Simply put, ethics is about appropriate behaviours. What is good or bad, right or wrong? What rights and moral duties do we have? What are our moral values and principles? It is when we are not clear about our values that we are most likely to act in ways we later regret.

Ethical Obligations and Conflicting Values

Ethical issues arise when there are conflicts between different values and responsibilities. For example, business leaders often experience conflicts between the value of, and commitment to, family life, and the value of hard work and commitment to their career; athletes may experience conflict between valuing their health and sense of obligation to the team. In general, ethical conflict is the result of competing obligations. We have obligations to ourselves, our families, friends, church or religion, profession, employer, clients, colleagues, local community, state, nation, future generations, etc. Ethical conflict can be very difficult to resolve. Leaders who are sensitive to the existence of conflict between values will anticipate problems and therefore make fewer mistakes. Awareness of our values, of what is important to us, is the first step in dealing with ethical conflicts.

Our values relate to how we view our role relative to the roles of others. For our discussion, therefore, we consider obligations we have to self, family, society, and organizations, such as our employer.

1. *We have an obligation to ourselves*. What we do has a direct and immediate impact on us. If we act contrary to our beliefs and values, we may experience serious internal conflict that could result in health problems, interpersonal conflicts or legal troubles.

2. *We have an obligation to family and friends.* What we do and how we act impacts our spouse, children, parents, other relatives and friends. Those who have a family should not make important decisions unilaterally but consult with their spouse, and consider the impacts of their decisions on family members.

3. *We have ethical obligations to the society we live in.* The most basic ethical principle to guide our actions relative to society is respect for the law, its spirit as well as its letter.

4. *We have legal and ethical obligations toward the organizations we serve.* For example, employees are expected to come to work on time and make a diligent effort to do their job well. They may not engage in activities that are harmful to their employer (unless to do otherwise would be harmful to more important ethical principles).

5. *Many people feel a sense of obligation toward their religion.* Following the rules of their religion is an important aspect of their lives. They may also feel obligation to other organizations, such as their professional associations, fraternal organizations, societal cultural groups, charitable organizations, etc.

Problems arise because values and standards of ethical conduct differ among individuals, organizations and societies. These differences create a potential for conflict. The study of ethics is in part the search for acceptable solutions to such conflicts.

Dealing with Ethical Conflict

The first step toward resolving a conflict is that of becoming aware of our most important values. To explore our most deeply held values and beliefs, it is useful to consider how we acquired them. For most of us, the influence of our parents and the home we grew up in shaped what we believe to be right and wrong. Others who shape our values are religious leaders, teachers and friends. Professional attitudes and ethics are often shaped during training and by our first employment experiences. Most of the time values are not taught explicitly but learned from the examples set by parents, teachers, religious leaders, supervisors, friends and colleagues. Because of this, we may not always be aware that we have internalized certain beliefs and attitudes, and instead assume some of these values to be objective truths that everyone should abide by. This causes problems when ethical conflict arises. It is very difficult for us to reach a balance between conflicting ethical principles when we regard some of them as truths. We can change values, but truths are unchangeable.

How is adherence to ethical standards enforced? Here we distinguish between our own values and those formulated by others, including the law, pro-

fessional codes of ethics and conduct, rules set by the employer, and the expectations others have of us. With regard to our own ethical standards and
beliefs, enforcement is internal. When we act contrary to what is important to
us, we feel guilty or otherwise uncomfortable; our actions bother us. This
internal control of our behaviour is powerful. As managers and leaders, we
should formulate rules and ethical principles that reflect the beliefs and values of employees. If we succeed in doing so, compliance will be high even
when enforcement mechanisms and efforts are rudimentary. When rules violate the beliefs of people, external controls are needed to obtain compliance.
External controls include formal and informal mechanisms. Loss of the respect or trust of family members or friends may prevent us from acting contrary to what they expect of us, even when doing so is tempting. Legal consequences or job loss are other enforcement mechanisms. Enforcement tools
can include physical means. This is particularly obvious in the case of theft:
locking up supplies reduces both opportunity and temptation.

The truly difficult ethical problems are not those where there is almost
universal agreement about what is right and what is wrong, but those where
important values are in conflict with each other. Even thieves know that steal-
ing is wrong and do not condone it when they are the victims. People steal or
commit other acts they know to be wrong because they give in to the temptation to gain a personal advantage, not because of unresolved ethical questions.

Over the last few years there have been several reports about researchers
forging the results of experiments. We suspect that the 'publish or perish'
philosophy prevalent at research universities and the rewards that come with
success – promotion, tenure, salary raises, prestige – created pressures and
temptations that were too much for some individuals. This interpretation suggests that managers need to consider the impacts of incentives. Great rewards
for success may encourage extraordinary effort *and* cheating. In the higher
education environment, the system of independent peer review of research
results was designed to ensure the quality and accuracy of results. In general,
this system of checks and controls seems to work quite well. Management
and leaders have an ethical obligation to devise systems of checks and controls because it is morally wrong to expose individuals to temptations they
may not be able to withstand. Systems that are not designed with human needs
and weakness in mind will not work well.

The key to resolving ethical dilemmas lies in considering the impacts of
different actions. In this vein, Pastin (1988) presents three approaches. In an
approach that he labels end-point ethics, he suggests that managers ask two
questions about possible outcomes: (1) 'What is in this course of action for
me?' and (2) 'What is in it for the others who are affected?' End-point ethics
and a benefit-cost analysis are similar except that benefit-cost analysis can
only incorporate factors that can be measured while end-point ethics tries to
consider all factors influencing the outcome (Pastin, 1988). The inclusiveness

of end-point ethics requires that all stakeholders be identified. This may be difficult to accomplish. Large organizations, in particular, impact the lives of many people. Stakeholders of a business enterprise include the owners/shareholders, executives and managers, employees, suppliers, customers, people in the community and local governments. In other words, the concept of a stakeholder is inclusive and usually goes beyond those who have a formal affiliation with the organization.

The second step in the recommended process is the identification of alternative courses of action. These alternatives can then be analyzed relative to their impact on different stakeholders. The advantage of end-point ethics is its rational approach to problem solving which results in excellent information on which to base the final decision. What it does not do, however, is provide guidelines for what is a just or good decision (Pastin, 1988). To address the need for ethical guidance, Pastin (1988) suggests that we should establish ethical principles. There is no universal agreement on all ethical principles. Our laws prescribe some principles and others may be widely accepted. This still leaves many areas where firm ethical guidelines do not yet exist.

Example 14.1

The ethical conflict concerning abortion is a particularly bitter one. The law in most countries is clear. What we do not have is agreement over what ethical principles should guide the resolution of the conflict between those who seek to ban abortion and those who wish to make or keep it legal. It seems that there is even disagreement over the nature of the conflict. It involves the question, 'When does life begin?' There is no hope at the present time that the competing values can be reconciled.

The third step in Pastin's process, called the rule-ethics approach, builds on the end-point ethics process. From the completion of steps one and two we have a list of the alternative courses of action and their outcomes and effects on different stakeholders. These alternatives can now be compared against the ground rules established by ethical principles. To make the comparison, Pastin (1988) suggests that we consider two questions: (1) 'Which of my ground rules are potentially in conflict with this action?' and (2) 'Which of the ground rules of stakeholders are potentially in conflict with this proposed action?' The second question is particularly relevant for organizations that are engaged in activities in different countries and cultures, as some ground rules differ significantly from culture to culture.

Pastin (1988) reminds us that most ground rules are not categorical, i.e. they will sometimes be compromised. For example, telling the truth is important. There are situations, however, when it may be permissible not to tell the truth. Ground rules can also be in conflict with each other. For example, a manager of an organization may have a ground rule that implies an obligation to avoid actions that may have a negative impact on the well-being of the community. This rule may sometimes conflict with another ground rule that requires loyalty to the organization and acting in its best interest. For managers, the ethics of dealing with employees is very important. Unless ground rules result in treatment that is considered consistent and fair by the employees, managers will lose the respect and support of their followers. Fairness concerns not just the outcomes of personnel decisions but also the processes. Procedural fairness is very important. Employees will be much more likely to accept an unfavourable decision if they believe that the process was fair. The code of ethics of Lockheed Martin Corporation (1997) contains general ethical principles of personal honesty, integrity and citizenship.

> *Honesty*: to be truthful in all our endeavours; to be honest and forthright with one another and with our customers, communities and shareholders.
>
> *Integrity*: to say what we mean, to deliver what we promise and to stand for what is right.
>
> *Citizenship*: to obey all the laws of the United States and the other countries in which we do business and to do our part to make the communities in which we live better.

One of the most serious ethical problems is that of conflict of interest. Such conflicts are frequent but usually not serious. Most of them, therefore, are handled without explicit thought given to them because we are so used to them. When deeply held personal values conflict with the wishes or values of the organization, however, the resulting situation can be very difficult. The following example illustrates such a situation.

Example 14.2

A consulting firm employed Paul. A year ago, his employer had bid on a project that was of great professional interest to some of the firm's principals. They were so eager to submit the winning bid that they underestimated the cost to complete the project. A year later, most of the funding for the project had been exhausted but the work was not yet completed. Rather than acknowledge their mistake and accept the resulting business loss, Paul's supervisor, one of the firm's principals, told him to charge some of the time for working on this project to other projects. Paul was aware that clients, who were funding those other projects, had not been consulted and that it was extremely unlikely that they would give their permission if they were consulted. It was also not clear that those other projects would generate surplus income beyond the profit margin budgeted into the fees charged.

The order caused a very serious conflict for Paul. His sense of personal honesty and integrity told him that charging his time on the project to other projects was dishonest; he wondered if it was not also illegal. Although, he would have liked to disobey his supervisor, he dared not do so because he had been hired fairly recently, and only after a long and frustrating job search. The job market in Paul's profession was depressed and it would not be easy to find alternative employment. He was very concerned, therefore, about his financial status and the future of his career.

Situations similar to the one described in this example are not uncommon. There are no clear ethical rules. We strongly suggest, however, that an employee refuse to participate in an illegal activity. If an employee is not sure whether or not an activity is legal, a consultation with a lawyer may be advisable. Over time, participation in illegal activities is likely to be more detrimental to one's career than disobeying an order by a supervisor. If discovered, it may lead to loss of income and reputation and, in some professions, loss of professional certification or registration required to practice in that profession. If charging another project would not violate the law, the conflict between the firm's wishes and Paul's personal values would be less serious. He might be comfortable to stay with his current employer until he finds employment with an organization that supports values more closely aligned with his own.

When there is a conflict between personal interests and the interests of the organization, the conflict should be resolved whenever possible. When it is not possible to reach an acceptable solution, the conflict should be disclosed. This is particularly important for individuals working in public sector and not-for-profit organizations. The effectiveness of such organizations depends on the trust the public has in them.

Example 14.3

A few years ago an executive officer of the national United Way office was using a large amount of money from the organization's funds for his private benefit. Publicity around this case seriously harmed the fund-raising success of the United Way campaign. It harmed not only the national office but also state, regional and local chapters who were legally independent of the national office.

The experience of United Way demonstrates the importance of separating private interests from those of the organization. When this is not possible, conflicts of interest should be disclosed. Disclosure is not a remedy, but at the very least it demonstrates recognition of the problem. Making a conflict of interest public invites scrutiny that tends to deter serious violations of ethical obligations. Sometimes the only resolution of conflict of interest is avoidance. Avoidance may mean something as simple as abstaining from participating in decisions that result in a conflict of interest or it may require separation from the organization.

Resolving ethical problems is often difficult. It is useful to reflect on values before ethical problems arise. How we deal with ethical problems and what criteria and values we use is determined by five major sources:

(a) personal values and ethics;

(b) laws and regulations;

(c) cultural norms and expectations;

(d) the values, cultural norms and expectations of the organization;

(e) the code of ethics of our professions (e.g. the code of ethics for architects, accountants, lawyers, medical doctors and other medical professionals, social workers, etc.).

We lead by example, and this requires awareness of the values that determine our conduct. Reflecting on values and expectations is best done when there is no immediate need to do so. It can take time to resolve some issues, such as how to deal with difficult personal problems. When such problems are upon us we do not have the luxury of time to think things through carefully or consult with others who may have more experience. Unless we are clear about our values and ethics, we may make decisions that will undermine our credibility. The danger to our credibility and integrity is particularly great if our actions are perceived as self-serving or demonstrating lack of respect or consideration for others.

Leaders also face an ethical obligation relative to their followers. The relationship between leaders and followers is one of trust. Followers cede some control over their professional or personal lives to their leaders; leaders depend on their followers to support them. When followers come to believe that their leaders use their positions for personal gain and to the followers' detriment, they will lose respect for and trust in them. The result is an organization that no longer functions well.

PART IV

STRATEGIES FOR ADVANCING LEADERSHIP

Seek ye counsel of the aged, for their eyes have looked on the faces of the years and their ears have hearkened to the voices of life. Even if their counsel is displeasing to you, pay heed to them. Also seek ye counsel of the learned, for their eyes have looked on the pages of their books and their ears have hearkened to the words of their teachers. A person who does not seek advice from the learned is a fool. His folly blinds him to truth and makes him evil, stubborn and a danger to his fellow human being.

Kalil Gibran

CHAPTER FIFTEEN

THE POWER OF NETWORKING

Things may come to those who wait,
but only the things left by those who hustle.

Abraham Lincoln

Organizations consist of two kinds of hierarchies, one formal and expressed by organizational charts, the other informal and unwritten. Formal networks reflect the organizational hierarchy; they reflect the responsibilities and duties of formal organizational positions, delineate reporting relationships, and describe the organizational chain of command. The formal organization is concerned primarily with the activities of employees as they perform their job functions. Yet no complex organization can control all aspects of the work to be done and personal relationships that exist in any organization. Whenever people come together, informal relationships develop that affect the effectiveness of the formal organization. Informal networks differ from formal networks in that they emerge from personal interactions among employees, that is, their emotions, feelings, communications, and values. Although informal networks are primarily concerned with interpersonal relationships and are characterized by links and connections not necessarily reflecting the organizational hierarchy, they can add flexibility that makes the organization more adaptable to changing needs (Barge, 1994).

Organizations are comprised of people working together to accomplish common goals. Their activities can be described as a form of collective action. Through collaboration and co-operation, people form links with readily identifiable clusters or groups, commonly called networks. The formation of networks occurs for a variety of reasons. People create some networks on the basis of friendship. Other networks are constructed based on the nature of a common interest or task. In this type of network, members talk to one another, exchange technical information, and otherwise collaborate to accomplish their work. Networks are also established to enhance, serve, and protect the influence and status of their members. The different purposes of networks are not mutually exclusive.

Informal networking begins with the primary group, or the people with whom an employee works most closely. Within this group, as in the larger organization, relationships develop as the result of status, power and politics. Status is the social rank or position of a person in a group. Status and status symbols exist in every group. Symbols may include title, age, experience, physical characteristics, knowledge, possessions, authority, location, privileges, acquaintances and a host of other factors. Earned status is a reward by a group to its members and can serve as a motivator for employee performance. Earned status is highly regarded. By contrast, unearned status, i.e. status that is given on the basis of personal relationships rather than accomplishments or other merit-based criteria, can be divisive. Status comes from official or formal and informal sources. Examples of official status are titles, corner offices, a company car, a personal secretary, etc. The symbols of unofficial status may be subtle. For example, a senior employee with good interpersonal skills may frequently be asked to serve as the spokesperson for a group of employees. An employee whose skills are admired may be asked for advice when other employees experience a problem. A third employee may be entrusted with the introduction of new employees to their job.

Power is the ability to influence another person's behaviour; it is related to status. Power may come from formal authority or may have been obtained because of special skills, a proven track record or other factors. Power is correlated with rank, but employees with a low rank sometimes hold surprising amounts of power. This is particularly true for employees who control access to important resources. It also holds for secretaries who schedule meetings for important leaders and screen their mail and phone calls. The power that they derive from their position is often larger than their official authority. Their goodwill can decide how soon you obtain a meeting with the managers or how quickly materials you requested will be made available. People who respect their power will receive an extra effort; others will be treated 'by the book'.

Position centrality is correlated with power. Since leaders are typically the most centrally located individuals within a network, they usually possess a high amount of power. Their location within the network gives them access to critical information, and they also control some processes and dissemination of information. The information obtained through official network involvement concerns not only task-related issues, but information about other leaders' priorities, opportunities within the organization, upcoming events, etc. Access to the information generation and distribution network also gives greater power to influence other leaders, i.e. official leaders can communicate to a greater number and diversity of people related to the organization than other members of the organization.

Effective leaders recognize the importance of power. They recognize their own power and that of others in the organization. The more power a leader has, the more he or she can contribute toward the objectives of the organization. In Chapter 14 we discussed the obligation to use power responsibly. Leaders who abuse their power to pursue selfish interests will lose respect among their followers and other leaders. In the long run, the abuse of power will diminish power, not enhance it. Employees who lack respect for their leaders can exert a great deal of unofficial power by withholding co-operation beyond customary norms (Barge, 1994). The process by which this is often accomplished is by 'shutting down' unofficial networks and groups. The result is that employees will not take initiatives but ask for permission, check back with the leader on anything but routine tasks, use the chain of command rather than informal networks and otherwise work strictly 'by the book'.

When we argue that leaders should not act selfishly, we do not suggest that they sacrifice their self-interests. What we are warning against is the use of the power of the office or position for purposes other than those intended by the organization.

Example 15.1

Tim is the manager of a department. A good friend asked him if he could help his daughter to obtain a position with Tim's employer. On several occasions Tim and his family had used this friend's vacation home in Colorado free of charge. They had already been invited to use their friend's vacation home again for a skiing trip. When a position opened in Tim's department, he reviewed the credentials of his friend's daughter. Although she was qualified for the position, other applicants were more qualified. Tim felt uncomfortable, but in the end decided to lobby for his friend's daughter.

The mechanism through which we pursue legitimate goals is politics. Politics is defined as the "methods or tactics involved in managing a government or state" (*Webster's II New Riverside University Dictionary*, 1984). This definition is also applicable to organizations. Like any method, it can be practiced well and with skill, or poorly. Politics that manipulate people and situations to accomplish a particular goal is almost always poor practice; people do not like to be manipulated. Politics is a process of give and take, the formation of coalitions and negotiations. The organization's goals and objectives are defined and revised through this process. Politics is the method for getting things done that are beyond our authority. It offers a method for accomplishing things that would be cumbersome to handle through purely formal channels. While politics may seem manipulative or even unethical to some people, it is a fact of life in all organizations. Effective leaders recognize its existence and deal with it realistically.

Leaders enhance their power and influence by being involved within a network. Leadership influence is positively associated with leaders' level of involvement in networks inside and outside the organization. Within organizations, the perceived influence of leaders is positively related to their centrality in the flow of work, communication and friendship networks. Between organizations, leaders' reputations and influence increase as they cultivate more links with influential people outside of the organization. At a community level, leaders who are able to influence community opinion regarding public issues tend to be better linked to the media than those who do not have such influence. Regardless of the reasons people have for creating or participating in networks, however, networks serve as an important thread in the fabric or organizational life. Without networks, leaders would not be able to organize themselves toward accomplishing goals because necessary information, materials, goods, and services would not flow freely through organizations (Barge, 1994; Downey and Erickson, 1987).

Although networks are important, it is possible to spend too much time and effort on networking. For networking to contribute to power, the activity must meet two criteria. First, not everyone who is prominent in the public's eye is a good contact. Individuals who can help organizational goals are often of a relatively low rank. An example is a journalist who writes for the local newspaper's business section. A good relationship with this journalist may result in more concrete and frequent positive coverage of the organization's activities than strong ties to the editor. While the editor can direct the effort, others do most of the writing. The second criterion is that of mutual interest. We will do occasional favours for others without necessarily expecting a payback. However, if we are frequently approached for such favours, our willingness to honor the requests will quickly decline. Therefore, the best contacts in the long-term result from mutually beneficial relationships with individuals and organizations.

Benefits of Informal Networking

Informal networking involves establishing relationships with other organizational members. Networking is a skill that facilitates the gathering and processing of information and gaining knowledge of central problems in need of resolution. Networking encourages leaders to enlarge their knowledge of the organizational environment and its members as well as to understand the processes that are considered appropriate within the organization. This enhanced knowledge base allows leaders to identify problems, develop solutions and select and implement policy measures more efficiently and effectively (Barge, 1994).

Informal networking contributes to the fulfillment of personal needs. Leaders who cultivate positive informal networking will discover that an informal organizational structure will be much more productive. No formal organizational diagram can anticipate all future events and needs. Informal networks result in additional pathways for the transfer of information and knowledge. Having alternatives is beneficial if formal pathways fail. The following example illustrates this benefit.

Example 15.2

Victor was responsible for the operation of a small branch office of a large company. Part of his responsibilities included transferring critical information to the main office. He had a part-time assistant who helped him but who, because of her limited and mostly secretarial responsibilities, had no official contacts to the main office. This assistant, Louise, had started her career with the company working at the main office. She had transferred to the branch office only two years ago and had maintained contacts with her former colleagues. She would call them when she had technical questions and her supervisor was out of the office. The branch office was responsible for most customer contacts in the region. The branch office relayed orders and customer concerns to the main office. Victor was out of the office when a client called in a large order. Normally Victor left instructions for Louise when he was absent, or she would call him if something unexpected came up. This time however, Victor had left in a hurry. He was called away with the message that his father had to undergo emergency surgery and he left without taking the time to leave instructions or a phone number where he could be reached. Louise, therefore, did not know what to do with the order. It was clear that the order was urgent and that the client wanted to take delivery as soon as possible. Louise remembered that one of the people she often ate lunch with when she still worked in the main office was based in the order department. She called her and asked if she could help with this important and lucrative order. Her colleague in the main office contacted her supervisor, and together they were able to process the order.

The example shows how informal networks can handle gaps in the formal network that are caused by unexpected situations. When the informal organization is ignored, flexibility is lost and employees may spend considerable time in activities to make up for the lack of flexibility. Informal networks can also be used to advance legitimate self-interest.

Example 15.3

Robert was uncomfortable with decisions made by his new supervisor. The supervisor was making decisions that previously had been delegated to Robert. Robert did not want to talk to his supervisor because he was not sure how she would react. Instead of talking to her, he went to see Carl, a senior manager who had once served as Robert's supervisor. Carl's position required him to interact regularly with Robert's supervisor. Robert told Carl of the cause of his frustration and asked for his help. Carl mentioned that the new supervisor had occasionally asked him for advice. He thought that he might have an opportunity to talk informally with her about decision making in her department without offending her.

Leaders who ignore the informal organization, who dictate without regard to interpersonal factors, may even experience 'malicious obedience' among employees. Rules that prevent the resolution of stressful situations will evoke negative feelings among employees and create situations that are detrimental to achieving organizational goals and objectives.

When leaders are isolated from informal networks, their ability to gain insight into organizational problems and alternative solutions is reduced. This causes a problem for junior managers who lack management practice and leadership experience because they joined the management only recently (Barge, 1994). Prejudice against women and ethnic minorities also causes problems by excluding them from informal organizations, with the result that their chances for success are reduced. Organizations that wish to encourage the full participation of women and ethnic minorities should, therefore, create a culture that is inclusive and respectful of gender and cultural differences.

The political aspects of organizations are tied to the informal network, personal power and the influence of interest groups. Leaders influence others, compromise, and collaborate to achieve personal and organizational goals. To be effective, new managers need to learn how to develop networks of mutual interests and obligations with others. Management is a 'team sport'. It is working with other people and organizations to accomplish common goals. Good managers understand the team aspects of their work. They rely on others not only to accomplish organizational goals and objectives, but also for moral support, guidance, direction and advancement. They use the formal and informal networks and participate in organizational politics in appropriate ways. Knowledge of the organizational culture is important because it defines acceptable and unacceptable behaviours. Those who learn how to function effectively will be able to build coalitions and gain support for decisions and activities. Managers who understand the organizational culture and know how to participate in and utilize networks will be successful because they enhance their personal power beyond the power given to them by virtue of their position. Most personal power comes from the ability to persuade others of the value of our ideas, and we cannot persuade others if we are insensitive to their needs, values and attitudes. In short, we need to understand their culture. Within organizations, success requires working with other individuals and groups of people. The organization wins when such co-operation is accomplished with little friction. Managers who have learned co-operative behaviours will be more effective and they will earn recognition and professional advancement (Barge, 1994; Miller, 1988).

In summary, the informal interaction comprises networks that will not be found on the formal organizational charts. It is where real action resides and objective realities prevail. Many things get done, or done more efficiently, through informal networking. The most effective networks are based on reciprocal obligations. They add flexibility to decision making, provide for improved flows of information, create opportunities for leadership beyond the official leadership positions, facilitate interaction across hierarchical barriers and create beneficial redundancies (Miller, 1988).

How to Establish Informal Networks

Many goals are accomplished through informal networks. As discussed earlier, informal networks add to the channels of communications, facilitate coordination between different units, promote adaptability to change, and meet personal needs of members of the organization. Informal networks are the result of communication. They are often started because members of the organization find that the formal networks do not give them timely access to information that is important to them. This can be information that is of personal interest to them (including gossip) or professional information. Leaders are particularly dependent on information for decision making and designing courses of action. They need to have access to information and communication with others. One of the keys to effective leadership, therefore, is involvement in communication networks. If formal networks are not sufficient, leaders should establish informal networks. According to Goldhaber (1993), leaders who foster innovations and adaptations are involved in informal communication networks because they are sometimes more accurate and reliable sources of information than the organization's formal networks.

Establishing relationships is a prerequisite for gaining access to communication networks. Meetings, social gatherings, and other events that bring people together are opportunities to establish relationships. It is much easier to contact someone with a question or request if we have met that person before. Trust is a prerequisite for access to many informal networks. Some managers who pride themselves on their efficiency view socializing after meetings as a waste of time. They also have no patience with people who talk to them and take up 'too much' of their time. However, personal relationships are often the result of such seemingly wasteful discussions. Trust is built in small steps and informal chats are often the first step in the trust-building process. While managers must protect their time, they should be sensitive to different communications styles and personalities or they may miss opportunities to establish and strengthen personal relationships that could give them access to informal networks. Leaders who are involved in informal communication networking are more likely to understand the political and cultural aspects of the organization, identify organizational problems successfully, recognize possible threats and take advantage of opportunities (Barge, 1994).

How can you learn to use the informal network and establish a reciprocal network system for you and your organization? The following is a step by step approach to accomplish this network system (Miller, 1988).

1. Move around the organization. Look for groups that can provide your department with necessary resources (information, services, personnel, etc.) and consider what you could offer that would be useful to them.

2.　Become acquainted with people in other groups and departments.

3.　Always express your appreciation when someone is helpful to you and your department.

4.　Be attentive and do favours for others; build goodwill and obligations.

5.　Conduct yourself in a friendly, professional, and confident manner and be sincere in your reciprocal actions.

6.　Look for indications of informal leadership or power so that you learn who the organization's informal leaders are.

How to Acquire Personal Power

Many people are suspicious of power. The constitution of the United States of America is designed to prevent the accumulation of too much power in the hands of government and its individual branches. There is probably good reason to worry about the accumulation of too much power. Historical experience teaches us that it usually leads to dictatorial behaviours. Personal power, however, is interpersonal influence; it is not taken from others but is earned. To obtain personal power you must learn what others might want. In other words, it requires sensitivity to the needs of others. Successful politicians demonstrate this characteristic very well. They employ professional pollsters to learn what issues are of most concern to their constituents. Politicians are often excellent communicators. Credibility is another characteristic that contributes to personal power because credibility is the foundation of leadership. The fall from power of politicians who are caught in illegal or immoral acts demonstrates the importance of credibility. There are many different sources of power. We will distinguish between six of them (Barge, 1994; Miller, 1988).

1.　*Legitimate power* is sometimes referred to as position power. Legitimate power comes from one's formal position within the organization and is based on the rights and privileges or authority attributed to the position one holds. *Example*: you have influence because you have the job – Department Head, Director, General Manager, etc.

2.　*Reward power* is the ability to provide desirable outcomes and compensate and give rewards for completed tasks or good performance. *Example*: supervisors have reward power because salary adjustments and promotions may depend on their appraisal of employee performance.

3.　*Coercive power* is power based on the ability to punish employees who do not conform. Withholding rewards or emotional support and making working conditions difficult and unpleasant are examples of punishments. Dismissal from a job is a particularly strong form of punishment. Coercive power may be held not only by managers, but also by employees.

Example: a data processing expert exercises at least some control over the timely release of valuable information.

4. *Referent power* is based on the attractiveness of individuals that causes them to be liked personally. A leader has referent power when employees identify with or like the leader; thus, the relationship formed between leader and employees creates the power base. Some leaders with referent power are respected for their personal characteristics, regardless of their formal authority.

5. *Expert power* is the influence held by those who have special knowledge or superior skills. This power base can be derived from innate talents, training, experience or access to information.

6. *Information power* is the influence people have when they hold information that others need and want at a certain point in time. *Example*: The executive secretary who schedules meetings with the boss and has some control over how soon you can see the supervisor has power and influence over you.

Managers need authority and power to be effective and to advance in their careers. Personal influence is in many ways more important than formal authority because it is based on achievement, integrity and credibility. Personal power enhances formal authority, and lack of personal power devalues it. Junior leaders should recognize the value of power and that it must be accompanied with competence and integrity or it will quickly be lost.

How to Become a Member of Informal Networks

Some informal networks are a narrow, exclusive circle or group of persons held together by common interests, views or purposes. Women still find it difficult to break into networks that have traditionally been dominated by men. Ethnic minorities also find access to some networks difficult. Entry into some networks may be by invitation only. For example, entry into Rotary Club requires that a current member act as the sponsor to the new member. While organizations such as Rotary Club have made efforts to be inclusive, there remain informal organizations that exclude women and ethnic minorities.

It is difficult to become part of informal networks if you are never invited to formal or informal social functions frequented by members of the network. However, it is not impossible to gain access. Not all members of exclusive networks are of the same mindset. Some members may welcome the addition of new members, including women and ethnic minorities. Many influential leaders believe that merit should be the most relevant criterion for advancement and are willing to serve as mentors or otherwise assist individuals who demonstrate talent, ambition and drive. With such help, access can be obtained, although the 'pioneers' may often find the process difficult and frustrating.

It makes no sense to try to become part of a network to which you have nothing to contribute. Inclusion requires participation, and that is possible only if you can make contributions that are valued by other members of the network. Individuals who benefit but do not contribute will be resented and eventually excluded. As in any social grouping, a person must have a utility or exchange value to be included. The following are eight ways that can be used in getting into the informal network (Miller, 1988).

1. Demonstrate self-confidence, self-respect and initiative at work.

2. Model your behaviour after those of successful managers you admire. Be a team player and develop strong communication skills.

3. Become familiar with the organization, its formal and informal networks, goals and objectives, plans, and how to get things done.

4. Get to know as many of the formal and informal leaders of the organization as you can. An association with such individuals helps in accelerating growth and development.

5. Establish multiple reciprocal relationships.

6. Seek moral support from other informal groups inside and outside your organization.

7. Get involved in activities that get attention, such as highly visible projects, task forces, etc.

8. Become indispensable to the success of key projects. For example, you are the best planner or organizer and they need you; you add an extra quality to the project; they value your sense of humour and interpersonal skills that keep everyone motivated, etc.

Entrance into an informal network can be obtained through a network member or as the result of personal power and influence. The reasons why members admit you to their network are diverse:

- they like and admire you;

- they want you on their side;

- you have something that is of value to them;

- they rely on your expertise to accomplish their goals and objectives;

- you have a position that gives you power;

- your membership will add to their prestige.

If you find that it is difficult to be admitted to a network, be persistent! Use opportunities to do favours for other members. If you create an obligation, members may repay you by helping you become accepted. Find out what qualities are valued by the network and try to demonstrate that you possess many of those qualities. Members should perceive you as a person who has something to contribute.

Example 15.4

Martha is an upper level manager of a post office in West Virginia. She is competent, effective and a high achiever. She has acquired good management skills and a style she is comfortable with. She is equally comfortable working with men and women. When she started her career she was the only woman employer in her unit but managed to be accepted into her colleagues' informal network early on. Her acceptance made work more pleasant for her and contributed to her success. She has been promoted several times since she first started working for the post office.

How did she accomplish this? Her obvious skills and talents earned her respect. She also made it a point to learn about the interests of her colleagues so that she had something to talk about with them during breaks or at informal gatherings. She was always interested in sports, so it was not difficult for her to become reasonably informed about sports teams. Her colleagues liked her and she was included when they went to lunch together. They talked about their families, sports, holidays, etc. From these discussions she learned what was really important to her colleagues. Her colleagues liked her and, over time, she became one of the informal leaders. She is well informed on what is going on around her organization, and she and her department get things done more easily because of her leadership skills.

Example 15.5

Sarah is a manager in a bank. Like Martha, Sarah is competent, productive and effective. Unlike Martha, however, Sarah has a reserved personality. She does not enjoy socializing with her colleagues outside of work and is more comfortable keeping work separate from her social life. Nevertheless, she was accepted into the informal network and is advancing in her professional career. Although Sarah is not a very outgoing person, she is always friendly and sensitive to others. Her supervisors respect her skills and noted that she was a good judge of the talents of others. Therefore, she was given responsibility over work assignments. Because she is observant and a good listener, she is skillful at putting together teams that work harmoniously and effectively. Because she controls important work assignments, and because her sensitivity to employees has earned her their trust, employees come to her to talk about their concerns and interests. The information has often been useful in making assignment and on several occasions she has been able to accommodate employee interests. The mutuality of her relationship with employees has been beneficial to all involved. Her acceptance into the informal networks was based on her skills and the respect her employees and colleagues felt for her.

CHAPTER SIXTEEN

THE STRATEGIES FOR CAREER PROMOTION

The greatest thing in this world is not so much where we are, but in what direction we are moving.

OW Holmes

Success is achieved one step at a time. Individuals who aspire to advance in their profession should remind themselves that earned advancement is based on merit, i.e. on skills and talents and the past record of accomplishments. Since accomplishments are more easily judged than talent, they tend to be given more weight, particularly in the case of experienced professionals. In the case of a new manager, education, skills, and promise may be given more favourable consideration. Since the past record is so important to advancement, professionals should concentrate on doing the best possible job in their current position. While there is nothing wrong with aspiring to advance to the next higher position, they should be careful not to create the impression that they lack commitment to their current position and responsibilities. If such a perception exists, it is likely to affect negatively letters and statements of recommendation.

Managers should reflect on their reasons for wanting to advance carefully. An egocentric desire for a higher position as a means to win prestige is unlikely to result in a satisfying experience for all concerned. There must be more substantive reasons. Modern approaches stress the service component inherent in successful leadership. Those who pursue positions of leadership for their own aggrandizement will often fail to serve others, and therefore fail one of the responsibilities of leaders. A strategy that improves a manager's chances to win promotions must include an honest evaluation of strengths and weaknesses. The strategy should be designed to take advantage of strengths, improve areas of weaknesses, and minimize the impact of weaknesses that cannot be addressed. Actions developed as part of the strategy must be responsive to, and the results of such actions should contribute to, the goals and objectives of the organization.

Reasons for Promotion Denial

If there is a proper structure and procedure of evaluating employees for promotion, performance evaluation can be the major source and base for consideration. Based on the merits of these evaluations and proper performance management procedures, an employee may be denied or accepted for promotion. There should be logical reasons for granting or denying a promotion. Although promotion denial is always a disappointment, it should not be regarded as the final word. We can learn from failure by asking, 'Why did it happen?' We may find out what should be done to achieve a positive result in the future. Ask your immediate supervisor why you did not get the job. Sometimes the response will be, 'No one had any idea that you wanted to be considered for the promotion.' If you receive this answer, you have failed to communicate effectively your desire to those who are in a position to help you.

Those who can help are not limited to those directly associated with the position to which you are aspiring. For example, your current supervisor is almost always an important ally. Make sure the supervisor knows of and supports your aspirations. Before you submit an application, talk with her and ask for advice. Provide her with a brief statement describing your interest in and qualifications for the desired position. There is a very good chance that she will be contacted for a reference; after all who else can give a more informed and independent assessment of your current responsibilities and performance? You want to make sure, therefore, that your supervisor is on your side.

Another reason why promotions or new positions are denied is insufficient understanding of position requirements. Usually this happens when a candidate does not do 'their homework'. Before submitting an application, try to find out what is expected of the person holding the position. The person who most recently held the position is usually the best source of this information. If he is leaving the position on his own accord, he will usually be willing to talk with you about it.

Once you learn what the required qualifications are, make a realistic assessment. Are you qualified? Do you have some special qualifications that might set you apart from other applicants? The answer to this last question is particularly relevant if the number of applicants is large. It may not be wise to apply for positions where the chances of success are very low. Individuals who apply to every open position without regard for how well their qualifications match the position requirements will generally be unsuccessful. Applying for jobs and/or promotions is not like the lottery where chances of winning improve the more tickets you buy. Those who often apply for positions for which they are not qualified or are only marginally qualified will eventually earn a reputation as being poor judges of position requirements. This reputation undermines the credibility of those candidates even when they apply for positions for which they are well qualified.

Thus, communication is one of the keys to success. Make sure that those who can help you are aware of your aspirations. Collect information about the position you desire and realistically assess your chances of winning it. If you are not successful, try to find out why. It is possible that your qualifications were as strong as those of the person who obtained the position, and you were just unlucky. In such a case, try again when another opportunity presents itself. If you learn that your qualifications were judged to be deficient, either address the deficiencies or find opportunities that make better use of your strengths and where your deficiencies matter less. Feedback may often feel like criticism, but it is good information to assess your strategy and improve your chances to succeed. Ignore vague comments, such as 'the other candidates were better suited for the job'. They contain no real information. If possible, probe and ask for specifics. Whatever information you get, evaluate it to see if you can increase your chances to advance your career (Miller, 1988).

Choosing a career is a key decision for promotion and advancement. Some individuals do not know the difference between a job and a career, and as a result they experience a conflict within themselves. Unresolved conflict is stressful, hinders effectiveness and can make you appear uncommitted and indecisive. Career orientation is a long-term commitment to oneself. It is a desire to map out a path that guides your future. Without a clear direction, preparing for professional advancement is difficult at best. Choosing a career and defining career goals help determine what knowledge and skills are most important. If you know where you want to go, you can find out how to get there. In addition to knowledge and skills, this includes appropriate career steps. What are the most promising entry-level positions for the career you would like to have? In short, career choice and career planning are the conscious avenues to advance through the ranks of management by acquiring skills, attitudes, and behaviours that will be recognized and rewarded. Its orientation is long-term. By contrast, the nature of job orientation is short-term and narrowly focussed on technical skills, task completion, and job performance. Job and career orientations are not mutually exclusive. However, job orientation without career orientation is more likely to result in opportunities missed. Combining job orientation, i.e. a focus on excellent performance at the current job, with career planning, is most likely to result in professional advancement.

Without a career choice and without career planning, skills and knowledge are more likely to be acquired in a somewhat haphazard fashion, usually in response to immediate job needs. Investments in human capital that are oriented toward the future are less likely to occur. Therefore, making a career choice is the first step toward having a successful and satisfying career. Some individuals find it difficult to choose a career. Miller (1988) identified six barriers to making a career choice.

1. *Neglect of personal needs.* Some people, out of a sense of guilt and obligation or because of the distaste for confrontation, are locked into satisfying others at the expense of satisfying their own needs. Some may not have really thought about their needs and therefore may not be consciously aware of them. To overcome this barrier, think carefully and deeply about

what you enjoy about work. Think also about your goals, both personal and professional. If you have a family, you should involve your spouse and other family members in your thinking and discuss together your aspirations and personal needs. Do not expect to resolve your difficulties in a short time. It may be necessary to ask for advice from senior colleagues or supervisors who may be willing to act as mentors or you may wish to consult a career counselling service.

2. *Lack of career role models in your organization.* Individuals in responsible positions can inspire you, advise you and serve as mentors.

3. *Short-term thinking.* Your current financial requirements or family problems may hinder you from looking beyond today.

4. *Confusion or misunderstanding about the difference between a job and a career.* It should be clear that a job is not a career, but a career can be a job.

5. *Uncertainty about your private life.* Where will you be next year? What will be the effect of your career aspirations on your family life? Because your career affects you and your family, it is important that your family be a part of your career planning. If professional and personal goals (which will involve your family) are not co-ordinated, conflict is almost inevitable. While your career could be very successful, your family life could be in shambles.

6. *Extreme risk aversion.* It is fear of failure or making mistakes, fear of the unknown, fear of taking risks and making commitments, and fear of role shifting and changing. People who are afraid of taking risks, who want security at almost any cost, tend to have a short-term orientation. Only the present is known, the future is uncertain. Fear of the unknown and of making mistakes renders them incapable of making commitments. Few challenging and interesting careers, however, are open to those who are not willing to take some risks and make commitments.

The Basis for Promotion

What is the basis for promotion? This is a particularly relevant question for an employee aspiring to enter the ranks of management but has no prior management experience. As discussed earlier, while managers and employees share many of the same qualities, the orientation of managers differs significantly from that of employees without management responsibilities. Managers must have a broader perspective, have less need to know and be informed about every detail, but need to understand connections ('the big picture') and focus on the accomplishments of their team or department, rather than limiting their concern to their own performance. Thus, some of the behaviours that are appropriate for an employee may not be appropriate for a manager. The following are key characteristics of successful non-management employees (Miller, 1988).

1. *Hard working.* Success comes when they enjoy what they do, and when they enjoy what they do, they willingly commit themselves to their work.

2. *Technical expert.* Expertise in an area is often the foundation on which a successful career can be built. Experts are given opportunities to provide leadership. If they carry out their responsibilities well, they earn the respect of their peers and superiors.

3. *Relies on internal motivation.* Intrinsic rewards are ultimately more important than extrinsic rewards, such as a higher salary. Those who perform well only if they receive material rewards are less likely to show initiative and take on new tasks for which no reward system has yet been established.

4. *Follows rules and procedures.* By following rules and procedures, employees contribute to a harmonious work environment.

5. *Performs relatively routine tasks.* In every job there are less interesting tasks. The willingness to carry out such tasks contributes to overall success. Those who look down on routine work also belittle those employees who are assigned such work.

6. *Has knowledge of the departmental requirements and goals.* Unless employees know requirements and goals, they cannot be efficient contributors to the team effort.

7. *Follows instructions of supervisor.* A successful employee is willing and able to accept directives and advice.

8. *Task-completion oriented.* If employees enjoy their work and believe that what they do is important, then they take pride and want to make sure that they complete tasks assigned to them.

9. *Job-performance oriented.* This is related to the previous point. Not only do highly motivated individuals want to complete their assignment, they want to do the job well.

10. *Attends to details of job activities.*

Example 16.1

Daniel has the characteristics listed above. They are the reason why he was promoted to supervisor. However, he did not adjust his behaviour to reflect his new role. His behaviour was still that of a very good employee and therefore he was not effective as a supervisor. Daniel kept working hard and his knowledge of technical aspects of the department was very useful. His perspective, however, was still focused on his own work; he did not

> show interest in his employees, except when there were problems. He also
> was slow to learn more about the organization, and how his department
> contributed to the overall goals and objectives. Fortunately, one of the sen-
> ior managers recognized that Daniel had the qualities to become a very
> effective manager but needed some help. He offered advice and recom-
> mended him for a training scheme that taught some of the skills that Daniel
> needed.

It is instructive to compare the characteristics of effective non-management
employees with those of effective managers. The basic characteristics of effective managers are listed below (Miller, 1988). The list reflects the change
from an orientation on one's own work to one of responsibility for the work of
others.

1. Enforce policies, rules and regulations.

2. Plan and carry out action steps to accomplish departmental or team goals.
   Departmental goals reflect the goals and objectives of the whole organization.

3. Organize work groups and engage in team building. Develop group co-
   hesiveness.

4. Assign jobs to employees.

5. Delegate projects to prominent employees.

6. Direct tasks, jobs and projects.

7. Lead and motivate employees.

8. Solve routine problems.

9. Conduct performance appraisals of employees and the department or team.

10. Discipline and reward employees.

In summary, the transition from a non-management to a management position
requires a change from following to leading, reacting to planning, specialization to a broad perspective, and executing and doing to delegating. Addition-
ally, managers assume responsibility for compliance with policies and rules
and regulations.

Step by Step Strategy for Advancement

What do you need to know to win promotions? Professional competence,
although important, is only one set of necessary characteristics. Some very
talented individuals do not win management positions because they lack interpersonal and/or communication skills. Others get promoted but are unsuc-

cessful because they do not learn new skills and fail to adjust their behaviours from those appropriate for non-management employees to those appropriate for a manager. The first step in the strategy to advancement requires honest and realistic self-assessment. You need to have a clear idea of where you are and where you want to go. The following steps include suggestions for the development of a strategy for advancement (Miller, 1988).

Learn High Level Management Skills

(a) The skills of planning, controlling, organizing and leading are still required, but the emphasis is changed from short-term to long-term; from routine to non-routine; from grouping tasks to organizing people into teams in a department; from departmental level to a broader perspective; from enforcing policies to making policies; from observing performance to checking progress through reports; from managing down to managing up, down and laterally; from reliance on positional authority to reliance on personal power, influence and interpersonal persuasion; and from physically supervising to monitoring and evaluating reports.

(b) Some new skills have to be learned. They include co-ordinating the efforts of several departments, negotiating for co-operation between groups, resolving and managing inter-departmental and interpersonal conflicts, analyzing complex, non-routine problems and making decisions that affect a large number of people.

(c) Methods of management involve a greater use of political influence and informal networking. Junior managers must rely on bases of power and influence other than positional authority because often they actually have little authority over some of the people they must work with (such as other departments or managers on the same or higher levels). Credibility becomes a prime concern and behaviour, track record and image become the primary sources of influence. 'Doing' may occupy 30 to 40 per cent of the time and 'delegating and checking' 60 to 70 per cent. The 'doing' part of the job involves planning, controlling, organizing, leading, co-ordinating, negotiating, resolution of conflicts, solution of complex problems and also routine work, such as paperwork, writing reports and analyzing available information.

Develop a Career Plan

(a) Where do you want to be in ten or twenty years? What do you want to be doing? What is feasible based on your skill and experience? As Peter Drucker indicated, "The best way to predict the future is to invent it."

(b) Where do you need to be in five years? How are you going to get there? What positions do you need to get to in four, three and two years? What is the next position you will get promoted to if everything goes as expected?

(c)	Target your next position. Chart your course of action. Start getting ready for it. If you need qualifications such as a degree or more management or leadership training, go get it. It is important to remember that there are no shortcuts to any place worth going. As David Johnson said, "There are no speed limits to the road to excellence." As long as you are persistent in trying to improve yourself, it does not matter if it takes a long time. "Persistence is the twin sister of excellence. One is a matter of quality; the other, of time" (Marable Morgan).

(d)	You have your goals for promotion established. Now implement your strategy for getting the visibility to improve your chances. A successful visibility campaign requires good performance. Take on projects that have high visibility. Get on a task group that includes influential members. Ask questions, be interested in the total organization and show initiative. Demonstrate high performance.

Learn from an Experienced Mentor

There will be obstacles in your path to advancement. Some of these obstacles may be your own values and attitudes. Lack of self-confidence and an overly critical attitude towards oneself are among the most common self-imposed obstacles. While you need to determine your strengths and weaknesses as objectively as possible, you must avoid falling into the trap of thinking that you are the only one who may have deficiencies in your background. Do not assume that you are the only one with insecurities and doubts. All people need help. It is being able to ask for help that separates the effective from the ineffective leaders.

In recent years, scholars and practitioners have recognized the value of having a mentor. Some organizations even make formal arrangements for new team members to be assigned to a senior staff member who serves as a mentor to the junior member. A mentor can be another supervisor, an organization executive, an associate, a university professor, a spouse or a friend. There is no fixed list of what a mentor should do. A mentor who is part of the same organization can be very helpful with opening doors to informal networks, meeting the formal and informal leaders, giving advice on protocol, serving as a professional advisor, and being an advocate for you with the organization's senior leadership. A mentor who is not part of the organization will usually not be able to serve all of these functions. What is common to all mentors, however, is their role as advisors. A good mentor is someone you can go to with problems that you find difficult to resolve. The mentor's most valuable service may not be the offer of a solution, but simply asking some questions and giving you the opportunity to reflect on the problem with the assistance of a sympathetic listener.

The value of a mentor is not limited to your professional life. Sometimes you need more help with your personal life, or with resolving conflicts between obligations to your family and yourself and career aspirations and the pressures that come with the desire to achieve professional success. Such conflicts, if unresolved, will be a drain on your emotional energy. Without help, divorce is often the only remaining resolution, usually at a very high personal cost to all involved.

Know your Organization and its Key Leaders

Obtain your institution's organizational chart. Learn the parts and how they fit together. Know the names of the people in key positions. Look at people who are advancing; study and learn from them. Be visible and effective. Learn what each department does and how it co-ordinates with other departments. Find out your organization's long-term strategy. What are its major goals? Know the nature and structure of the organization from top to bottom. Know how it works inside and out. Show that you understand the 'big-picture'. Investigating and researching often impresses senior managers/supervisors.

Get Rid of Old Habits that Keep you from Succeeding

1. *Take some chances; do not avoid reasonable risks.* "Daring ideas are like chess pieces moved forward; they may be beaten, but they start a winning game" (Anonymous).

2. *Welcome and accept critiques; do not react defensively.* Information from feedback helps you identify areas of strength and areas in need of improvement.

3. *Constantly seek to improve your performance but realize that perfection is impossible.* Do the very best possible with available resources and skills. Don't use perfectionism as an excuse for not trying. Set high standards for yourself. "If you refuse to accept nothing but the best, you very often get it" (William Somerset Maugham).

4. *You cannot please everyone.* It is part of human nature that we like to be liked. Therefore, be sensitive to constructive critiques but ignore petty criticisms. Do not take them personally and do not change decisions just to please someone. You should reach your decisions based on careful consideration of all available information; apply the same standard to those who wish to influence your decisions. Your reward will be the respect of your employees and the success that comes with carefully planned decisions. Do not trade being respected for being liked.

5. *Communicate clearly.* Be sensitive to the feelings of others. Formulate statements that focus on issues, not personalities. Do not use allusions to

spare someone's feelings. Instead, be honest and direct. Others will not know what you want or expect if you do not express it clearly.

6. *Do not hold grudges*. Avoid personalizing disagreements or conflicts. If you are unable to resolve a conflict on your own, ask for help from someone who has the skills and experience to act as a mediator. Unresolved conflict that lingers continues to absorb some of your energy and is more likely to turn into a personality conflict.

Learn to Manage your Immediate Supervisor

You know you must lead and manage your employees. You know peer relationships need some of your time and attention. Your supervisor is also important to you and your career. You should, therefore, get to know her. What are her background and interests? How did she arrive at her current position? What are her strengths and weaknesses? What motivates her and what does she value in those who work for her? Sometimes small things can be big irritants.

Example 16.2

Andy is well known for his creativity and outgoing personality. He likes to use meetings to brainstorm, think out loud, and explore ideas. His new supervisor prefers structured meetings with a formal agenda and follow-up memos. The first meeting between Andy and his supervisor, therefore, did not go very well. Andy was frustrated because his supervisor wanted to know how he would implement his ideas and pressed him for detailed information he did not have. His supervisor was dissatisfied with what appeared to her as lack of organization and planning on Andy's part. Fortunately, Andy had a friend who had worked for his supervisor at her previous position. He called his friend and discussed his experience at the meeting with him. His friend told him that the supervisor was very open to new ideas, but that she seemed to like a much more structured approach for dealing with them. Therefore, in preparation for his next meeting, Andy submitted an agenda with an appendix that explained the nature and status of the ideas he wanted to discuss with his supervisor. At the meeting itself he was prepared to answer specific questions on projects that were ready to be implemented. Andy also had prepared questions to obtain feedback on projects that were still ideas in his head. The meeting went really well, and at the end of the meeting, Andy's supervisor thanked him for the careful preparation and commented on how valuable that meeting had been for her. Andy was pleased. He had not only obtained the information he needed but also the support of his supervisor to conduct research on the feasibility of a new project.

The example illustrates that it is possible to be sensitive to the needs of others without giving up your own. By getting to know your supervisor, you can better meet their needs and you can communicate your own needs more effectively to make sure they are met.

Some supervisors expect that those who work for them have the same style as they do, and others prefer a complementary style. Some leaders have creative minds that dream up new ideas and are looking for individuals to follow up, work out the details, and implement the ideas. Supervisors have personal and professional goals and objectives. They will react positively to those who can help them reach their goals and objectives. How do you get to know your boss? The following are suggestions on how to establish and maintain an effective relationship with your boss.

1. *Be assertive.* If you have a problem, idea, or suggestion, talk to your supervisor about it. How would she prefer it to be handled? Be prepared to offer options or suggestions of how you can work together.

2. *Communicate regularly.* In particular, keep your supervisor informed of current and anticipated problems and progress.

3. *Do not hesitate to be firm when you need your supervisor's time and attention.*

4. *Do your homework.* Always be prepared to discuss agenda items with your supervisor.

5. *Be sensitive to the fact that your supervisor is ultimately responsible for your department's performance.*

6. *Be loyal and do not talk behind your supervisor's back.* It will eventually get back to her.

7. *Your supervisor is a human being and enjoys the pleasant aspects of positive feedback.* Thank her when she helps you. A compliment in front of her supervisor may be particularly appreciated. Be sincere; most people appreciate an honest compliment but are uncomfortable with flattery.

Learn to Cope with Career Change

You have done everything you were supposed to do but you are not satisfied with your career. Maybe it is because your interests have changed. What seemed like a great career a few years ago is no longer appealing to you. Or maybe your employer has changed. Maybe the firm you started with has been bought by another company which brought its own values and culture with it, values with which you are not comfortable. Or maybe in spite of all your planning and efforts to acquire leadership and management skills, your career did not develop as you had hoped. Regardless of the reason, you have analyzed your situation and concluded that you wish to change careers. How should you go about changing your career?

In today's dynamic environment, jobs change more frequently and whole industries have shifted their practices. The growth in the number of global companies is also changing business practices and typical career paths. Career change, therefore, has become common. There are no fixed rules on how to identify and start a new career. The initial steps are just plain common sense to assess situations. Here is a list of questions that can help you get started with the process of self-assessment.

1. *What do you know and what skills and experiences do you possess that might be of value in another career?*

2. *What are your interests?* For example, do you enjoy working with people or do you prefer a job with limited contacts with clients and/or other employees?

3. *What contacts do you have that might be helpful for starting a new career?* Do you know people who could help you find an appropriate new job? Do you have contacts with people who could help you start your own business (e.g. lenders, partners, and potential clients)?

4. *What are your constraints?* How long can you afford to be without a steady income to prepare yourself for a new career? Do you have the funding to start a business of your own? Do you have constraints where you can/want to live? Do you have any health constraints?

5. *Do you feel well informed about career opportunities?* Do you need to conduct some research to find out what types of careers are possible? Should you consult a career counselor?

It is difficult to start over and it can be a humbling experience for someone who once held a position of significant responsibility and income. Let go of the past. You cannot expect to get back into a similar position in a new career. Those who manage to change careers without a loss in status or income are the exception, not the rule. In every organization, you have to earn your status and rank. You will do better if you find a new career that values the skills and experiences from your previous career. The further away you move from your previous career, the more fundamental will be the adjustments you should be prepared to make. This may be discouraging, but there are role models of individuals who have successfully moved into new careers. Examples are retired police officers who are working as security consultants; military officers who are employed by defence contractors; business leaders managing a not-for-profit organization; geography teachers who are leading guided tours to foreign countries; professors who became consultants; or professional athletes using their fame to start a business, broadcasting or movie career. What can we learn from those who have changed careers? A few guidelines emerge.

1. *Explore opportunities that bear some relationship to your current career.* This will make it more likely that you can transfer knowledge, experi-

ence, and contacts to a new career to get a higher lifetime return on your human capital investment and start the new career at above the entry level.

2. *Adjust your expectations.* A new career is a new beginning. Be prepared to invest in new skills and networking.

3. *Do not limit yourself to careers that are known to you.* There may be opportunities available you do not know about. Be creative, consult career guides (available at public libraries) and consider career counseling.

Example 16.3

Dr Smith was a faculty member at a large land grant university. When his university offered faculty members an incentive package to retire early, he felt it was too good a deal to ignore. He was not really ready to retire yet, however. In his mid-fifties he considered what other careers might be available to him. He had no recent professional experience that he could have marketed other than serving as a faculty member. The academic job market for senior professors was so depressed, however, that full-time employment at another university or college was out of the question. Dr Smith really enjoyed teaching and, therefore, was thinking about ways to continue his teaching career. He noticed that many departments had short-term teaching needs to fill in for lectures who were on leave or to temporarily cover courses when people left but were not replaced right away. He decided to offer his services to universities and colleges anywhere in the United States. His requirement was that he be permitted to schedule the courses in a non-traditional fashion, so that he could fly in every two or three weeks only and teach the course in a concentrated format. He would stay for two days. This gave him two days to teach and enough time to meet with students individually. This idea proved successful. Soon he was not only offering his own services, but had recruited other faculty to teach in a similar fashion. Through risk taking he was not only able to continue his teaching career but to build a successful business.

---

4. *Be patient.* It takes time to develop a new career. Unless you have the financial security to wait for just the right opportunity, you may have to find a job just to support yourself and your family. Do not allow that to stop you from looking for better opportunities.

APPENDIX

He who knows not and knows not that he knows not is a fool, shun him.

He who knows not and knows that he knows not is a child, teach him.

He who knows and knows not that he knows is asleep, wake him up.

He who knows and knows that he knows is a wise man, follow him.

Gabriel Solomon Ibn, *Choice of Pearls*

CASES FOR
ANALYTICAL DISCUSSION

Mindfulness must be engaged.
Once there is seeing, there must be acting.
Otherwise, what is the use of seeing?

Thich Nhat Hanh

1. George and Linda both work for the Environmental Protection Agency. Mr Hackett, the director of the agency, was originally the leader of a project team for which he interviewed and hired George. Linda, another project team member, also interviewed George but strongly opposed hiring him for the project because she thought he was not competent to do the job. One year after George was hired, the director left the project to devote more time to his administrative duties and proposed that George and Linda serve as joint project leaders. Linda reluctantly agreed but stipulated that it would be made clear she was not working for George. The director agreed that George and Linda were to share the project leadership. Within a month Linda was angry because George was representing himself to others as the leader of the entire project and giving the impression that Linda was working for him.

   Linda and George are meeting with you to see if you can help them resolve their conflict. As they meet with you, they explain their situation to you individually as follows.

   Linda explains, 'Right after the joint leadership arrangement was reached with the director, George called a meeting of the project team without even consulting me about the time or content. He just told me when it was being held and said I should be there. At the meeting George reviewed everyone's duties line by line, including mine, treating me as just another team member working for him. He sends out letters and signs himself as project director, which obviously implies to others that I am working for him.'

   George replies, 'Linda is all hung up with feelings of power and titles. Just because I sign myself as project director does not mean that she is working for me. I do not see anything to get excited about. What difference does it make? She is too sensitive about everything. I call a meeting and right away she thinks I am trying to run everything. Linda has other things to do and other projects to run, so she does not pay too much attention to this one. She mostly lets things slide. But when I take the initiative to set up a meeting, she starts jumping up and down about how I am trying to make her work for me.'

Now, put yourself in the role of a mediator between George and Linda. What is the nature of the conflicts occurring between George and Linda? What are the conflict resolution strategies or possible methods for managing the conflict between George and Linda? Given the benefits of retrospection, what could or should have been done to avoid this conflict?

2. Lisa is promoted to a supervisory position in a male-dominated line of work, the Department of Highway Construction. There are a couple of men (Scott and Mark) in the same department who are very hardworking and productive. They are well respected and liked by their former male supervisors and co-workers. However, when Scott and Mark learned about the new female supervisor, they reacted negatively and indicated that they did not want to be supervised by a woman. Whatever decisions Lisa made, Scott and Mark were not supportive or co-operative. How should Lisa deal with Scott and Mark? If she considers firing them as one option, what are the implications?

3. Solomon is the General Manager of Oil and Petroleum Company, and Joseph is the Manager of the Department of Marketing and Distribution. Customers are complaining about the inefficiency and irregularities of Joseph's department. Employees of the department also are not happy with the way Joseph runs the operation. Solomon tried to make Joseph aware of his management deficiencies, particularly with how he interacts with both his employees and customers. Joseph does not seem to have the skills to manage and lead the department efficiently and effectively. However, Joseph has very close contacts and friendship with high officials at the ministerial level. Solomon is in a serious dilemma. If he decides to fire Joseph, he will lose the respect and acceptance of those at the high level. If he does not fire him, the work will not be properly managed. What do you think Solomon should do?

4. You recently attended an important meeting. In that meeting, one of the senior managers announced that within six months the company would downsize its labour force by at least 25 per cent. You are ordered to keep this information confidential. Today, one of your employees asked for your advice. She had received a job offer from another company and was trying to decide whether or not to accept it. She had heard some rumours that cutbacks might occur, but no official announcement has been made yet. She is asking you, therefore, about her future in the company. If you tell her that her job is secure she will turn down the job offer from the other company; otherwise she will leave. What would you do?

5. Sophia was promoted to Head of the Research and Information Depart-

ment. Now she must supervise Craig, a good friend from her college days and a former peer in the same department. For the past couple of weeks, she has noticed that Craig has been absent for several days without permission. He also chats excessively with co-workers during work hours. Sophia worries about showing favouritism if she does not confront Craig about unacceptable work-related behaviours. What would you recommend that she should do? How should she resolve the problem?

6. Susan is a member of a management team. Every time she gives work to a secretary she shares with other team members, the secretary claims to be too busy to do the work by the desired deadline. The secretary always seems to have time for work submitted by Susan's male colleagues. How can Susan address this issue to gain respect and consideration without being seen as a complainer?

7. The company you are working for is preparing a proposal for a project for the government. You are part of the team preparing the bid. Last month you ran into an acquaintance from college whom you had not seen for several years. He asked what you were doing and you mentioned your work, including the project for the government. It turns out that he works for the agency to which the proposal will have to be submitted. You did not ask him for any information or otherwise request his assistance with preparing the proposal. The proposal is due in just a few days and your company is getting ready to submit it. Last night you received a call from your college friend who gave you unsolicited information about the bids and proposals that have already been submitted to the agency. What should you do?

8. During the weekend you ate dinner at a restaurant. At a table close to yours, two individuals you did not know were talking about the business strategy of a company that is a competitor of your employer. You could hear everything they said and the information was very helpful. Should you use the information? Is there a difference between this case and case number 7?

9. David is a Director of Sales and Promotion of a shoe factory. Penny is a poor performer on his team. He would like to address her performance problems or fire her, but David is afraid of being perceived as the 'bad guy' and is also worried about possible fall-out from firing a woman. How can David bring Penny back in line or terminate her without adverse departmental reactions?

10. On your team you have discovered that one of the members has a drinking problem. The policy of your organization is unclear about how to deal with employees with a drug or alcohol problem. In some instances, employees have been dismissed from employment without any explanation.

In other cases, they have been offered counselling and rehabilitation. How would you approach this problem if the team member were one of your peers? How would you act if you are the team member's supervisor?

11. One of your employees has lost his temper when you pointed out a problem with a project you had assigned to him. He started to yell at you in front of other employees and blamed circumstances and others for the problems. As his supervisor, (a) how would you handle the situation and (b) how would you deal with the employee?

12. At a meeting with your supervisor, she lost her temper and blew up at you. The dispute was over a memorandum she claims to have sent to your office last week and in which she asked you to contact an important client. You are certain that you did not receive the memorandum and you did not contact the client; (a) how would you deal with the client and (b) how would you respond to your supervisor?

13. You have recently been promoted to manager of a small department. Within a few weeks you knew the names of all employees. You would like to make some changes to how the department operates to improve efficiency and encourage greater teamwork. What process would you use to plan for and then implement the changes?

14. You are in charge of a very large department. There are too many employees for you to meet and get to know them all individually. Instead, employees are organized into groups. A group leader represents each group. Normally you interact with the group leaders to address issues concerning a particular group. The group leaders together form your administrative team to address issues concerning the whole department. If you were to make changes in this department, how might the process differ from the process employed in case number 13?

15. You have probably seen it happen many times in your professional career: two people with similar abilities are working in the same organization. One grows in his career, gains new responsibilities and prospers financially. The other does not advance far. What reasons could explain the difference between the two individuals?

16. You have been charged with leading a task force to determine ways to increase awareness of and sensitivity to gender issues in your organization. The group is to determine programmes for promoting awareness of gender issues. To focus the discussion, what specific issues should the task force address?

17. What are some of the problems that you commonly encounter when leading others? List on one side of a piece of paper problems you have been able to solve. Then on the other side, list the leadership skills that allowed you to manage the problems.

18. List all management-related problems you have encountered in your organization to which you have not found workable solutions. What are the most appropriate steps to address the problems and become a more effective leader?

19. The following statements are responses collected from a survey about the characteristics of leadership. Discuss the merits and demerits of these statements.

    (a) A good manager knows at all times what is going on in the department.

    (b) A good manager should have more technical expertise than the employees.

    (c) A good manager should be able to solve any problem that comes up.

    (d) A good manager should be the primary (if not the only) person responsible for how the department is working (the success and failure of the organization).

    (e) A good leader should always know the goals of an organization in advance.

    (f) Someone who is an effective leader in one environment should also be able to lead in other environments.

    (g) Effective leadership is nothing more or less than manipulation of followers to do what the leader wishes.

20. Some people have a negative attitude towards an informal network. They believe that its disadvantages are greater than its advantages. Explain in detail the positive and negative impacts of informal networks in the contemporary business environment.

REFERENCES

Adler, Nancy J, *International Dimensions of Organizational Behavior* 2nd edn (Belmont, California: Wadsworth Publishing Company) 1991.

Barge, J Kevin, *Leadership: Communication Skills for Organizations and Groups* (New York: St Martin's Press) 1994.

Becker, Gary S, *Human Capital: A Theoretical and Empirical Analysis* (Princeton, New Jersey: Princeton University Press) 1964.

Beierlein, James G, Kenneth C Schneeberger & Donald D Osburn, *Principles of Agribusiness Management* (Prospect Heights, Illinois: Waveland Press, Inc.) 1986.

Bennis, Warren, *On Becoming a Leader* (New York: Addison-Wesley Publishing Company, Inc.) 1989.

Bennis, Warren, *Why Leaders Can't Lead: The Unconscious Conspiracy Continues*. San Francisco: Jossey-Bass Publishers, 1989.

Bennis, Warren & Burt Nanus, *Leaders: The Strategies for Taking Charge* (New York: Harper & Row, Publishers) 1985.

Bennis, Warren, Jagdish Parikh & Ronnie Lessem, *Beyond Leadership: Balancing Economics, Ethics and Ecology* (Developmental Management, Cambridge, Mass: Blackwell Publishers) 1994.

Birdsall, Nancy, David Ross & Richard Sabot, "Inequality and Growth Reconsidered: Lessons from East Asia" *The World Bank Economic Review* (1995) 9, 3 pp. 477-508.

Blanchard, Ken, John P Carlos & Alan Randolph, *Empowerment takes more than a Minute* (San Francisco: Berrett-Koehler Publishers) 1996.

Bogardus, E S, *Leaders and Leadership* (New York: D Appleton-Century Company, Inc.) 1934.

Bolton, Robert, *People Skills: How to Assert Yourself, Listen to Others and Resolve Conflicts* (New York: Touchstone/Simon & Schuster, Inc.) 1979.

Bradford, David L & Allan R Cohen, *Managing for Excellence: The Guide to Developing High Performance in Contemporary Organizations* (New York: John Wiley and Sons Inc.) 1984.

Browne, C G, *The Study of Leadership* (Danville, Illinois: Interstate Printers and Publishers, Inc.) 1958.

Castle, Emery N, Manning H Becker & A Gene Nelson, *Farm Business Management (The Decision-Making Process)* 3rd edn (New York: MacMillan Publishing Company) 1987.

Chaleff, I, "Followers: The Key to Leadership" *Industry Week* (1995) pp. 28-31.

Coase, Ronald, "The Nature of the Firm" *Economica* (November 1937) 4, pp. 386-405.

Conger, Jay A, *Learning to Lead: The Art of Transforming Managers into Leaders* (San Francisco, California: Jossey-Bass Publishers) 1992.

Covey, Stephen R, *Principle-Centered Leadership* (New York: A Fireside Book, Simon and Schuster Publishers) 1992.

Downey, W David & Steven P Erickson, *Agribusiness Management* 2nd edn (New York: McGraw-Hill, Inc.) 1987.

FAO, *Women in Agricultural Development* (Rome: FAO's Plan of Action) 1990.

Fairholm, Gilbert W, *Leadership and the Culture of Trust* (Westport, Connecticut T: Praeger) 1994.

Fiedler, Fred E & Martin M Chemers, *Leadership and Effective Management* (Glenview, Illinois: Scott, Foresman and Company) 1974.
Fisher, Roger & William Ury, *Getting to Yes* (Harmondsworth, England: Penguin Books) 1981.

Fromm, Erich, *The Art of Loving* (New York: Harper and Row) 1974.

Gebremedhin, Tesfa G, *Beyond Survival: The Economic Challenges of Agriculture and Development in Post-Independence Eritrea* (Lawrenceville, New Jersey: The Red Sea Press) 1996.

Gebremedhin, Tesfa G & Luther G Tweeten, *Research Methods and Communications in the Social Sciences* (Westport, Connecticut : Praeger) 1994.

Gini, Al, "Moral Leadership: An Overview" in William E Rosenbach & Robert L Taylor (eds), *Contemporary Issues in Leadership* 4th edn (Boulder, Colorado: Westview Press) 1998.

Gmelch, Walter H & Val D Miskin, *Leadership Skills for Department Chairs* (Bolton, Massachusetts: Anker Publishing Company) 1993.

Goldhaber, G M, *Organizational Communication* 6th edn (Madison, Wisconsin: WCB Brown and Benchmark) 1993.

Heasley, Daryl K, "What is Rural Leadership: It is Establishing, Maintaining and Enhancing Credibility" (Northeast Regional Center for Rural Development, Pennsylvania State University) 1997.

Heifetz, Ronald A, *Leadership Without Easy Answers* (Cambridge, Massachusetts: Belknap Press of Harvard University Press) 1994.

Hollander, EP, *Leadership Dynamics* (New York: Collier Macmillan Publishing) 1978.

Holton, Susan A, "Cracks in the Ivory Tower: Conflict Management in the Classroom – and Beyond" *Teaching Excellence* (1996-1997) 8, 4.

International Labor Organization (ILO), "Foundations for Sustained Employment in Eritrea" report of an ILO Employment Advisory Mission in Eritrea (Addis Ababa: Eastern Africa Multidisciplinary Advisory Team (EAMAT) ILO) revised 1995.

Kelley, Robert E, "In Praise of Followers" in William E Rosenbach & Robert L Taylor (eds), *Contemporary Issues in Leadership* 4th edn (Boulder, Colorado: Westview Press)
1998.

King, Larry, *How to Talk to Anyone, Anytime, Anywhere: The Secrets of Good Communication* (New York: Crown Tradepapers) 1994.

Kohn, Alfie, *Punished by Rewards: The Trouble with Gold Stars, Incentive Plans, A's, Praise and Other Bribes* (Boston: Houghton Mifflin Company) 1993.

Kolb, D, *Learning-Style Inventory* (Boston: McBer and Company) 1985.

Kotter, John P, "What Leaders Really Do" in William E Rosenbach & Robert L Taylor (eds), *Contemporary Issues in Leadership* 4th edn (Boulder, Colorado: Westview Press) 1998.

Kouzes, James M & Barry Z Posner, *Credibility: How Leaders Gain and Lost it, Why People Demand It* (San Francisco, California: Jossey-Bass, Publishers) 1993.

Kouzes, James M & Barry Z Posner, *The Leadership Challenge: How to Get Extraordinary Things Done in Organizations* (San Francisco, California: Jossey-Bass, Publishers) 1987.

Kouzes, James M & Barry Z Posner, *The Leadership Challenge: How to Keep Getting Extraordinary Things Done in Organizations* (San Francisco, California: Jossey-Bass Publishers) 1995.

Krueckeberg, Donald A & Arthur L Silvers, *Urban Planning Analysis: Methods and Models* (New York: John Wiley and Sons) 1974.

Lee, Chris, "Performance Appraisal: Can we Manage Away the Curse" *Training* (May 1996) pp. 44-59.

Lee, Chris & Kelly, R, "Good Followers are Worth Training" *National Business* (September 1988) pp. 54-55.

Lockheed Martin Corporation, *Setting the Standard: Code of Ethics and Business Conduct.* (Lockheet Martin Corporation, Office of Ethics and Business Conduct, Westlake Village, California) 1997.

Lynch, R, *Lead* (San Francisco, California: Jossey-Bass Publishers) 1993.

Mallory, L, *Leading Self Help Groups* (New York: Family Service America) 1984.

McCroskey, James C & Virginia P Richmond, *Fundamentals of Human Communication: An Interpersonal Perspective* (Prospect Heights, Illinois: Waveland Press, Inc.) 1996.

McGregor, Douglas, *Leadership and Motivation* (Cambridge, Massachusetts: The MIT Press) 1966.

McIntosh, Jennifer, "Sexual Harassment Awareness" Notes from a workshop for faculty,
administrators and supervisors (West Virginia University, Morgantown) 21 August 1996.

McLean, J W & William Weitzel, *Leadership: Magic, Myth, or Method?* (New York: Amacom, American Management Association) 1992.

Miller, Patricia Murdock, *Powerful Leadership Skills for Women* (Shawnee Mission, KS: National Press Publications) 1988.

Myers, I B & K C Briggs, *Myers-Briggs Type Indicator* (Palo Alto, California: Consulting Psychologists Press, Inc.) 1993.

Nelson, Richard & Edmund Phelps, "Investment in Humans, Technological Diffusion and
Economic Growth" *American Economic Review* (1966) 56, pp. 69-75.

Pastin, Mark, "The Thinking Manager's Toolbox" in Elizabeth K Kellar (ed.), *Ethical Insight-Ethical Action: Perspectives for the Local Government Manager* (Washington, DC: International City Management Association) 1988.

Posner, Barry Z & James M Kouzes, "Ten Lessons for Leaders and Leadership Developers" in William E Rosenbach & Robert L Taylor (eds), *Contemporary Issues in Leadership* 4th edn (Boulder, Colorado: Westview Press) 1998.

Richmond, Virginia P & James C McCroskey, *Communication: Apprehension, Avoidance, and Effectiveness* 5th edn (Boston: Allyn and Bacon) 1998.

Rogers, Brenda, *How to Solve your Problems* (London: Sheldon Press) 1991.

Romer, Paul M, "Endogenous Technological Change" *Journal of Political Economy* (October 1990) 98, S61-S102.

Rosenbach, William E & Robert L Taylor, "Followership: The Under-appreciated Dimension" in William E Rosenbach & Robert L Taylor (eds), *Contemporary Issues in Leadership* 4th edn (Boulder, Colorado: Westview Press) 1998.

Rosenbach, William E & Robert L Taylor, "On Becoming Better Leaders" in William E Rosenbach & Robert L Taylor (eds), *Contemporary Issues in Leadership* 4th edn (Boulder, Colorado: Westview Press) 1998.

Schultz, T Paul, "Education Investment and Returns" in Hollis B Chenery & T N Srinivasan (eds), *Handbook of Development Economics* (Amsterdam: North Holland) 1988.

Schultz, Theodore W, "Investment in Human Capital" *American Economic Review* (1961) 51, 1, pp. 1-17.

Stenmark, Marea, *The Creative Communicator* (A New Approach to Successful Communication in Your Personal and Professional Life) (New York: Harper Collins Publishers) 1994.

Strauss, John & Duncan Thomas, "Human Resources: Empirical Modeling of Household and
Family Decisions" in T N Srinivasan & Jere Behrman (eds), *Handbook of Development Economics* Vol. 3 (Amsterdam: North Holland) 1995.
Terry, Robert W, *Authentic Leadership* (Courage in Action) (San Francisco, California: Jossey-Bass
Publishers) 1993.

Tjosvold, Dean, "Conflict Management in a Diverse World: A Review Essay of Caplan's Understanding Disputes: The Politics of Argument" *Human Relations* (1996) 49, 9.

Tweeten, Luther G, "Elements of Economic Growth in Rural Areas" in James S Plaxico (ed.), *Research Application in Rural Economic Development and Planning* Research Report P-665, (Stillwater Oklahoma: Oklahoma State University) 1972.

United Nations, *Women in the Changing Global Economy* 1994 World Survey on the Role of Women in Development (New York: Department of Public Co-ordination and Sustainable Development, United Nations) 1995.

Weaver, Timothy, "Linking Performance Review to Productivity and Quality" *Performance Management HR Magazine* (November 1996) pp. 93-98.

Wellins, Richard S, William C Byham & Jeanee M Wilson, *Empowered Teams: Creating Self-Directed Work Groups that Improve Quality, Productivity and Participation* (San Francisco, California: Jossey-Bass Publishers) 1991.

Wishart, J K, *Techniques of Leadership* (New York: Vantage Press, Inc.) 1965.

Zaleznick, Abraham, "The Leadership Gap" *Academy of Managment Executive* (1990) 4, 1, 12.

INDEX